DANCE OF LIFE

The Novels of Zakes Mda in Post-apartheid South Africa

Gail Fincham

OHIO UNIVERSITY PRESS • ATHENS

Ohio University Press, Athens, Ohio 45701
ohioswallow.com

First published 2011 by UCT Press
an imprint of Juta and Company Ltd
First Floor, Sunclare Building,
21 Dreyer Street, Claremont, 7708, South Africa

First published in North America 2012 by Ohio University Press

Printed in the United States of America
Ohio University Press books are printed on acid-free paper ♾ ™

20 19 18 17 16 15 14 13 12 5 4 3 2 1

Library of Congress Cataloging-in-Publication Data

Fincham, Gail.
Dance of life : the novels of Zakes Mda in post-apartheid South Africa / Gail Fincham.
p. cm.
Includes bibliographical references and index.
ISBN 978-0-8214-1993-9 (pbk. : acid-free paper) — ISBN 978-0-8214-4414-6 (electronic)
1. Mda, Zakes—Criticism and interpretation. 2. South African literature (English). I. Title.
PR9369.3.M4Z63 2012
823'.914—dc23

2012003609

For my husband, Jonathan Geidt,
and for Ed French,
in gratitude and celebration.
And in memory of my colleague
Stephen Watson, who died on
10 April 2011. His life and writings
will continue to inspire all
who knew him.

Work by the wood carvers of Montebello Design Centre in Newlands, Cape Town

Table of Contents

Acknowledgements

I am grateful to my readers for their searching commentaries. **David Attwell** insisted that I address the plagiarism issue between Mda's *The Heart of Redness* and Peires' *The Dead Will Arise*; tackling this project made me understand what Derek Attridge calls 'singularity' in relation to both works. **Johan Jacobs'** suggestions helped me reconfigure the introductory chapter and led to my consulting dozens of critical readings on Mda's texts that complicate my own. **Wendy Woodward** advised me to expand the section on diaspora, and to give as much attention to South African ecocriticism as to American ecocriticism. My readers' input has much improved this book. For remaining errors and infelicities only I am to blame.

The careful scholarship, patience and good humour of my research assistant **Jill Gribble** turned a chaotic manuscript into a well-organised manuscript. In the University of Cape Town's English Department **Isa Mkoka** and **Shihaam Peplouw** gave calm and frequent support to a panicking technophobe, while **Sue Buchanan's** friendship was always sustaining. We are grateful to the **staff of the African Studies Library at UCT** who did a sterling job of finding and supplying missing material.

As the manuscript went into production, the UCT Press/Juta team — **Sandy Shepherd**, **Corina Pelser** and **Glenda Younge** — were unfailingly efficient, meticulous and encouraging.

On the visual front, **Lesley Charnock** gave us permission to reproduce her vibrant painting of dancers on the front cover. **Theresa and Albio Gonzales** of Barcelona, who own the painting by Zakes Mda shown in the Plates and on the back cover, gave us permission to reproduce it. **The wood carvers of Montebello** in Newlands crafted depictions of humans and animals that might have been created by Mda's fictional protagonists; hence they appear opposite the Contents page. Grateful thanks to **Patricia Kotze** for capturing them in a photograph. Finally, **Dirk and Dominique Schwager** gave us permission to reproduce all the Claerhout paintings in this book from their publication *Claerhout: Artist and Priest* (1994).

For the use of previously published material the author and publishers thank **Russell West-Pavlov** of the Free University, Berlin, for Chapter Two, **Johan Jacobs**, editor of *Ways of Writing: Critical Essays on Zakes Mda*, for some of the material that appears on *The Heart of Redness* in Chapter Four and **Anne Collett**, editor of *Kunapipi* for Chapter Five, on Mda's *The Madonna of Excelsior* and the paintings of Frans Claerhout.

I gratefully acknowledge the assistance of **Tanya Barben**, in charge of Rare Books and Special Collections in the Jagger Library, UCT, who lent me her own books on Frans Claerhout.

On the history of paintings of the Madonna during the Renaissance, I am indebted to **Michael Barbour**, whose summer-school course at UCT in January 2008 explored 'Devotional Directions in Tuscan Art, 1300–1600', particularly the evolution of paintings of the Madonna and Child.

To **my students at UCT**, past and present, I owe many remarkable discoveries.

In the ecological vision, the salmon and the river weeds and the water insects interact in a great complex dance with the earth and the weather. The whole is greater than the sum of the parts. In the dance, each organism has a role: it is these multiple roles, rather than the particular beings who play them, that participate in the dance.

— J.M. Coetzee, *Elizabeth Costello*

I danced in the morning
When the world was begun,
And I danced in the moon
And the stars and the sun,
And I came down from heaven
And I danced on the earth;
At Bethlehem
I had my birth.

Dance, then, wherever you may be;
I am the Lord of the Dance, said he;
And I'll lead you all, wherever you may be,
And I'll lead you all in the dance, said he.

— Sydney Carter, *Lord of the Dance: Hymn 375 in Hymns Ancient and Modern*

Labour is blossoming or dancing where
The body is not bruised to pleasure soul.
Nor beauty born out of its own despair,
Nor blear-eyed wisdom out of midnight oil.
O chestnut-tree, great-rooted blossomer,
Are you the leaf, the blossom or the bole?
O body swayed to music, O brightening glance,
How can we know the dancer from the dance?

— W.B. Yeats, *Among School Children*

Introduction

Zakes Mda

Zakes Mda was born Zanemvula Kizito Gatyeni in 1948 in the Eastern Cape. He spent his childhood in Soweto, and then moved to Lesotho to join his father in exile. One of South Africa's foremost writers, he has produced plays, novels, poems, and academic articles in addition to being a musician and graphic artist. Mda is now Professor of Creative Writing at Ohio University, but he continues to make frequent trips to his native South Africa to launch his novels and to work in community initiatives such as the beekeeping project on the Pink Mountain described in his recent memoir, *Sometimes there is a Void.* This autobiographical work exhibits some of Mda's most striking characteristics: his sense of place, which enables him to create his characters, and his conviction that his writing cannot be separated from his commitment to building community.

His work in both theatre and fiction has been compared to that of leading African writers, including Chinua Achebe, Wole Soyinka, Ngugi Wa Thiong'o, Andre Brink, Njabulo Ndebele, J.M. Coetzee, Ivan Vladislavic, Antjie Krog and Etienne van Heerden.[1]

Mda's plays, which include *Dark Voices Ring* (1979), *The Hill* (1980), *We Shall Sing for the Fatherland* (1980), *Collected Plays* (1980 and 1990), *And the Girls in their Sunday Dresses* (1993), *Dankie Auntie* (1997), *Let us Play* (1998) and *Fools, Bells and the Habit of Eating: Three Satires* (2002) have been published by Ravan Press, Wits University Press, *Matatu: Journal for African Culture and Society* and Vivlia Press. His poetry is widely published, starting with a collection titled *Dance of the Ghost,* published in 1977 and culminating with the printing of *Slaughtered Gods* and *Uninspired Graffiti* in a 1996 issue of the literary magazine, *Staffrider.*

Mda's work has in recent years attracted worldwide critical attention. This is attested by the number of international scholarly journals that have carried articles on his fiction, such as *Kunapipi, Diacritics* and *Critical Quarterly.* South African journals that have published articles on Mda include *The English Academy Review, Current Writing* and *English in Africa.* In 2009 David Bell and J.U. Jacobs brought out the first collection of critical essays on Zakes Mda. The 19 South African and international authors contributing to this collection,

1 See the Introduction to *Zakes Mda: Ways of Writing* (Pietermaritzburg: University of KwaZulu-Natal Press, 2009) by Bell, David and Jacobs, J.U., 1.

titled *Ways of Writing: Critical Articles on Zakes Mda*, discuss Mda's plays and his novels. The editors have included lists of Mda's fiction, drama, poetry, scholarly works and published articles, and appended a critical bibliography of the most important articles on his work. Many of the essays in *Ways of Writing* are referenced in *Dance of Life*, which is the first single-author monograph on the fiction of Zakes Mda to be published to date.[2]

It is with Mda's novels that this book is chiefly concerned. Beginning in 1995, and ongoing in 2011, they mirror the establishment of post-apartheid South Africa, which began with the release of Nelson Mandela in 1990 and the election of the country's first ANC government in 1994. What makes a monograph on Zakes Mda particularly timely is the author's engagement in the cultural, historical and social complexities of the 'new' South Africa. Mda has had many years of experience in writing for theatre, and of using performance techniques to educate people for democracy. But his self-invention as a novelist experimenting with narrative techniques begins with South Africa's transition to democracy. He investigates the roles of history, community and memory in reforging a new national identity. His novels thus contribute to the many debates around nation-building, memory and reconciliation since 1994, and the way these influence the construction of narrative. In 'Memory, metaphor and the triumph of narrative', Njabulo Ndebele records 'the movement of our society from repression to expression' (Ndebele: 1998, 20) embodied in the hearings and writings of the Truth and Reconciliation Commission: 'These stories may very well be some of the first steps in the rewriting of South African history on the basis of validated mass experience' (*Ibid*, 20).

No less than the stories produced by the Truth and Reconciliation Commission, Mda's narratives dramatise the co-existence of competing versions of history. *Ways of Dying* dramatises creative autonomy versus disempowerment. *The Heart of Redness* juxtaposes colonial bigotry against Xhosa customs and traditions. In *The Madonna of Excelsior* official apartheid history contradicts non-racist, non-gendered artistic expression. *Cion* offers storytelling and quilt-making as alternatives to capitalist commodification.

The role of narrative in coming to terms with the past is emphasised by David Bell: '[I]n the reassessment of the past, the voicing of silences, the need is not to record, to witness and to represent, but to storify' (Bell: 2003, 63). Bell talks

2 In a research project undertaken in 2009, the following figures for students working on Mda texts in South African universities were compiled: University of Cape Town, 500; University of the Witwatersrand, 450; University of Fort Hare, 110; University of Pretoria, 580; Walter Sisulu University, 400. Figures were not available for readers of Mda texts in postcolonial courses around the world, but are assumed to be much higher than those for South Africa.

about Paolo Freire's distinction between *dialogic* and *anti-dialogic* societies. It is Mda's rejection of the anti-dialogic society, whatever its political or racial constitution, that accounts for his 'even-handed' fictional treatment of black, white and coloured protagonists from diverse backgrounds. This depiction is both compassionate and humorous. Essential to Mda's capacity to speak to the needs of the 'new' South Africa is the tool of satire he frequently uses in his fiction. Ralph Goodman observes: '[Mda] sets up a dialectic which does not allow for absolute categories of oppression or collusion' (Goodman: 2004, 63). This refusal to be ideologically proscriptive is born of Mda's empathy, his identification with both the perpetrators and the victims of apartheid. This is why his fiction is so important in South Africa today.

Why 'Dance of Life' ?

This book is about Zakes Mda's fiction and explores the performative dimension of his novels in particular. His protagonists are involved in writing, speaking, acting, singing, playing instruments, creating sculptures and dancing. Mda's fiction also involves both author and reader in performative responses. This book's title, *Dance of Life*, dramatises this performative dimension: Mda creates narrative designs that his characters perform and his readers construe. It also links with the epigraphs that preface this book. The 'dance' metaphor alludes to J.M. Coetzee's notion, explored in *Elizabeth Costello*, of the interconnection between humans and non-humans as celebrated in the metaphor of the dance. The hymn of the second epigraph links the moon, stars and sun to the inhabitants of earth in a cosmic dance, while in Yeats' *Among School Children* the chestnut tree's roots, trunk and flowers together represent a somatic unity in which dancer and dance become indistinguishable.

The 'dance' metaphor is useful to the understanding of Zakes Mda's fiction, because it involves author, characters and readers in a kind of performance. This is reflected in the book's representation of visual images. The front cover shows Lesley Charnock's striking painting of dancers, while the painting of intertwined figures on the back cover and on Plate XVI is by Mda himself. The Frans Claerhout paintings on which Mda builds *The Madonna of Excelsior* are reproduced so that readers can see how Mda's story-world in this novel dialogues with that of Claerhout. Mda says that all his artwork explores the 'dance' motif, either realistically or in abstract terms.[3] Crucial to the performative dimension into which Mda inducts his readers is the visual

3 Grateful thanks to Teresa and Albio Gonzales in Barcelona, who own the painting by Zakes Mda displayed on the back cover and on Plate XVI, and who gave me permission to reproduce it.

repertoire orchestrated in all his novels. Mda's strong painterly imagination teaches his readers how to see anew by creating changed spaces in memory and culture, which redress the negativity of the colonial experience. Mda uses authorial and figural points of view, perspective and focalisation to induct the reader into an altered understanding of socio-historical realities. *Ways of Dying* transforms the horror of death and the pain of mourning into artistic commemoration. *The Heart of Redness* translates the chiaroscuro of Conrad's novella into the vibrant colours of an Africa rich in culture and tradition. *The Madonna of Excelsior* turns the context of repressive legislation into an occasion for artistic expression, while *Cion* interweaves the sufferings of slaves in the American deep South with the liberating art of their descendants. Mda's saturation in the visual enables the construction of a dynamic postcolonial subjectivity.

This emphasis on the visual in Mda's writing is never merely aesthetic. It is above all a way of rewriting history. Even as he exults in the new narrative freedoms that South African writers are able to celebrate after 1994, Mda insists on social and historical accuracy. His characters are represented in the specificity of their cultural moment and their geographical positioning in his stories of both pre-and post-apartheid South Africa.

Towards an ethics of performance

Mda's new fictional practice is continuous with his previous experience of writing and directing plays. Critics have commented on the Brechtian focus of Mda's plays, which weight the ethical over the psychological and the social over the individual.[4] Mda has himself insisted that his work with the Maratholi Travelling Theatre was aimed at producing critical awareness and self-education amongst communities participating in development activities: 'Consciousness is raised from inside, by group analysis of social reality and power relations' (Mda: 1990, 355). Mda's theatre provides a voice for the voiceless and redresses the circularity in which 'the most marginalised sections of society, trapped in a "culture of silence" ... remain passive consumers of the ideas and values of more powerful classes' (Mervis: 1998, 39).[5] Underlying Mda's thematic and narrative preoccupations as sketched

4 Carolyn Duggan 'outlines the ways in which Mda's plays mirror the social and political contexts of apartheid and the struggles of ordinary people to retain some freedom and humanity under an oppressive regime'. See Duggan's article, 'Betrayal and the search for empowerment in the early plays'. In Bell & Jacobs (eds) (2009) *Ways of Writing: Critical Essays on Zakes Mda.*

5 See Margaret Mervis, 1998 'Fiction for development: Mda's *Ways of Dying*'. *Current Writing* 10 (1).

in the previous paragraph — his powerful presentation of the visual and his emphasis on performance — is a hybrid world-view. Through a combination of magic realism, orature, intertextuality and deployment of the conventions of disparate genres, Mda undermines the dualistic thinking characteristic of our Western heritage, whether between the past and the present, the human and the non-human, the living and the dead, the rural and the urban, the realistic and the imaginary, or the local and the global.

In his new autobiography, *Sometimes there is a Void*, Mda describes living in Johannesburg as a 12-year-old who was soon to be banished by his anxious parents from the seductions of city life to a small country town. His father was serving articles under George Matanzima in the Transkei; his mother was working as a registered nurse and midwife at the Dobsonville Clinic. Instead of concentrating on his schoolwork, Mda entertained himself with music and drawing:

> *While [my mother] was at work in the clinic which was just across the street from our four-roomed home, or cycling in the township delivering babies, I was playing truant from school and hanging out at shop verandahs where I played the pennywhistle with other delinquent youths … On the occasions when I did go to school I spent most of the class time drawing pictures. My talent was recognized when the teacher asked me to illustrate the poetry we were studying with appropriate pictures and I drew the Zulu warrior, uPhoshozwayo, as an illustration for a poem in his praise. With crayons I brought his traditional dress of leopard skins and a shield to life. Then I signed the picture at the bottom right, 'by Zakes the Artist'.* (Mda: 2011, 5–6.)

Mda also writes of how, revisiting Lesotho in later years, he re-encountered the vinyl records that were his father's legacy to him:

> *Frank Sinatra, Marion Anderson, the Beatles, King Kong (the South African musical), Ella Fitzgerald, Satchmo, Handel's Messiah, Dark City Sisters, Jim Reeves, the Mormon Tabernacle Choir and thirty or so [other vinyl records] that [my father] used to collect when he was a member of a record club from 1963 to 1966* (Mda: 2011, 14).

Art and music were, therefore, central activities for Mda from his early childhood. They spill over effortlessly into his writing life, as is recognised in this citation for winning, in 1997, the Olive Schreiner Prize:

> *The prize is presented for excellence in prose, poetry, and drama … in 1997 it was presented for prose to Zakes Mda for his first novel* Ways of Dying. *Sharply conscious that Mda last year won the prize for drama, the adjudicators nevertheless deemed this novel their first choice, in a close-run race, for literary merit. They felt it served to bring together African and occidental structures, forming the foundations for a new 'music' in South African writing.*

J.U. Jacobs points out that not only are cultural and artistic performances *described* in Mda novels, they are '*enacted* by the narrative' (Bell & Jacobs: 2009,

356, author's emphasis). In the chapters that follow, I will try to demonstrate these enactments by showing how Mda designs narrative forms that illustrate his thematic preoccupations — just as an artist chooses the colours, forms and textures of his brush-strokes.

From play-writing to novel-writing

In his aptly titled article, 'A theatre for democracy', David Bell writes about Mda as theatre practitioner in the years 1979 to 1989, when he worked with the Maratholi Travelling Theatre in Lesotho. Bell points out that the Latin-American writers Paolo Freire and Augusto Boal, whose work encouraged participatory democratic practices, inspired Mda to create plays '*with* the people, not *for* the people'. (Bell: 2009, 18). Intended, like the work of his Latin-American counterparts, to involve the rural poor and urban slum dwellers, and drawing on 'popular indigenous modes of performance' (*Ibid*, 22), Mda's theatre for development underwent a three-phase process 'from a theatre of protest via a theatre of resistance to a theatre of reconciliation' (*Ibid*, 21.) Mda's theatre work, Bell argues, is driven by 'a belief that theatre can help people change their lives through a process of conscientisation, naming, reflecting and acting, that leads to critical awareness and self-reliance' (*Ibid*, 34). Therefore, an obvious starting-point for anybody writing about Mda's fiction is its relation to his earlier writing for theatre, where he worked closely with communities in order to educate largely non-literate audiences. Like his plays, Mda's novels are about 'ordinary people doing ordinary things'.[6]

When Mda and I met to talk in November 2009, I commented that Mda has always insisted on the relationship between art and politics. I quoted the interview in which he stated: '[T]he role I hope my work plays is that of social commentator ... I want [my art] to rally people to action' (Bell & Jacobs: 2009, 3). I asked how his work in the different areas of theatre, fiction and cinema writing connected in relation to this *desideratum* of social commentary. He replied:

> *In answer to your question about the 'trajectory' of my writing first for theatre, then novels, and most recently scriptwriting for film, this was never a planned 'trajectory'. My MA was in writing for film and television, so I've been doing this, combining different kinds of writing, for many years. On the issue of social commentary and*

6 Margaret Mervis links Mda's theatre with his fiction. She speaks of his project of giving 'a voice to the voiceless' and shows how this is extended to *Ways of Dying*. She comments that '*Ways of Dying* is ultimately a combination of Brechtian didacticism and indigenous African participatory story-telling in which the difference between "artist" and "audience" is virtually non-existent' (Mervis: 1998, 55).

> *rallying people to political action ... I was talking about my plays, about educating people for democracy, not about my novel-writing now. Now I am a storyteller. In the past, we didn't have the luxury of writing one work over many months. The plays I wrote had to be produced under pressure, for an immediate political purpose. Fiction-writing is much more leisurely.*

Asked how his fiction creates participatory processes analogous to those that his plays demand, Mda replied: 'I want to tell a story, like my grandmother told it when I was a child.' Questioned about how his most recent novel, *Black Diamond*, positions its reader as performer, Mda replied: 'How does it position the reader as performer? Well, that's up to you critics to decide. I tell a story that is driven by the needs of its characters in their situations and contexts, in the places where they live. I'm not conscious of "positioning" the reader.'

Perhaps what this exchange illustrates is that my preoccupations as critic, and Mda's preoccupations as storyteller, don't always overlap, a fact that allows us both greater freedom to explore divergent areas. But the relationship between Mda's earlier theatre writing and his current novel-writing is of course a crucial question.[7] A link here is his use of proverbs and of an extensive African resource base in both his novels and his plays. These cross-cultural allusions 'capture the reconciliatory spirit of a South Africa striving to heal the wounds of the past' (Warnes: 2009, 89).

If theatre-writing involves a bodily present spectator interacting with the performers, fiction-writing presupposes an absent reader. Yet even in the activity of reading, a performative dimension comes into play, as Derek Attridge explains:

> *Among all the inventions that can be so characterised, works of art are distinctive in the demand they make for a performance, a performance in which the authored singularity, alterity and inventiveness of the work as an exploitation of the multiple powers of language are experienced and affirmed in the present, in a creative, responsible reading* (Attridge: 2004, 136).

7 Shane Graham describes how the play *The Bells of Amersfoort* (2002) foregrounds issues of space-time to dramatise trauma and memory. This play '[forges] new modes of constructing and interacting with social space' (Graham: 2009b, 70), a project which is extended into Mda's novels. Linking the temporal and spatial coordinates of his plays with his novels, Rogier Courau and Sally-Ann Murray discuss *Ways of Dying* as a novel in which 'two states of transition, one temporal and the other spatial, come together in a plot of extreme violence and morbidity' (Courau & Murray: 2009, 95). Their argument complements Graham's analysis of dramatic space-time as connecting with fictional space-time to represent trauma.

In the same way that theatre requires a performance based on the collaborations of a director, actors and an audience, so too does the act of reading require a collaborative performance between the text's author and its readers.

Written texts and oral storytelling

Mda's knowledge and use of a wide range of intertexts derives from a Western tradition. This is more fully discussed in the section on hybridity as a postcolonial strategy in Chapter Three, titled 'The cross-border reader'. It is also foregrounded in Chapter Four, which deals with Mda's flexible deployment of intertextuality.

If Mda's writing dialogues extensively with other writers' texts, it is also steeped in African oral storytelling features. In interview with me Mda said that he wanted to tell stories as his grandmother told them when he was a child. Childhood memories of communal storytelling, long before the beginning of formal education, are frequently crucial to the development of African writers. Ngugi Wa Thiong'o recalls how in his native Kenya children's voices participate in and extend storytelling:

> *I can vividly recall those evenings ... around the fireside. It was mostly the grown-ups telling the children but everybody was interested and involved. We children would re-rell the stories the following day to other children who worked in the fields picking the pyrethrum flowers, tea-leaves or coffee beans of our European landlords* (Ngugi: 437).

Ngugi continues:

> *There were good and bad story-tellers. A good one could tell the same story over and over again, and it would always be fresh to us, the listeners. He or she could tell a story told by someone else and make it more alive and dramatic. The differences really were in the use of words and images and the inflexion of voices to effect different tones* (*Ibid*, 473).

The power of stories to involve their listeners thus turned on the storyteller's use of language:

> *Language was not a mere string of words. It had a suggestive power well beyond the immediate and lexical meaning. Our appreciation of the suggestive magical power of language was reinforced by the games we played with words through riddles, proverbs, transpositions of syllables, or through nonsensical but musically arranged words* (*Ibid*, 437–438).

The spoken word, no less than the written word, thus shapes Mda's development as a creator of fiction. Far from communicating a timeless world, it intersects with the social and cultural realities that he invokes in his novels. Frantz Fanon draws readers' attention to the potential subversiveness of the spoken word: '[T]he oral tradition — stories, epics and songs of the people, which formerly were filed away as set pieces' began to change as Algeria prepared for independence:

> *The storytellers who used to relate inert episodes now bring them alive and introduce into them modifications which are increasingly fundamental. There is a tendency to bring conflicts up to date and to modernise the kinds of struggle which the stories evoke, together with the names of heroes ... Colonialism made no mistake when from 1955 on it proceeded to arrest these storytellers systematically* (Fanon: 1993, 48).

Writing about contemporary postcolonial fiction, Elleke Boehmer points out how writers

> *justify their choice of language by emphasising how the various conflicts and anomalies of the postcolonial condition are vibrantly displayed within the hybridised medium itself... the point on which they agree is the need to dismantle the authority once commanded by English. If a colonial language embodies a colonial vision, then the aim must be to dislodge that vision ... It is a process which can also be termed cultural boomeranging or switchback, where the once-colonised take the artefacts of the former master and make them their own* (Boehmer: 1995, 210).

This 'cultural boomeranging or switchback' is achieved in Mda's novels both by his ability to reconfigure other writers' texts and by his deployment of the linguistic resources of the spoken word. No less than literate thinking, the oral tradition feeds into the development of national consciousness, on which nation-building in a newly democratic South Africa depends.[8]

Social realism or magic realism?

Mda's settings are historically and geographically accurate, whether in the cityscapes of apartheid-designed 'locations' or in the indigenous flora and fauna of such places as Nongqawuse's Valley in *The Heart of Redness.* Yet his accurately

8 Douglas Killam and Ruth Rowe sketch the evolution of oral history in South Africa, and relate it to the country's current political situation:

> In addition to folkloric and prose narratives, oral poetry has been an important feature of South African society since the development of the first human communities in the subcontinent, from the lyric songs of the Khoikhoi and Bushmen, expressing complex mythological and social understandings, to the praise poems (*izibongo, lithoko*) of African societies, which serve to negotiate relations of power between ruler and ruled... The study of oral poetry in South Africa has received impetus recently from the far-reaching political changes in the country, which have emphasised the need for the creation of inclusive cultural histories, the broadening of the scope and methodology of literary studies to include 'popular' non-canonical forms, and developments in oral theory and critical practice. Areas which have received particular attention recently include orality and history, oral forms and conceptions of gender, oral poetry and political power, and the adaptation of performance genres to contexts of modernity (Killam & Rowe: 2000, 201–202).

historicised and acutely observed realism sometimes alternates with what has been described as 'magic realism'. This genre is associated with the supernatural and with Latin-American writing, particularly that of Gabriel Márquez. Mda, however, explicitly rejects the notion that his use of magic realism is influenced by such writers as Márquez. Rather, he insists that magic realism is an *African* storytelling tradition: 'I wrote in this manner from an early age because I am a product of a magical culture. In my culture the magical is not disconcerting. It is taken for granted. No one tries to find a natural explanation for the unreal. The unreal happens as part of reality' (Mda, in Naidoo: 1997, 281).

Yet magic realism is a mode little used by South African writers. Why is this? In his Jerusalem Prize acceptance speech, J.M. Coetzee asks what prevents the South African writer from following the example of Don Quixote and entering 'the realm of faery'. Coetzee replies:

> *What prevents him is what prevents Don Quixote himself. The power of the world his body lives in to impose itself on him and ultimately on his imagination, which, whether he likes it or not, has its residue in his body. The crudity of life in South Africa, the naked force of its appeals, not only on the physical level but at the moral level too, its callousness and its brutalities, its hungers and its rages, its greed and its lies, make it as irresistible as it is unlovable* (Coetzee: 1992, 98–99).

Mda's story-worlds include plenty of the 'power, crudity, naked force … callousness, brutalities, hungers, rages, greed and lies' described by Coetzee. We need only think of *Ways of Dying*, in which children of five are killed by 'necklacing' because they are accused of being informers, or *The Madonna of Excelsior*, where women like Popi and Niki are thrown into prison by a government blind to their humanity and impervious to their civil rights. Yet Mda casts these characters into story-worlds that are potentially transformed by what Warnes calls 'the redeeming qualities of the aesthetic' communicated 'not through magic means, but through ordinary acts of imagination' (Warnes: 2009, 82). He remarks that *The Madonna of Excelsior* juxtaposes its characters and situations with those of the symbolist/expressionist world of the painter Frans Claerhout because '[Claerhout] represents a force that numinously rejoins the religious, the aesthetic and the possibilities of healing the wounds of the past' (*Ibid*, 83). What Mda's 'magic realism' achieves, therefore, is 'an affectivity and a dignity denied for generations by the impositions of colonialism and apartheid' (*Ibid*, 83–84). Mda's magic realism is thus connected much less with the supernatural than with the transformative potentials of the human imagination.

A striking number of critics[9] see magic realism as characteristic of a *transitional* or *transformatory* category of writing. Brenda Cooper describes the

9 Barker cites Mervis, Van Wyk, Bell, Cooper, Durrant, Steinmeyer, Jacobs, Mazibuko, Courau and Barnard.

genre in African literature as 'thriving on transition, on the process of change, borders and ambiguity'. She remarks: 'such zones occur where burgeoning capitalist development mingles with older pre-capitalist modes in postcolonial societies, and where there is syncretising of cultures' (Cooper: 1998, 15). For Derek Barker, Mda employs magic realism 'wherever the subject matter deals with extreme and inexplicable inhumanity or ontological rifts' (Barker: 2008, 17). The critical debate around the function of magic realism in African writing, and particularly in Mda's fiction, is thus lively and extensive. My own sense is that Mda's magic realism has to be understood as an *extension of*, rather than a *contradiction of*, his social realism. I am here in agreement with Marita Wenzel, who remarks that 'the presence of magical realism in Mda's fiction underlines and illustrates the essential duality of existence by suggesting other possible interpretations of reality' (Wenzel: 2009, 131).

Vision/focalisation

Mda's explorations of the I/eye relationship challenge his readers to reconstitute individual and collective identity through the changed spaces in perception, memory and understanding which pervade his fiction. His deployment of the visual as an authorial strategy may be referred to as 'focalisation'. It is defined by Mieke Bal as 'the relationship between the "vision", the agent that sees, and that which is seen' (Bal: 1997, 146). The author's design of focalisation affects both fictional characters, whose processes of vision are described in the narrative, and the readers of the narrative, who '[watch] with the character's eyes and will ... be inclined to accept the vision presented by that character' (*Ibid*, 146). Every one of Mda's novels — except perhaps *Black Diamond* — makes telling use of vision and focalisation. By changing the way we *see*, Mda aims to change the way we *think* about the world.

His first post-apartheid novel, *Ways of Dying*, dramatises the reappropriation of urban space by the former victims of apartheid. In focalising the urban space inhabited by Toloki the Professional Mourner, Mda makes us see the astonishing complexity and diversity of life in what middle-class readers would otherwise see only as an impoverished and culturally marginalised space. Mda's project here is complemented by Jacob Dlamini, who in *Native Nostalgia* (2009) writes about his memories of growing up in the township of Katlehong. These memories fundamentally deconstruct the ignorance of apartheid and of colonial discourses that discriminate against township-dwellers:

> *Townships tend to be seen as zones of deprivation that can only ever be defined in a negative sense, in terms of what they do not possess. In the telling of most histories, townships are poor places, full of poor people, who often make poor choices in life* (Dlamini: 2009, 105).

But Dlamini shows that there is nothing inevitable or innocent about seeing townships in these terms, since our perceptions are culturally mediated. He points out:

> *In the case of a township and the way we see it, what is apparent to a viewer (that what she has in front of her is row upon row of unimaginative houses on dusty streets) may be as much a function of what her brain has been taught to 'see' as what she sees in front of her* (*Ibid*, 121).

If in *Ways of Dying* Mda uses focalisation to challenge dominant ways of seeing typical of apartheid ideology, his use of focalisation in each of his subsequent novels is equally subversive, surprising us into new ways of understanding what we had previously taken for granted. In each of the chapters that follows, I shall attempt to demonstrate how Mda uses the visual to destabilise the reader's preconceived notions.

Place/setting/landscape

> *[There is] an elaborate frame through which our adult eyes survey the landscape. Before it can ever be a repose for the senses, landscape is the work of the mind. Its scenery is built up as much from strata of memory as from layers of rock* (Schama: 1996, 10).

Mda's story-worlds are both rooted in specific carefully observed places and suffused with the memories of those who have inhabited those places: 'I have written elsewhere that I usually see a place and immediately decide that it is so beautiful or so ugly that it deserves a novel. The next question is: what character would live in a place like this and what memories are contained in this landscape? I see the trees and the rocks and the grass and the hills and the rivers as storing places of memory' (Mda: 2009a, 3). In his use of setting, therefore, Mda mutually imbricates memory, history, landscape and culture. His attitude to landscapes has little in common with Western perspectives that perceive geographical settings as mere expressions of human mastery. Rather, settings and landscapes in his storytelling derive from African oral genres, which refuse to separate people from land. Writing of the characteristics of oral praise poetry, Liz Gunner comments: '[T]he land frequently becomes the person, and becomes part of the body's text; the social and the historical self is perceived through the land' (Gunner: 1996, 120). Like the praise singers', Mda's settings '[collapse] linear time and [allow] the past to sit within the ambit of the present' (*Ibid*, 123). They also '[break] down the categories of land, body and being' (*Ibid*, 127).

Where Western mental categories separate, indigenous peoples' conceptions of geography join: 'History, science, spirituality and aesthetics are all tied together by these peoples' oral, or recently written, bodies of local knowledge … In contrast to the observation of specialised professional scientists, indigenous knowledge is local, intensive, long-term, and based on intimate, shared experience that is dynamic, complex and recursive' (Allison: 1999, 273). Landscape therefore functions as an integral part of an indigenous group's sense of identity. For Aboriginal Australians as well as for Native Americans, social identity cannot be separated from the ancestors whose past life created the topographical features inherited by their descendants. These links with the past are strongly present too in Mda's story-worlds. They deconstruct many of the binaries on which Western history is built. Memory takes the place of the topographic documentation created by Western maps. As Barbara Bender remarks:

> *Past and present elide. The topographical details — dune, hill, lake, shoreline — are the site of memory. Where ... spatial maps reflect a Western sense of personal autonomy, these are the memories of ancestral wanderings that are also contemporary songlines, ancestral exits and entrances that are also contemporary sacred places ... In Aboriginal society, [the] divide between nature and culture, something 'out there' as opposed to something socially and culturally constructed, is, quite literally, inconceivable* (Bender: 1999, 41).

This nature/culture binary is inconceivable also in the world-views of Mda's characters. Their relationship to the lands they inhabit is shot through with the African concept of *ubuntu*,[10] an inter-relatedness that both unites different people and places them in dynamic relationship to their environment.

I have been arguing that the sense of place so central to Mda's fiction is both the product of accurate observation of topographical details on the author's part and the repository of remembered experience of those who inhabit these places. It has therefore both a real and an imagined dimension. Into this rich and evolving sense of place feed both the strategies of focalisation already touched on and the discursive blending reflected in a given novel's narrative structure, which will be made up of authorial, narratorial and figural elements. As the authors of the earlier quotations argue, nature and culture, divided by Western thought, fuse in African storytelling. In Mda's novels place is dynamic and transformative.

In this brief introduction, I have attempted to sketch the contexts of Mda's novel-writing, in relation both to the political and social worlds of post-apartheid South Africa in which they are set, and in relation to some of the narratological features of his writing. I have repeatedly emphasised the importance of the performative in the author's interactions with his characters and his readers. This performative dimension will be more fully explored in each of the subsequent chapters.

10 The concept of *ubuntu* or African humanism is discussed in Chapter One.

Chapter One

Zakes Mda's construction of the 'cross-border' reader

Introduction

This chapter concentrates on the readership that Mda creates for his fiction, and considers particularly Mda's construction of the 'cross-border' reader. What does the term 'cross-border' mean? Does it refer primarily to the characteristics of an author's works or to the cultural positioning of the works' readers? Are we to understand the concept geographically, psychologically or generically? Borders define the boundaries of real spaces as politically and topographically constituted. Equally, borders can invoke culturally constructed notions — conceptual spaces that shift. Nowhere is this shape-shifting more apparent than in the genre of the novel, for Mikhail Bakhtin teaches us that the novel is a protean genre, staging dialogues between older, conventionally accepted literary forms and newer forms born of changing socio-political conditions. Generic instability is thus a defining characteristic of the novel.

This chapter seeks to unravel some of the complex and often contradictory meanings of the term 'cross-border' in relation to the novels of Zakes Mda — playwright, painter, musician and literary performer of the 'new' South Africa.

Maps, writers, readers and communities under apartheid

Writing in 1994, on the eve of the creation of the 'new' South Africa, Lewis Nkosi doubts that black writers are in a position to construct a 'cross-border' readership:

> *Black writers have had very restricted access to institutions of higher education and until recently enjoyed almost no contacts with the outside world through travel and other cultural exchanges ... even in their own land such public facilities as libraries and writers' workshops, elsewhere taken almost for granted by many aspiring writers, have until recently been denied to black South Africans* (Nkosi: 1994, 39).

Reading this cultural exclusion as the inevitable consequence of the rigid imposition of apartheid boundaries, he quotes John Stotesbury:

> *[A] map of South Africa can be read, like any map, in terms of a complexity of ambivalences. For example, it consists of a combination of geopolitical spaces separated by geopolitical divisions. In addition, the spaces its borders separate may conventionally be described in terms of inclusion (national territory) and exclusion (foreign territory). The anomaly of South Africa's self-created dilemma … is the degree to which its inclusive space has been designated exclusive space* (Nkosi: 1994, 42).

Pursuing the question of how South African authors construct their readers, or 'what kind of audience they envisage', Nkosi remarks: 'South Africa emerges … as a country of borders, existing both internally and internationally, separating it from the outside: a network of "geopolitical lines" carving up "geopolitical spaces"' (Nkosi: 1994, 45). Just as the black writer under apartheid had been excluded from effective communication with the oppressed in the 'geopolitical spaces' of South Africa, so white writers opposed to apartheid have turned to a readership largely outside the country:

> *Any literature which lays claim to being 'contra' apartheid within the South African conditions, especially the realist 'protest' text, can never be exclusively addressed to [the] internal community of oppressed readers for that would make no sense: such a text would be continuously telling people who already know it that they are oppressed* (Nkosi: 1994, 47).

He concludes: 'The character and identity of South Africa is determined somewhere else, by people outside of the community in whose name the writer claims to be speaking' (Nkosi: 1994, 48).

From pre- to post-apartheid South Africa

Nkosi was writing in 1994. From the time of Zakes Mda's first South African novel, *Ways of Dying* (1995), the situation of black writers in South Africa and the audiences they target began to undergo a radical change. I will be arguing that in all of the novels written between 1995 and 2009, Mda situates himself both outside and inside the communities for whom he speaks. In arguing that Mda creates a 'cross-border' readership, I do not underestimate his commitment to a style of writing that frequently incorporates non-standard English, nor to his insistence that international readers must learn to interpret a South African context. Andrew van der Vlies notes that Mda writes 'primarily for the South African audience'. When challenged by an editor about the particularly South African nature of some expressions, Mda replied that his overseas readers 'were not morons'. If they did not understand 'South African expressions in a South African novel they would go and find out'; he 'certainly was not going to refashion [his] novels to suit American and European tastes' (Van der Vlies: 2007, 162).

What is a 'South African' readership?

The claim that Mda writes chiefly for a 'South African readership', but also for an international readership, needs to be explored in the context of the linguistic, cultural and racial complexities of South African identity. In November 2009 Mda returned to Johannesburg from Ohio to launch his latest novel, *Black Diamond*, with his publishers, Penguin (Johannesburg). He granted me a series of interviews in which we discussed his novels. Asked about his childhood and his earliest writing experience, Mda explained that he was in the process of writing an autobiography. Entitled *Sometimes there is a Void* (the title of one of the chapters in *The Madonna of Excelsior*), it was published early in 2011. Three chapters had been written at the time I was working on this manuscript; these he was kind enough to share with me. They deal with his school days and early adolescence. The son of a lawyer who was also a political activist, Mda spent his early childhood in two South African locations: Soweto and Sterkspruit. When his father's political activism put him in danger of imprisonment under apartheid, father and son fled to Lesotho, where they joined many intellectuals exiled from South Africa. Here they encountered a wide spectrum of political affiliations as Lesotho moved towards independence from British administration: the Basutoland Congress Party (BCP) which was aligned with the Pan Africanist Congress (PAC) in South Africa, and therefore supported by Mda; the Basotho National Party (BNP) which was supported by the Catholic church in a predominantly Catholic country; the Marematou Freedom Party (royalists, supported by King Moshoeshoe II) and the Communist Party.

As a Xhosa-speaking South African, Zakes was teased in Lesotho by the Sesotho-speaking children at Mohale's Hoek Government Controlled School. They called him *mothepu* (a derogatory name for any Nguni-speaking person) and *moketa* (a Sesotho word for an emaciated cow: Zakes was a thin child). His first published writing was a short story originally composed in his Sterkspruit school days for a magazine called *Wamba*. By the time it was published, Zakes had moved to Lesotho, where the story was not understood:

> *I wanted everyone in my class at the Mohale's Hoek Government Controlled Primary School to look at my name just below the title 'Igqirha IaseMvubase'. But no one shared my excitement. The story was in a strange language that no one could fathom. My name also was written as Zanemvula Mda, whereas since my arrival in Mohale's Hoek I was going under the name of Motlalepula, a direct translation of my first name into Sesotho. With a Sesotho name I would not stand out as a foreigner, or so I thought* (Mda: 2011, 76).

Thus the relationship of 'inclusive' to 'exclusive' space, which Stotesbury discusses in the geopolitics of contemporary South Africa, is problematised in Zakes Mda's own life story, where black anti-apartheid resistance is not the same in South Africa as it is in Lesotho. The distinction between 'exclusive' and 'inclusive' space is also multiply problematised in the fictional strategies of Mda's novels, which I go on to discuss. The notion of the 'cross-border' reader is therefore complex and elusive; it cannot be essentialised. It includes rootedness in one place and the experience of diaspora — divergent spaces that Mda inhabits in his autobiography and continues to orchestrate in his narrative designs.

The concept of *ubuntu* as constitutive of the cross-border writer and reader

Probably the most crucial notion to understand in relation to the elusive 'cross-border' writer and reader is commitment to the African humanist conception of *ubuntu*. This notion links an individual to the community that defines him or her:

> *Though it is a broad cultural concept,* ubuntu *is effectively expressed by the proverb common to most South African languages,* motho ke motho ka batho *(Sotho), or* umuntu ngumuntu ngabantu *(Nguni). This proverb, translated as 'a person is a person through others', establishes a perception of the world in which the self is not created through self-determination, but primarily through the sacrifices of others (birth, protection, support) and through the interaction of self with others* (MacDonald: 2009, 134–5).

Significantly, *ubuntu* is shown here to bridge Nguni and non-Nguni speakers — the linguistic constituencies that Mda experienced as divided in Lesotho. Mda draws on the philosophy of *ubuntu* in the perspectives orchestrated by the communal narrator in his first South African novel, *Ways of Dying*: 'We are the all-seeing eye of the village gossip. When in our orature the storyteller begins the story "They say it once happened...", we are the "they". No individual owns any story; the community is the owner of the story, and it can tell it the way it deems fit' (Mda: 1995, 12). This notion of loyalty to community transcends race and nation. It is a cultural concept with strong ethical resonances, for the cross-border reader is necessarily a believer in *ubuntu*.

From 'interstitial' space to the space of novel-writing

Like the late Edward Saïd, Zakes Mda occupies, culturally and biographically, an 'interstitial' space. His position as Professor of Creative Writing at Ohio University allows him to speak from within the authority of the educational institution. Yet, as Saïd spoke for the Palestinians, so Mda speaks for the marginalised and dispossessed in his native South Africa. Mda's protagonists are typically poor and ordinary people whose voices have been silenced under apartheid. His writing thus speaks directly to those constituencies of 'class, gender, location, race, caste or ideology' (Loomba: 2005, 19) which in Anya Loomba's view have been largely overlooked in postcolonial theory. There are analogies, too, between Saïd and Mda in the worldliness of their writing, which draws the reader's attention to who addresses us in the text. Like Saïd, Mda eschews a 'politics of blame' (Saïd: 1986, 45), maintaining freedom from party politics in order to 'speak truth to power'[1] (Saïd: 1994, 75). Saïd's discussion, in *The World, The Text and The Critic*, of the relationship between culture and place, exile, diaspora and home-coming applies also to Mda: 'It is in culture that we can seek out the range of meanings and ideas conveyed by the phrases *belonging to* or *in* a place, being *at home in a place*' (Saïd: 1983, 8). Like Saïd, Mda situates identity within transcultural displacement; like Saïd he perceives the *constructedness* of human identity.[2]

If culture constructs boundaries or borders, it also deconstructs them. So Mda, post-1994, moves from his earlier commitment to writing theatre for development — the aim of which was to prepare his audiences for democracy — to the less didactic and more experimental arena of novel-writing. In this move he both embraces what Ndebele describes as 'rediscovery of the ordinary' and embarks on new narrative challenges. Mda has recorded his gratitude to the example of J.M. Coetzee's *Waiting for the Barbarians* because that novel's refusal of geographical and historical specificity offers the black writer escape from the straitjacket of 'struggle' writing:

> *What others saw as a failure to represent lived experience appeared to me — I was then in exile — as a refreshing way to re-imagine South Africa and transcend the repetition of the horrors reported every day in newspapers* ... Waiting for the Barbarians *awakened me to new possibilities for writing fiction. Here was a first among South African authors: a writer with an imagination that creates worlds rooted in immediate reality while also transcending it* (Mda: 2008, 1).

Mda then goes on to write *Ways of Dying* — a novel 'rooted in immediate reality while also transcending it'. *Ways of Dying* therefore marks the first border-

1 Mda's critique of African National Congress party politics is reflected in his characterisation of Camagu in *The Heart of Redness,* while *The Madonna of Excelsior* demonstrates the suffering both of blacks under apartheid and whites in the 'new' South Africa. In *Cion,* Mda mounts a scathing attack on the aggressive militarism and social conservatism of the Bush administration.

2 Saïd's phrase 'contrapuntal ensembles' (Saïd: 1993, 60) also strikingly applies to Mda, in whose novels musical analogies, and the performance of music, are central. Saïd's term 'affiliations' (1983), describes both writers' positioning within history and culture. Their experience of exile contributes to their 'plurality' of vision (1984). Both writers, in their complex worldliness, demonstrate Robbins' (1994) idea of reconceptualising geography.

crossing in Mda's fictional practice: from the communal and participatory activity of writing, directing and performing plays with the Maratholi Travelling Theatre in Lesotho in the 1980s and 1990s to writing novels about the 'new' South Africa. Just as Mda's protagonist, Toloki, invents for himself the role of Professional Mourner in *Ways of Dying*, Mda reinvents himself as a novelist centrally concerned with the issues of community, history and memory for the construction of identity in post-1994 South Africa. This concern with community, history and memory links Mda's novels with the recent narratives of the Truth and Reconciliation Commission. Writing about the turn from 'repression to expression' (Ndebele: 1998, 20) embodied in the stories collected by the TRC, Ndebele remarks: 'In few countries of the contemporary world do we have a living example of people reinventing themselves through narrative. Only now has South Africa succeeded in becoming metaphor, in becoming a true subject of philosophy.' For Ndebele, it is only post-TRC that South Africans 'can [create] new thoughts and new worlds ... Only now does our experience resonate with moral import' (*Ibid*, 27). This passage from intense trauma recorded in documentary evidence to imaginative transcendence is strikingly captured by Mda's first novel of the 'new' South Africa, *Ways of Dying*.

Mda's novel-writing in the 'new' South Africa is marked by narrative innovation. This is not to claim, however, that it represents a deliberate departure from his earlier, more didactic use of theatre for democracy with the Maratholi Travelling Players. There are many points of overlap between Mda's previous work in theatre and his current novel-writing.[3] But his shift from theatre to novel is more an incidental result of his personal circumstances than a deliberately planned trajectory. In a recent interview with me, Mda emphatically denied that his novel-writing was designed to overlap with the birth of a democratic South Africa:

> *I never thought of my fictional work as beginning with, or corresponding to, the birth of the new South Africa. It was Christmas Day. My wife had gone to church, leaving me with our 4-month-old baby. I had a job at Yale which left me lots of time and a brand new computer. Up to this time I had always written my manuscripts in longhand. I started trying to use the computer, wrote 'There are many ways of dying', decided I liked writing prose fiction, and by the time my wife returned had written*

3 See Carolyn Duggan on the plays of 1979–1989. She points out that Mda 'iterates the plight of the colonised and the struggles, and pitfalls, of post-colonial society' (Duggan: 2009, 39) and concludes: 'Questions are raised about the importance of individuals, about the need to change our lives and the need to be active in this process. Equally, Mda explores the idea of integrity and asks how loyal we are to our fellow humans and our ideals' (Duggan: 2009, 55). Many of these issues are also explored in Mda's novels.

> *the first few pages. So that was, quite fortuitously, the start of my novel-writing career in the 'new' South Africa* (unpublished interview, November 2009).

Fortuitous as the transition from play-writing to novel-writing may have been for Mda, his current novel-writing is experimental in ways that his earlier work could not afford to be, given the urgency of using plays to educate a predominantly non-literate audience for democracy. Now Mda as novelist speaks to a readership, both in South Africa and abroad, that assumes familiarity with the canon of European and African literatures. Though his novels frequently deploy aspects of performance and response derived from African orature, their recipients are necessarily literate.

Refiguring temporality

Central to the issue of identity in the 'new' South Africa is its relationship with history. David Attwell remarks: 'The axis has been shifting ... from an emphasis on how to write about sameness and difference, to writing about *temporality*, which is to say, writing about one's own place in history or one's place in the present and future' (Attwell: 2005, 8). Mda's narrative structures frequently imbricate time with space. Here Bakhtin's concept of the chronotope is particularly useful. Explaining Bakhtin's ideas about the relationship of language to culture, Pam Morris defines the chronotope as the 'spatio-temporal matrix which shapes any narrative text. Specific chronotopes correspond to particular genres ... which themselves represent particular world-views. To this extent, chronotope is a cognitive concept as much as a narrative feature of texts' (Morris: 1994, 246). In Bakhtin's own words: 'The chronotope is the place where the knots of narrative are tied and untied. It can be said without qualification that to them belongs the meaning that shapes narrative' (Morris: 1994, 187).

In *The Heart of Redness*, Mda reconfigures South African history. He takes the nineteenth-century colonial story of the Xhosa prophetess, Nongqawuse, whose prophecies resulted in the Cattle-Killing and the division of the Xhosa nation into Believers and Unbelievers, and juxtaposes this story with the late twentieth-century story of the descendants of the Believers and Unbelievers in the Eastern Cape. The modern chronotope plays out in the same place that witnessed the Cattle-Killing. But what is omitted from the novel's historiography is the story of the 'Middle Generations' — the story of the people who suffered from starvation and dispossession after the Cattle-Killing and from racial discrimination under several decades of white dominion. Mda emphasises instead, the *reterritorialisation* of Qolorha-by-Sea in the Eastern Cape. The district is now freed from the colonial demarcations of Sir George Grey, the 'Man Who Named Ten Rivers' and imposed on the

South African landscape the character of the European coloniser. Now, post-apartheid, Qolorha-by-Sea is ablaze with colour and Xhosa names replace the names given to local people and places by the coloniser. Agency replaces instrumentalisation as the inhabitants of Qolorha-by-Sea, whose practices and beliefs remain linked to those of their ancestors, take control of their future in planning their new ecological development.

In *The Madonna of Excelsior*, Mda again uses temporal juxtaposition as a central narrative technique. The novel is constructed around two conflicting discourses — that of the popular journalism of the media reports of the Miscegenation Trial as it unfolds in the Free State town of Excelsior and that of the visionary artistic language of the expressionist/symbolist painter Frans Claerhout. These conflicting discourses describe the same period in apartheid history from radically divergent perspectives. Where the discourse of journalism perpetuates apartheid's most callous and barbaric legislation, Claerhout's paintings celebrate the formerly instrumentalised, allowing Mda's two main protagonists, Niki and Popi — who have served as models for *Madonna and Child* in Claerhout's studio — to access a new autonomy, or to assign themselves new places in history.

The conceptual and temporal juxtapositions effected by alternating between popular journalism and visionary art are illustrated in the following examples. In *The Madonna of Excelsior*, Frans Claerhout's paintings, whose characters and settings are linked to the story-worlds of Mda's protagonists, are described by an omniscient narrator. The reader is shown the inside of the Claerhout studio:

> *Madonnas all around. Exuding tenderness. Burnt umber mother in a blue shirt, squatting in a field of yellow ochre wheat. Burnt sienna baby wrapped in white lace resting between her thighs. Mother with a gaping mouth. Big oval eyes. Naked breast dangling above the baby's head. Flaky blue suggesting a halo. Unhampered bonding of mother and child and wheat* (Mda: 2002, 11).

The omniscient narrator also describes Niki's perception of the value of the Trinity's paintings, and the way they influence her life and that of her daughter. Niki, the Madonna of Excelsior

> *...closed her eyes and silently prayed for the trinity's long life. For his hands that must stay strong. For his vision that must continue to find joy in cosmos, donkeys, women and sunflowers. For his passion for colour that must never fade. And for his muse that occasionally flung him into a mother-and-child mode. She pleaded with whatever spirits drove his passions to immerse him in more Madonna moods before Popi grew too big to model as the child* (Mda: 2002, 112).

The contrast between this egalitarian, non-sexist and non-racist vision and the apartheid-generated accounts of the Miscegenation Trial as reported in the local newspaper (*The Friend*) could hardly be starker:

> *The Friend, 3 February 1971:*
> *The Minister of Justice, Mr P. C. Pelser, said in the Assembly yesterday that as long as he was Minister of Justice and as long as the Nationalist Party governed the country, the Immorality Act would not be 'scrapped'.*
> *He also said that the reason why the police had acted in the Free State town of Excelsior was because Whites and non-Whites had complained that there were too many half-caste children walking the streets.*
> *The consequences of the implementation of section 16 of the Act were actually as a result of the abhorrence which the people felt against miscegenation* (Mda: 2002, 101).[4]

Cion is once again constructed around juxtaposed discourses deriving from timeframes that occur in the same place. Mda takes Toloki, the protagonist of his first novel, *Ways of Dying*, and transports him to the poor Appalachian community of Kilvert, Ohio, whose inhabitants trace their ancestry back to the plantation slaves of the South. The slaves' dreams of escape and freedom via the Underground Railroad, which were figured in the designs of the tapestries made by women like the Abyssinian Queen, mother of the escaped slaves Nicodemus and Abednego, are continued in the tapestry-making of the current inhabitants of Kilvert. Toloki learns to weave tapestries himself; through his relationship with the Quigley family and their socioeconomic location in contemporary America, he is enabled to achieve a sense of his own present, as well as of the past to which his career as Professional Mourner had connected him.

What is striking in these stories of transformation is the geopolitical context in which historical agency is dramatised. Mda insists on *the politics of place or locatedness.* This locatedness is the starting point of all his writing:

4 My research assistant, Jill Gribble, and her husband, James Gribble, who grew up in Bloemfontein, query Mda's implicit dismissal of *The Friend* newspaper as a pro-apartheid organ. They comment: 'It was the daily newspaper we grew up with in Bloemfontein; compared with *Die Volksblad*, it was a very liberal paper. It had a succession of fine editors among whom were Rudyard Kipling and, much later, René de Villiers, who in time became a Progressive Party MP.' They provide the following information from the Internet: 'Originally published in both English and Dutch, in 1894 [*The Friend*] began publishing in English only, while affirming its commitment to "fighting for the interests of everyone without regard to race or colour" … *The Friend* maintained a liberal stance throughout its publication, and news stories were frequently sympathetic to blacks and "coloureds" in Africa. The paper became aligned with the United Party, the ruling party from 1934–1948. *The Friend* came under the control of the Argus group of newspapers and continued publication until July 1985.' Given this history, readers may wonder why Mda quoted this newspaper rather than *Die Volksblad*, and why its embedding in his narrative does not hint at editorial irony.

Place is key. To me place is not just background, for my characters are suggested by the place. I ask, what kind of character would be in a place like this? And what would they be doing here? What happens is determined by who that character is and what that place is all about (Mda: Interview, 25 May 2004).

Pechey remarks that J.M. Coetzee's narratives 'speak to the world by speaking from their own ineluctable chronotope to the chronotopes of their potential readers abroad' (Pechey: 1998, 67). The same could be said of Mda.

Crossing textual boundaries

I have spoken of Mda's autobiographical positioning between the American academy and grassroots communities in South Africa, and about his use of chronotopes that dramatise agency in their juxtaposition of the times and spaces of his story-worlds. In this final section I want to consider the textual parameters of Mda's novel-writing. In addressing a readership made up of both South Africans and international readers, Mda's works draw on a richly intertextual reading experience that frequently crosses generic boundaries — between romance and realism, between history and modernity, between metafictional and factual storytelling modes, between individual and communal consciousness.

Hybridity as postcolonial strategy

Mda's novels are thus hybrid in the sense which Bakhtin originally defined:

[A] hybrid construction is an utterance that belongs, by its grammatical (syntactic) and compositional markers, to a single speaker, but that actually contains mixed within it two utterances, two speech manners, two styles, two 'languages', two semantic and axiological belief systems. We repeat, there is no formal — compositional and syntactic — boundary between these utterances, styles, languages, belief systems; the division of voices and languages takes place within the limits of a single syntactic whole, often within the limits of a simple sentence (Bakhtin: 1981, 304–5).

In current postcolonial theory, hybridity has a central importance because of its deconstruction of colonial authority. Homi Bhabha writes:

[H]ybridity is the sign of the productivity of colonial power, its shifting forces and fixities; it is the name for the strategic reversal of the process of domination through disavowal (that is, the production of discriminatory identities that secure the 'pure' and original identity of authority). Hybridity is the revaluation of the assumption of colonial identity through the repetition of discriminatory identity effects. It displays the necessary deformation and displacement of all sites of discrimination and domination. It unsettles the mimetic or narcissistic demands of colonial power but reimplicates its identifications in strategies of subversion that turn the gaze of the discriminated back upon the eye of power. For the colonial hybrid is the articulation of the ambivalent space where the rite of power is enacted on the site of desire,

> *making its objects at once disciplinary and disseminatory — or, in my mind's mixed metaphor, a negative transparency* (in Ashcroft *et al*: 1995, 34–5).

Hybridity, a crucial term in postcolonial discourse, is also a frequently contested term, with many critics rejecting what they see as its political naïveté. Radhakrishnan (1996) for instance critiques celebrations of difference which are to him at odds with the actual experience of difference as undergone by diasporic peoples, while Gayatri Spivak warns against the dangers of 'triumphalist self-declared hybridity on the part of the postmodern postcolonialist' who deploys this hybridity 'in the service of neo-colonialism' (Spivak: 2003, 361).

Although for some theorists, critical responses to the hybridity of postcolonial texts may risk overlooking the political in favour of the textual, it seems to me that the hybrid nature of Mda's texts is essential to their construction of new socio-political perspectives. Mda's narrative strategies are frequently double-voiced, to return to a Bakhtinian category. By alternating between authorial and figural perspectives they teach the reader to recognise and evaluate competing discourses. These competing discourses combine African orature, folklore and mythology with European literary traditions.

Hybridity and intertextuality in Mda's novels

Hybridity as defined above frequently refers to the ways in which a text may simultaneously inhabit several genres. Nearly always, hybridity also involves intertextuality. Here I draw on Jeremy Hawthorn's definition:

> *A relation between two or more texts which has an effect upon the way in which the intertext (that is, the text within which other texts reside or echo their presence) is read ... The term transtextuality is reserved for more overt relations between specific texts, or between two particular texts, while intertextuality is reserved to indicate a more diffuse penetration of the individual text by memories, echoes, transformations of other texts* (Hawthorn: 2000, 182).

Mda's use of intertextuality with Western and African stories encompasses both formulations given above. Sometimes it establishes precise thematic connections between his fiction and the intertext; sometimes it refracts these connections through 'memories, echoes, transformations'. Mda's novels borrow, appropriate, interrogate and transmute other authors' works in order to reposition the reader in a reshaped historical and cultural tradition.

Mda's intertexts

Any discussion of the texts with which Mda's fiction resonates draws attention to the different domains of writer and critic. For in numerous interviews Mda has denied conscious engagement with other writers. Such comparative analysis, he insists, is the critic's prerogative; his prerogative is that of the storyteller. But of course the storyteller's art is shaped by his listening and reading practices: 'I come from a family of readers. I strongly believe that to be a good writer you need to read. Actually, reading made me a writer, because when you read stories, you are fascinated by these stories, and you want to create your own stories.'[5] As writers create story-worlds inspired by — even if not consciously modelled on — other writers, so critics look at these convergences. We are free to explore the multiple intertextual resonances that Mda's fiction orchestrates without expecting him to enter into these explorations.

Ways of Dying (1995)

Mda's first novel set in South Africa remarkably combines documentary realism — the horrors of township life under apartheid — with visionary empowerment. Through his Professional Mourning, Toloki learns to become a creative subject in his own right, rather than a passive object of others' gaze or design. As David Attwell puts it:

> *Mda dramatises the power of non-instrumental art to awaken listeners to their precariousness, to stir up affective capacities, and to remind them that despite the brutalisation that is their daily lot, they are still agents of culture* (Attwell: 2005, 194).

With its use of the grotesque, its fusion of colloquial with literary registers, its emphasis on the body and its enactment of carnival, *Ways of Dying* is the most Bakhtinian of Mda's novels. Rita Barnard comments: 'Mda may be consciously importing and rewriting a number of tropes from *Rabelais and his World*' (Barnard: 2004, 283). Barnard also draws attention to 'the peculiar and productive ambivalence' of the grotesque as literary mode in the postcolonial context of 'the volatile and violent years between the unbanning of the resistance movements and the inauguration of the democratically elected ANC government' (*Ibid*, 279). Bakhtin's central thesis that human existence is 'a ceaseless battle between centrifugal forces that seek to keep things apart, and centripetal forces that strive to make things cohere' (Bakhtin: 1981, xviii) is of course particularly applicable to an interregnum, a time of cultural and historical crisis such as that experienced by South Africans in their transition from apartheid to democracy.

In 'Discourse in the Novel' Bakhtin says that 'the prose writer makes use of words that are already populated with the social intentions of others' (Holquist: 299–300). So Mda throws his protagonist Toloki into a heteroglot world in which he has to develop his own voice amid the clamour of competing

5 Interview with Venu Naidoo (Naidoo: 1997, 247).

voices that surround him in the township: the Nurse's voice, the voices of the Street Committee, Noria's voice, the memory of voices of the rural village from which he and Noria originate. The narrator explains Toloki's development of his profession:

> *[T]he people are not yet used to the concept of a Professional Mourner. It is a fairly new concept, and he is still the only practitioner. He would be willing to train other people though, so that when he dies the tradition will continue. Then he will live in history as the founder of a noble profession* (Mda: 1995, 17).

Laughter, folk humour, carnival: these elements are present everywhere in Bakhtin's exploration of the Rabelaisian world-view. Here is an example of a similar world-view in *Ways of Dying*. Toloki, *flâneur*-like, wanders through the city's central business district during the Christmas-New Year celebrations. His perspective is reported by the communal narrator:

> *He alights and walks in the familiar streets.*[6] *They are decorated with lights of different colours, and with banners and bunting — all in preparation for the parades that will take place in the afternoon to celebrate the New Year. Over the years, Toloki has watched many of these parades of colourful dancers with painted faces, dressed in silk suits. Their childish antics and their funny songs always make the spectators on the pavements laugh. This is one of the highlights of the year, when we are all carefree and forget about the problems that live with us the whole year round* (Mda: 1995, 195).

6 Courau and Murray draw attention to Mda's use of Walter Benjamin's figure of the *flâneur*: 'Toloki's wandering is reminiscent of Walter Benjamin's *flâneurs*, those urbane, mid-nineteenth century, male urban strollers, who revealed the lives of the bourgeois margins through voyeuristic observation, with Benjamin clearly overwhelmed by the city's theatricality, its passion for improvisation and its ironies' (Courau and Murray: 2009, 99). Sarah Nuttall sees the *flâneur* figure as inviting us 'to read the city from its street level intimations, to encounter the city as lived complexity, to seek alternative narratives and maps based on wandering' (Nuttall: 2004, 731–748). Kudzayi Ngara reads Mda's use of the *flâneur* motif as a postcolonial strategy: 'As Toloki journeys across the city he is able to fashion links that transcend the binary limits or divides of apartheid, demonstrating at the same time how even in spaces dominated by poverty, grief and conflict — such as the informal settlement — there is always room for the expression of the most sublime beauty' (Ngara: 2009, 23). Chris Lazley comments: '[F]or Toloki to "strut like a king" in the city, for him to imaginatively take ownership of its spaces, is more than simply progressive. Mda has contrived a protagonist who is black, foul-smelling, and impecunious; he is dismissed throughout his life as ugly, a constant reminder, as Nofolovhodwe tells him, "that we are all going to die one day" (WD, 133). His only real possessions are an increasingly threadbare Halloween costume and a shopping cart, and yet he is a "king"' (Unpublished MA thesis: 2008, 62).

The Heart of Redness (2000)

I have written elsewhere about intertextuality between *The Heart of Redness* and Conrad's *Heart of Darkness.*[7] In summary, the narrative design of Mda's text shares features of Conrad's narrative in challenging conventional Eurocentric ways of reading. It also undermines teleological readings of 'progress' in the colonial context. Like *Heart of Darkness, The Heart of Redness* frustrates readers' desires to find either a textual centre or definite closure to the story's multiple ironies. Like Conrad, Mda dramatises the mapping and naming strategies by which the coloniser controls the colonised. Where Mda's text departs strikingly from Conrad's is in his presentation of the interiority of the thoughts of the inhabitants of Qolorha-by-Sea in both the nineteenth century and the contemporary chronotope. Marlow lacks access to the language, customs and beliefs of the indigenous Congolese he meets on his upriver journey, and therefore his presentation of them depends on stereotypes that privilege the West over 'Others'. Hence, Conrad ironically reverses the conventional European binaries of light/darkness; illumination/blindness; idea/idol; civilised/savage; conqueror/conquered; vital/dead and dream/nightmare. Finally, Mda's text shows the richness of the cultural life of its African protagonists by exploring dimensions that *Heart of Darkness* can only obscure or repress, such as those of the dance and dreaming. Through his use of magical realism, Mda achieves psychic liberation from Old World domination and its cognitive codes. His depiction of African landscape restores Africa to its full-colour vibrancy where Conrad's chiaroscuro depiction of Africa reduces it to black and white. I conclude my exploration of both texts by remarking that Mda, as postcolonial writer, appropriates a profoundly colonial incident that he recontextualises. Where Conrad's text problematises the concepts of agency and of community, Mda creates agency by reconfiguring history. Through invoking memory he insists on the possibility of meaningful community.

The Madonna of Excelsior (2002)

In Section 3 of this chapter ('Refiguring temporality') I have attempted to show how *The Madonna* is the most intertextual of Mda's novels because of its interconnectedness with Frans Claerhout's paintings. A Jesuit priest, Claerhout came from Belgium to found a mission station in the Orange Free State. Mda's novel juxtaposes the two opposing chronotopes of apartheid-driven

7 See Fincham, Gail (2009) 'Community and agency in *The Heart of Redness* and Joseph Conrad's *Heart of Darkness*'. In Bell, David & Jacobs J. U. *Ways of Writing: Critical Essays on Zakes Mda*, 191–206. This chapter is reproduced in the first section of Chapter Three.

journalism[8] and the visionary art of Claerhout's paintings. This structuring of the story-world around two opposing world-views reveals the power of art to return dignity and significance to individuals silenced under apartheid. Claerhout's work is itself a striking example of intertextuality. Owing much to the Flemish primitive painters Pieter Breughel and Constant Permeke, Claerhout's mystical protest art depicts ordinary people doing ordinary things. It also has affinities with the work of Vincent van Gogh, Paul Gauguin, James Ensor, Edvard Munch, Marc Chagall and Georges Rouault — 'all artists whose work is both expressionist and symbolist'.[9] Frans Claerhout is himself a striking example of transgressive hybridity. Devoted to his peasant non-literate parishioners and to the 'threeness that has tamed the open skies, the vastness and the loneliness of the Free State', Claerhout as 'man, priest, and artist' (Mda: 2002, 2) refuses Christianity's binary constructions. He rejects the demonisation of female sexuality that has resulted in the opposing stereotypes of virgin and whore. Instead, his paintings fuse the secular with the sacred to celebrate both fertility and maternity. In Claerhout's work, Mda finds the perfect expression of a vision that deconstructs the political, social and gender violence perpetrated by apartheid.

The Whale Caller (2005)

This novel continually draws attention to the fact that its grounding intertexts belong to a lost world. With all its comic elements it is therefore bleakly dystopian. A story about the triangular relationship between the unnamed Whale Caller of Hermanus, Saluni 'the feisty village drunk, a passionate but self-destructive woman who frequents the taverns and consorts with passing sailors'[10] and a Southern Right whale named Sharisha, it is also a story of that loss of ecological balance that guarantees the survival of all species on earth. 'Primitive' people such as the Khoikhoi of Southern Africa or the Aborigines of Australia lived in equilibrium with the animals on whom their livelihood depended. But our commodifying ethos in the twenty-first century endangers the ecological equilibrium on which all species depend. The contrast between an ecologically balanced past and an ecologically unbalanced present is clear in the following extract:

8 See my footnote on page 9, which argues that *The Friend* was never a pro-apartheid organ. *The Madonna* juxtaposes visionary art with politically reactionary thinking; that this thinking is reported in *The Friend* does not mean that the newspaper itself was reactionary.

9 As pointed out by J.U. Jacobs in *Ways of Writing* (Bell & Jacobs: 2009, 285).

10 Quoted from the novel's dust jacket.

> *When the Whale Caller is in a happy mood he can see the weather-beaten fishermen shrouded in the mists of time, taking to sea in their fleet of small boats. Some are rowing back with their catch, while others are gutting the fish or drying it on the rocks. He can see even deeper in the mists, before there were boats and fishermen and whalers, the Khoikhoi of old dancing around a beached whale. Dancing their thanks to Tsiqua, He who Tells His Stories in Heaven, for the bountiful food he occasionally provides for his children by allowing whales to strand themselves. But when there are mass strandings the dance freezes and the laughter in the eyes of the dancers melts into tears that leave stains on the white sands* (Mda: 2005, 2).

In this depiction of the relationship between hunters and hunted, there is a strong spiritual component in the dance that celebrates the whale's existence and in the mourning accompanying the mass stranding of whales.[11]

Similarly, the Whale Caller tells Saluni of the myths that celebrated whales 'way back in the Dreamtime of Australian Aborigines' (Mda: 2005, 200). The Aborigines combined reliance on the natural world with a spiritual or mythological relationship to the hunted — as did the stories of the Khoikhoi of Southern Africa who once lived on the Hermanus coast now inhabited by the Whale Caller. Both Aborigines and Khoikhoi practised not only exploitation but also protection of their fellow creatures. This protectiveness is expressed in the Aborigine story of the Strong Man 'who could sing to make a female whale and her calf escape the shallow waters' (Mda: 2005, 200). This is precisely what the Whale Caller of Hermanus cannot do when freak wave conditions result in the beaching of Sharisha, causing her death and endangering the life of her calf.

Cion (2007)

In *Cion*, Mda again draws on a range of intertextual sources: accounts from the 'ghost hunter' John Kachula, the work of writers and historians who researched the escapes of plantation slaves to the North via the Underground Railroad, and the history of quilt-making as a community activity. He also moves for the first time to auto-textuality or metafiction, designing a 'novel about novels' characterised by 'self-love, a tendency toward self-obsession' (Hutcheon: 1980, 10, 13). Toloki the Professional Mourner of *Ways of Dying* develops his craft to new heights. Discovering that the expression of mourning

11 While I see *The Whale Caller* as contrasting our modern technological world with the lost worlds of both Khoikhoi and Aborigines, Wendy Woodward believes that the Aborigines' stories about whales brought into play a spirituality lacking in the Khoikhoi relationship with whales: 'For Mda, what is implicitly lacking in Khoikhoi relationships with whales … is that they cannot account mythically for these mammals as the Australian Aborigines do in their story of Whale Man' (Woodward: 2009, 335).

and grief is an anthropological universal spanning many countries and many periods, he individuates himself from his creator the Sciolist, an authorial god-figure who stands in for Mda himself. *Cion,* like *The Madonna of Excelsior,* interweaves its story-world with art forms. In *The Madonna,* Niki and Popi grow towards fulfilment through their connection as Madonna and Child with the Claerhout paintings. In *Cion,* Toloki's adopted family in Kilvert, Ohio, develop new strength through their involvement in quilt-making. Both novels celebrate the protagonists' achievement of ecological balance. *The Madonna* ends with singing and dancing in the same sunflower fields that once saw the brutalisation of black women by Afrikaner farmers; *Cion* ends with the Quigley family's achievement of independence from the simultaneously consumerist and militarily aggressive ethos of Bush's America. Their closeness to the land and to the community link back to their slave ancestors.

Black Diamond (2009)

At first glance, Mda's latest novel seems to offer little intertextuality with other authors' story-worlds. Written like a detective or mystery novel, its plot is based on a simple, fast-moving storyline. *Black Diamond* is modelled on non-literary popular genres and the lingo of the media. It satirises the values of a black professional middle class whose lifestyles, homes and daily activities — buying clothes with designer labels, spending at the supermarket, keeping fit in the gym — are indistinguishable from the white middle classes who previously dominated suburban Johannesburg. But the real heart of the novel is the Soweto in which Mda himself grew up, and to which the novel's protagonists return nostalgically whenever they can. And at the heart of Soweto is the world of jazz, in which Don Mateza's father is an expert. Jazz, Ralph Ellison tells us, is the most complex of musical forms. It embodies tension between imitation and originality, individual and community:

> *There is a cruel contradiction implicit in the art form itself. For true jazz is an art of individual assertion within and against the group. Each true jazz moment (as distinct from the uninspired commercial performance) springs from a contest in which each artist challenges all the rest, each solo flight, or improvisation, represents (like the successive canvases of a painter) a definition of his identity: as individual, as member of the collectivity and as link in the chain of tradition. Thus, because jazz finds its very life in an endless improvisation upon traditional materials, the jazzman must lose his identity even as he finds it* (Henry Louis Gates: 1988, preface).

Embedded in the slick and glossy world of *Black Diamond,* then, is a continuously evolving hybridity. The jazz world provides a metaphor for the protean shapes that black identity already takes and will continue to take in post-apartheid South Africa.

Finally...

The notion of a 'cross-border' writer or reader is both complex and elusive. I have argued that the concept is far more culturally than physically constructed, and that it draws centrally on the ethical dimensions of an African humanism, or *ubuntu.* Zakes Mda's hybrid, intertextually challenging novels, written between 1995 and 2009, assume a readership familiar with both European and African canons. Rooted in the time and place of post-apartheid South Africa while profoundly concerned with the postcolonial experience of diaspora, Mda's fiction thus plays a significant role in constructions of identity in the 'new' South Africa.

Chapter Two

'Appropriating urban space': *Ways of Dying*

Introduction: Why Bakhtin?

This book explores Zakes Mda's novels in relation to the 'new' (post-apartheid) South Africa. It picks up on the dynamics of performance[1] in particular, which Mda carries over into novel-writing from his experience of acting, directing and writing for the Maratholi Travelling Theatre in Lesotho during the 1980s and 1990s when he worked in Theatre for Democracy.[2] The dynamics of performance thus transfer from the context of theatre to the context of writing and reading novels and involve author, characters, narrators and readers. African oral traditions as well as Western texts contribute to these dynamics.

Ways of Dying (1995) is Mda's first novel about South Africa. A text about transition and cultural crisis, it fuses Mda's ongoing commitment to social realism with the liberating potentials of the creative imagination. While the novel is set in an apartheid squatter community characterised by violence and

1 In his concept of the 'imagined city' Kudzayi Ngara stresses Toloki's performative role in the search for self-identity: 'In *Ways of Dying* … Toloki does not sink into faceless and anonymous conformity, disappearing into the mass that is the city and becoming forever indistinguishable in the seething human morass. On the contrary, he embarks on a process of self-definition by looking at all that he can potentially be in the city — and it is this that enables him to survive in the city (Ngara: 2009, 17).

2 On the relation of Mda's theatre work to his novel-writing, Margaret Mervis is particularly illuminating. Discussing Mda's work with disadvantaged protagonists trapped in a 'culture of silence' she comments: 'They must be motivated through art to raise themselves to an awareness of their problems and capabilities' (Mervis: 1998, 40). Toloki in *Ways of Dying* takes over the role of catalyst to provoke both individual awareness and community consciousness. He thus builds 'a more humanistic ethos' free of the evils of apartheid ideology. Toloki takes the place of the 'facilitators' or 'catalysts' in the plays. Like them, he is 'different (heterophilous) from the community in attributes such as beliefs, values, education and class position' (*Ibid*, 43). Like the facilitators of the plays Toloki — despite his naïveté — has a higher level of critical awareness than that of the community. In *Ways of Dying*, Mervis contends, Mda moves beyond anger at apartheid to 'a transitional stage in which individuals and communities have to reconstruct themselves and their societies' (*Ibid*, 44).

horror, its protagonists are nevertheless capable of imaginative transcendence. Bakhtin's ideas about the nature of discourse propose language as dynamic social interaction and connect closely with the performance dynamic explored in this book. Rita Barnard remarks that 'the whole novel has a dramaturgical quality' (Barnard: 2004, 282). Discourse participates both in what Bakhtin calls synchronic and diachronic dimensions; that is to say, 'it is of its own contextual moment [as well as] part of the long evolution of social change' (Bakhtin in Morris: 1994, 5). Bakhtin is particularly concerned to explain how new meaning is generated, just as Mda is concerned to explore how new social and political realities come into being. *Ways of Dying* graphically illustrates how Toloki as Professional Mourner learns to appropriate a new language through interacting with the many languages and discourses that surround him in the township, first under apartheid, then in post-apartheid South Africa.

Bakhtin draws our attention to the 'double-voiced' or dialogic character of language, which moves between author and characters and in which readers have to learn to interpret the social voices that structure our being: 'Each word, as we know it, is a little arena for the clash and criss-crossing of differently oriented social accents' (*Ibid*: 1994, 12). This struggle for dominance is a feature of all power, all hierarchy; it is through the generative dynamics of opposition that new meanings are born. The fictional genre of the novel orchestrates these new and dynamic possibilities through its complex ('heteroglossic') language. Through the introduction of laughter and comedy, it breaks down stratifications and makes for social equality. Words take on different meanings and connotations for different social classes at different times. They disrupt authority and privilege alternative voices. Central to this disruption of authority is Bakhtin's notion of carnival: 'The festivities associated with Carnival are collective and popular; hierarchies are turned on their heads (fools become wise, kings become beggars); opposites are mingled (fact and fantasy, heaven and hell; the sacred is profaned) ... Everything authoritative, rigid or serious is subverted, loosened or mocked' (Selden, Widdowson and Brooker: 1985, 43).

In her article 'On Laughter, the Grotesque and the South African Transition: Zakes Mda's *Ways of Dying*', Rita Barnard suggests that in *Ways of Dying* Mda may be consciously importing and rewriting a number of tropes from Bakhtin's 'Rabelais and his World' (Barnard: 2004, 283). She explores the novel's concentration on the body and the grotesque to dramatise the 'profound and regenerative connection between life and death, of the world of the living and the earthy netherworld' (*Ibid*, 284). She also investigates the function of carnival to liberate the formerly oppressed:

> *At the end of the novel, the traditional trappings of carnival are clearly in place, complete with drunken carousers in costumes and masks, and it is in the description*

of their revels that one of the most crucial elements of the Bakhtinian carnivalesque is foregrounded. This is, in a word, freedom: freedom from the fear and intimidation that was pervasive in the unpredictable world of the South African transition (Barnard: 2004, 288).

In the context of what Barnard sees as a recent sociological emphasis on 'squatter camps' or 'informal settlements' at the margins of wealthy African cities, this potential for freedom becomes critical: 'In situations where the usual benefits of urban life such as employment, legality and shelter cannot be relied on, a capacity for continual self-invention becomes an essential skill' (Barnard: 2004, 281). Rogier Courau and Sally-Ann Murray also address the creative reappropriation of urban space in *Ways of Dying*. They see the novel as 'Mda's attempt to give imaginative weight and historical context to the experience of the migrant labourer and the rite of passage from a poverty-stricken rural life to the even more severe conditions of urban existence' (Courau & Murray: 2009, 91). In *Ways of Dying* 'the rituals of death become a performance of the substance of community memory — a source of connection between the worlds of the living and the dead' (*Ibid*, 93). Their argument foregrounds the eclecticism of Mda's borrowings from both African and European traditions, and the importance of community history and community memory in both traditions.

The social realism of *Ways of Dying*

Set in the transitional period[3] of South African history between the last years of apartheid and the birth of democracy, *Ways of Dying* reflects the horrors of

3 Johan van Wyk remarks of transitional literature that it is produced 'when societies experience extensive ideological, political, economic and institutional changes. The transition is, in many ways, traumatic and productive' (Van Wyk: 1997, reprinted in *Kagablog*, 1). Sam Durrant also theorises the concept of transition: 'It is precisely because colonialism often involves both the destruction of traditional communities and the traditions by which those communities are remembered that literature becomes a crucial site not only for the recovery of communal traditions of remembrance but for the reinvention of community' (Durrant: 2005, 441). Speaking of funerals and rites of mourning, Durrant remarks: 'Rather than constituting a culture's most entrenched and unchanging traditions, mourning rites often reflect the instability and adaptability of colonised cultures, especially where communities are responding to new forms of death and dying. What anthropologists term mortuary rites usually relate to the so-called good deaths, where the death can be anticipated, preparations made and relations gathered around. It is under the pressure of dealing with what anthropologists call "bad" deaths, those which happen outside the home, in unexpected or unknown circumstances, that mourning rites undergo their most radical reinvention' (*Ibid*, 441–2).

apartheid legislation. Conditions in the settlement in which Toloki and Noria live are governed by the Group Areas Act, which also maintains the Pass Laws.[4] Xenophobia, made more oppressive by state and police intervention, is manipulated by the tribal chiefs; migrant hostel dwellers turn against the residents of the township. 'Street committees', such as the one that prevents Toloki from speaking to Noria at the funeral of her son, further police individuals. Bulldozers demolish shacks and the government moves people up to fifty miles from their workplaces. Labourers travelling to work are killed every day on the trains, while militants such as the Young Tigers indoctrinate children into political activism. Naïve and unaware of the consequences of their actions, these children — like Noria's five-year-old son — pay the price of death for being 'sell-outs'. In this climate of continuous political violence, funerals are as common as weddings, and mortuaries and cemeteries are overflowing. In such a situation of legislated brutality, what possibilities exist for freedom or community? Given the political barbarity of its setting, it is hardly surprising that numerous critics have found the ultimately hopeful storyline of *Ways of Dying* implausible. Underlying the negativity of their responses is the sense that this novel contravenes social realism by mingling fact with fantasy.

More than any of Mda's other fiction, *Ways of Dying* is illuminated by Bakhtin's ideas on the novel. One reason for this is that Bakhtin's notion of *heteroglossia* dramatises the coexistence of socio-ideological contradictions. Reflecting the ideologically fractured environment of apartheid, *Ways of*

4 The following background, all too familiar to South Africans, is provided for overseas readers:

> In the months leading up to the 1948 elections, the National Party (NP) campaigned on its policy of segregation, or 'apartheid' (an Afrikaans term for the state of being apart). It was voted in, in coalition with the Afrikaner Party (AP), under the leadership of DF Malan.
>
> Thus it was that apartheid, long a reality of life, became institutionalised under Malan. Within short order, legislation was passed prohibiting mixed marriages, making interracial sex illegal, classifying every individual by race and establishing a classification board to rule in questionable cases. The noxious Group Areas Act of 1950 set aside desirable city properties for whites, while banishing 'non-whites' into the townships. The Separate Amenities Act created, among other things, separate beaches, buses, hospitals, schools and even park benches.
>
> The existing Pass Laws were further strengthened: blacks and coloureds were compelled to carry identity documents at all times and were prohibited from remaining in towns, or even visiting them, without specific permission. Couples were not allowed to live together (or even visit each other) in the town where only one of them worked, and children had to remain in rural areas (Bainbridge: 2009, 40–1).

Dying is riven with such contradictions from its opening sentence. A second reason is that Bakhtin's formulations on the carnivalesque, grotesque realism, folk humour, laughter and degradation are particularly suggestive in the context of Toloki's self-created career as Professional Mourner. The first concept — *parodic* or *dialogised heteroglossia* — deals with the historical specificity of the competing utterances and competing discourses that Mda captures in the apartheid-governed squatter camp in which the novel is set. This is the *synchronic* aspect of the novel's construction. The second concept, the notion of the carnivalesque, refers to the novel's *diachronic* aspect, namely its relationship to much earlier developments in medieval Europe, where carnival, folk humour and laughter achieve the novel's 'fundamental liberation of cultural-semantic and emotional intentions from the hegemony of a single and unitary language' (Bakhtin: 1981, 367). While the first concept lends itself to political, cultural and historical specificity — the words and utterances deriving from a particular political situation at a particular time — the second concept refers to archetypal and trans-historical concepts, that is, to aspects of human response that remain relatively unchanged over time.

Heteroglossia and states of transition

I begin with the concept of 'heteroglossia', which refers to 'a perception of language as ideologically saturated and strained' (Morris: 1994, 15). 'The word in language,' Bakhtin remarks, 'is half someone else's. It becomes "one's own" only when the speaker populates it with his own intention, his own accent, when he appropriates the word, adapting it to his own semantic and expressive intention' (Bakhtin: 1981, 293). So an approach to *Ways of Dying* might be to trace the ways in which Mda's narrator tells the story of Toloki's and Noria's appropriation of language amidst the competing discourses amongst which their story is set. 'What is realised in the novel is the process of coming to know one's own language as it is perceived in someone else's language, coming to know one's own horizon within someone else's horizon' (*Ibid*, 365). *Ways of Dying* graphically illustrates this conflictual discursive complexity, as Mda shows the reader the fracturing effects of apartheid ideology on political thought and social cohesion.

Since *Ways of Dying* is his first South African novel and it takes place on the eve of the 'new' South Africa, this demonstration of discursive self-contradiction is a salient achievement. This does create problems for the novel's reader, however, as (s)he must decide whose voice to trust as the novel opens: the communal narrator's? The omniscient narrator's? Toloki's? But these voices are fundamentally incompatible. The communal narrator speaks for *ubuntu*, for a community awareness that dictates and owns the story. His attitudes as patriarch and member of the settlement are fundamentally at odds with the attitudes of the omniscient narrator, who orchestrates all the details of the story-world. To exacerbate this problem, no distinction is made between the communal narrator and the omniscient narrator whose voices blend into each other. Toloki's attitudes, as they emerge from the dialogues in which he is involved, must be distinguished from the narrator's, for Toloki is less worldly and less identified with tribal patriarchal values than the narrator.

These narrative tensions are enacted in the novel's opening page. We are at the funeral of Noria's child, an occasion for communal memory and communal mourning as the residents of the settlement express their solidarity with Noria. The Nurse is speaking about the life and death of 'this little brother ... our own child [who] was killed by those who are fighting to free us' (Mda: 1995, 7). But the voice of the communal narrator objects: 'We mumble. It is not for the Nurse to make such statements. His duty is to tell how this child saw his death, not to give ammunition to the enemy' (*Ibid*, 7). Revealing the true facts around the child's death would amount to 'parading our shame to the world', and result in retributive action by 'the enemy'. So sympathy and solidarity in grief are shown, from the outset, to be threatened in the context of this settlement, where the residents are intimidated by the ongoing likelihood of political violence. Toloki, the chief protagonist whose development the narration traces, 'belongs to the section of the crowd who believes strongly in the freedom of the Nurse to say it as he sees it' (*Ibid*, 7). So Toloki's sympathies are not aligned with the communal narrator's. This divergence in political views widens as the reader is shown Toloki's coming of age in the urban environment of the squatter camp. Yet Toloki's voice and thoughts are communicated throughout by the omniscient narrator who takes control of the trajectory of the narrative.

The Nurse's oration is soon drowned out by the din made by the bystanders, as funeral mourners and wedding celebrants mingle. Noria, aged 35, invites the 38-year-old Toloki to visit her at the squatter camp when the funeral is over, and the communal narrator relates their previous association in the rural village in which they grew up together. Toloki's and Noria's history, and their likely future connection, is thus sketched for the reader from the novel's opening pages. The narrative tensions demonstrated in the first chapter are particularly striking in the communal narrator's insistence that life in the country villages from which the novel's protagonists are drawn is not substantially different from life in this urban settlement: 'It is not different, really, here in the city. Just like back in the village, we live our lives together as one'. He continues:

> *We know everything about everybody. We even know things that happen when we are not there; things that happen behind people's closed doors deep in the middle of the night. We are the all-seeing eye of the village gossip. When in our orature, the storyteller begins the story, 'They say it once happened…' we are the 'they'. No individual owns any story. The community is the owner of the story and it can tell it the way it deems fit* (*Ibid*, 12).

Although the concepts of 'the all-seeing eye of the village gossip' and of communal responsibility and communal ownership have great narrative power in orchestrating the implications of African humanism or *ubuntu*, Mda creates a narratological impasse in his deliberate conflation, from the beginning of the story, of the roles of communal narrator and omniscient narrator. We are told: 'We would not be needing to justify the communal voice that tells this story if you had not wondered how we became so omniscient in the affairs of Toloki and Noria' (*Ibid*, 12). For of course the role of the communal narrator is different from that of the omniscient narrator. The communal narrator's voice reflects both the strengths and weaknesses of the collective, and so the perspectives he enacts are necessarily partial. The omniscient narrator's voice, by contrast, must orchestrate the author's understanding of the whole context of the story-world in which the communal narrator speaks, and must instruct the reader in how to interpret these conflicting discourses.

This is a problem that, by the time he writes *The Madonna of Excelsior*, Mda has solved by counterpointing descriptions of Claerhout's paintings against the communal narrator's accounts of life in Excelsior. Through *ecphrasis*, the incorporation of the contents of paintings into fiction, the authorial narrator vividly describes the subjects, colours and moods of Claerhout's eccentric symbolist/expressionist studies of the local people. The reader of *The Madonna of Excelsior* is taught how to distinguish between the communal narrator's perceptions — both valuable for, and limited by, their connection with the community — and the authorial narrator's perceptions. (S)he is taught to perceive both these voices as different from the values and attitudes communicated by the popular press reporting the Miscegenation Trial. *The Madonna of Excelsior* thus juxtaposes three disparate narrative levels, which the reader must recognise and compare in order to interpret the novel's story-world. *Ways of Dying*, in conflating the voices of the communal narrator and the omniscient narrator, makes no such discrimination available to the reader. This fusing and blurring of narrative perspectives sometimes makes the novel's story-world difficult to follow, contributing to the sense of implausibility on which critics have remarked.

The communal narrator insists on *ubuntu*, on the life of the community and the way in which the community shapes acts of storytelling. But the reader becomes aware of the existence of competing and dissenting voices underlying the narrative. For Toloki's and Noria's stories, as they emerge, deny the communal narrator's statements. Life in the country village from which Toloki and Noria originate is fundamentally dissimilar to life in the city, which is where we meet them. Both have come to the city with inflated hopes and expectations: Toloki of an 'odyssey to a wondrous world of freedom and riches' (*Ibid*, 59), where he will find 'love and fortune' (*Ibid*, 104); Noria of urban glamour and allure — 'the streets of the city were paved with gold and diamonds, after all' (*Ibid*, 135). Yet for both Toloki and Noria this *Bildungsroman* optimism is frustrated as they complete the transition from rural to urban. Noria's first child, Vutha, dies; worn down by drudgery in the shebeen in which she is working, Noria also loses the gift of laughter that has accompanied her from early childhood. Toloki's three-month journey to the city is equally traumatic, blighted by the torture and death of individuals who have helped him on the way. So the novel's story-world, as it is revealed to the reader, contradicts the communal narrator's celebration of *ubuntu* and his claim that the life of the country and that of the city are similar. Although Toloki and Noria experienced the range of emotional problems characteristic of adolescence in the rural village in which they lived, nowhere during this period were they confronted with the legislated violence of the city's 'ways of dying'.

'That stuck-up bitch' Noria

If *Ways of Dying's* narrative is shaped by the heteroglossia of competing ideas, like those expressed by the narrator and those expressed by Toloki, these reflect the many discordant voices of the novel's apartheid setting. Form and content thus merge in a structure that is both confusing and revealing to the reader[5] — confusing because the position of the narrator is not individuated, but bleeds into other characters' perceptions; revealing because it records the effect of communal prejudice and gossip on the construction of individual identity. For instance, Noria's story is initially always accompanied, in the narrator's account, by the epithet 'that stuck-up bitch'. As the novel unfolds, this epithet is revealed to have no connection with her behaviour. But because Noria is both loved and feared by the settlement dwellers — loved for her beauty and her seductive voice, feared for her sexual power — the narrator's account is infected and confused by patriarchal ambivalence. His prejudice is initially transferred to his account of Toloki's first dealings with Noria: 'He has no doubt that this is Noria, the beautiful stuck-up bitch from his village' (*Ibid*, 11). But it is not Toloki who finds Noria either beautiful or stuck-up at

5 'Along with the internal contradictions inside the object itself, the prose writer witnesses as well the unfolding of social heteroglossia surrounding the object, the Tower of Babel mixing of languages that goes on around any object' (Bakhtin: 1981, 278).

this point; these attributes have long been noted and conflated in the reactions of other people, first in her rural village, then in the city. Toloki is shown to be outside of these reactions.

So when the communal narrator moves into Toloki's mind, reporting thoughts as though they were Toloki's, he introduces a prejudice that does not emanate from Toloki, as in the comment that links him to the funeral of Noria's son: 'It was just sheer luck that there was a funeral yesterday: only because that stuck-up bitch was sensible enough to insist that her son be buried on Christmas day' (*Ibid*, 25). The epithet that the communal narrator at first insists on applying to Noria comes from his combined resentment of, and admiration for, her power. That the Street Committee acceded to her wish to hold the funeral on Christmas Day 'just shows how much power Noria still has — especially over men' (*Ibid*, 25).

The narrator's bias against Noria goes right back to the early days, when she and Toloki were growing up in their rural village. There Noria's voice had inspired Jwara's creativity in making his figurines; without her, he could not work. Noria's unconscious power stirs up jealousy in the community; others besides the narrator make disparaging remarks about her. Toloki's mother screams at her husband: 'You spend all your time with that stuck-up bitch, Noria, and you do not care for your family' (*Ibid*, 29). Toloki, by contrast, 'does not remember' that his own mother is the source of the epithet that clings to Noria for years. The communal narrator initially loses no opportunity to repeat the epithet, revealing the depth of his ambivalence: 'We all loved the stuck-up bitch, for she had such beautiful laughter' (*Ibid*, 31). His prejudice also attaches to That Mountain Woman because she 'had no respect for our ways, and talked with men anyhow she liked'. This resentment of her 'shamelessness' — her lack of respect for male authority — combines oddly with his admiration for her powers as healer.

Interestingly, the communal narrator's prejudice against Noria, fed by all the voices that have resented her since her childhood, begins to evaporate when he looks at her. Now we move from telling to showing, as the narrator begins to focalise Noria rather than describing others' opinions of her. He now transfers his new perception of Noria to Toloki. Despite the trauma she has suffered in the burning down of her shack, Noria is '[t]all and graceful. Sharp features. Smooth, pitch-black complexion — which in the village we call poppy-seed beauty' (*Ibid*, 50). When Toloki looks at her, '[s]he looks beautiful, this Noria, standing surrounded by debris. Holding flowers of different colours. For the first time in his life he sees her as a woman. Not just as Noria the stuck-up bitch, daughter of That Mountain Woman' (*Ibid*, 51). When Noria thanks Toloki for the zinnias he has brought her, which remind her of his drawings as a child, vision becomes linked to memory and triggers performance. Toloki will go on, at the end of the novel, to draw pictures of people that are valued by the community. This transition to creativity is enabled by his collaboration with Noria and by the mutual process of recognition, which enables an altered cognition.

From this moment onwards, the narrator moves away from the 'stuck-up bitch' epithet; like Toloki, he now sees Noria 'for the first time in his life'. Her behaviour is suddenly revealed to be grounded in respect; it is the opposite of 'stuck-up': 'Noria never refers to the area as a squatter camp, or to the residents as squatters' (*Ibid*, 53). As they work together to rebuild Noria's shack, the newly independent Noria — no longer willing to take money from men — and the Toloki who has reinvented himself in the city begin to reveal themselves to the reader. Recognising in himself the 'worms of jealousy' diagnosed by That Mountain Woman, the narrator's resentment of Noria recedes. He shows us instead the new closeness between Toloki and Noria as they build the shack together. Admiring the beauty he helped to create, Toloki is filled with wonder at the fact that he has accepted Noria's invitation for them to live together; he too has begun to see Noria anew. The narrator's celebration of Noria's 'knowing how to live' starts when he enacts processes of focalisation in the shack-building episode. These are graphically conveyed to the reader and replace the 'stuck-up bitch' epithet with which he introduced Noria.

By the end of the novel, we have crossed from the communal narrator's biased, patriarchal perspectives to Toloki's acute awareness that it is the women who work hardest for the community, although they get no recognition within the settlement. By making the reader see Noria through Toloki's eyes, and by showing the reader the miracle of their creative collaboration, the narrator teaches himself to see anew. He no longer needs to rely on the biased perspectives of a community that has taken out its resentment against Noria by calling her 'that stuck-up bitch'.

Bakhtin's demonstration of social and ideological conflicts embodied in the heteroglossia of a community's many languages can thus be seen in the context of the apartheid-generated prejudice against Noria, a woman disempowered by a system that marginalises blacks and women. This prejudice is strongly evident in the narrator's opening remarks about Noria, who is both admired and envied by the men in her settlement. But when the narrator brings the reader closer to Noria by focalising her, his perceptions, attitudes and values begin to undergo change. Bakhtin remarks that 'self-consciousness is arrived at dialogically by an inner polemic with the social values which inevitably first structure our social being' (Bakhtin in Morris: 1994, 16). The narrator's move from unthinking repetition of social prejudices to a process of vision that recreates Noria's identity is an example of this dialogism and this inner polemic — listening first to other voices and then to his own voice as he sees and records the developing identities of Noria and Toloki.

Carnival, grotesque realism, degradation

I move now to another set of Bakhtinian constructs that have relevance for Mda's creation of Toloki as Professional Mourner. These are *carnival, grotesque realism* and *degradation*. 'Carnival,' Pam Morris notes, 'is one of Bakhtin's most influential concepts, second only to "dialog[ism]". In one way it can be seen as yet another term for a centrifugal force that apposes the centralising imposition of the monologic word' (Morris: 1994, 20). In this concept of carnival 'Bakhtin stresses the sensuous, concrete forms of carnival gesture and ritual because its whole meaning derives from the physical materiality of the human body ... Bakhtin uses the term "grotesque realism" to describe the comically grandiose representation of the body. Such comical grandeur indicates the fundamental ambivalence of all carnivalesque meaning as Bakhtin sees it; it always simultaneously ridicules and celebrates, crowns and decrowns, elevates and debases' (*Ibid*, 21).

'Comical grandeur' well describes the Toloki we encounter in the novel's opening pages. His is a curious blend of naïveté and sagacity. He is naïve in his hope that he can become a Professional Mourner 'without becoming involved in human quarrels' (Mda: 1995, 23–4), a hope shown to be unrealistic in the quarrelsome world of the novel's opening. But he is sagacious in creating for himself a role that addresses the anthropological universals of death and bereavement and that draws together past and future, local and global, and living and dead. Toloki's functions or roles as Professional Mourner in his interactions with the township dwellers are deeply significant. Mda endows Toloki with an agency born of performance. Invoking Bakhtin's notions of carnival, grotesque realism and degradation helps the reader to understand this agency that counterpoints the themes of life and death on which the novel turns. 'Comical grandeur' captures the novel's central chronotope of the cemetery — a place where people congregate to support one another and remember the dead; a place of grief and hilarity, where memory reinvokes the past in relation to the present and future and where, in the narrow confines of the overcrowded township, wedding and funeral processions intermingle.

The novel is framed entirely by carnival, as it opens on Christmas Day and ends on New Year's Day. This carnival framing reinforces the central epiphany that 'our ways of dying are our ways of living' (*Ibid*, 98), for central to the meaning of carnival is an insistence on 'the body of all the people' (Bakhtin in Morris: 1994, 21). This communal body 'brings together in one sensuous image life and death as a continually renewing process of generation' (*Ibid*, 21). Carnival is associated with celebration, feasting, music, dancing. Enacting this celebration is the grotesque body that 'is not individualised; it is the undying body of all the people, comically debased so that it may be festively reborn' (*Ibid*, 194). Central to both carnival and grotesque realism is the concept of debasement or degradation: 'The essential principle of grotesque realism is degradation, that is the lowering of all that is high, spiritual, ideal, abstract; it is a transfer to the material level, to the sphere of earth and body in their indissoluble unity' (*Ibid*, 205). Bakhtin continues: 'Earth is an element that devours, swallows up (the grave, the womb) and at the same time an element of birth, of renascence ... Degradation here means coming down to earth, the contact with earth as an element that swallows up and gives birth at the same time' (*Ibid*, 206). He concludes: 'Finally, debasement is the fundamental artistic principle of grotesque realism; all that is sacred and exalted is rethought on the level of the material bodily stratum or else combined and mixed with its images' (*Ibid*, 239).

Toloki is immediately recognisable as a figure embodying the paradoxes of grotesque realism. As Professional Mourner he appeals to people's self-respect and the dignity that comes of understanding the past. He debunks 'all that is high, spiritual, ideal, or abstract' by insisting on the spheres of earth and body 'in their indissoluble unity'. In fact, Toloki's customers are always the poor, never the well-off, and he is happy to receive whatever poor people can afford. He is himself of the earth, earthy, as his smell attests. On the Christmas Day when we first meet Toloki, the narrator recounts that people back away from his body odour. Entering into Toloki's self-perception, he asks:

> *Why would anyone hate his sacred fragrance? It is the perfume that he splashes all over his body as part of the ritual of his profession before he goes to a funeral. On this fiery Christmas day, its strong smell is exacerbated by the stench of sweat, not only from his body, but from those in the crowd as well* (Mda: 1995, 8).

The grotesque realism of Toloki's smell calls to mind Bakhtin on the body and the Underworld: 'The downward thrust of grotesque realism affirms the material life of the body and of the earthly world. The conquest of fear [opens] the way ... for a new historical perception of human life' (Bakhtin in Morris: 1994, 227). Carnival and grotesque realism surround us from the novel's opening pages. The funeral crowd of the opening sequence blends with a 'wedding procession of many cars and buses, all embellished with colourful ribbons and balloons' (Mda: 1995, 10). There is loud singing and a comic stalemate as bridal and funeral etiquettes clash. Toloki is much in evidence through sight and smell, dressed as he is in his Professional Mourner's costume and exuding a strong odour. The costume, we learn, has only been rented once before, by some Americans who wanted it for a Halloween party. Its connection with carnival celebration is thus proclaimed. Toloki is focalised in comic mode by the narrator, who brings home his African appearance: 'Above his eyes rest thick eyebrows, like the hairy *thithiboya* caterpillar' (*Ibid*, 11). Toloki's characterisation is both somatic and sensory. The reader is drawn into his responsiveness to the sights and sounds of a Christmas setting:

> *At the window of the tower, perhaps in the belfry, Toloki can see a Christmas tree with twinkling lights of red, green, blue, yellow and white. The cathedral is a few streets away from his headquarters, as he calls the quayside shelter and waiting-room where he spends his nights. But since it is on a hill, he can enjoy the beauty of the lights, and tonight the bells will lull him to a blissful sleep with carols* (*Ibid*, 14).

The relationship of degradation to carnival is well illustrated by Toloki's responsiveness to the sensory stimuli of his environment and his imaginative connection with individuals such as the Oriental monks, whose spiritual devotion is linked to their connection with death and the excremental:[6]

> *He sees himself in the dazzling light of the* aghori sadhu, *held in the same awesome veneration that the devout Hindus show the votaries. He spends his sparse existence on the cremation ground, cooks his food on the fires of a funeral pyre, and feeds on human waste and human corpses. He drinks his own urine to quench his thirst* (*Ibid*, 15).

At the same time as he imagines these privations, Toloki savours the taste of Swiss roll and green onions: 'The food is singing in his mouth' (15).

The carnival context on which the novel opens on Christmas Day is repeated in the closing sequences, which take place on New Year's Day. Now teenagers cross-dress and go from house to house asking for cakes and sweets, as on Halloween night in America. Toloki as *flâneur*, relaxed and at ease in the city, experiences a sensory explosion made up equally of the visual and the auditory:

> *The taxi stops in the central business district. He alights and walks in the familiar streets. They are decorated with lights of different colours, and with banners and bunting — all in preparation for the parades that will take place in the afternoon to celebrate New Year. Over the years, Toloki has watched many of these parades of*

6 Toloki manages to spiritualise his connection with the excremental by placing it in the realm of the imagination. A less edifying example of grotesque realism is that of the drunk in the shelter where Toloki initially lives: 'He takes a long swig from a bottle wrapped in brown paper, and drifts into a noisy snooze. His toothless mouth moves all the time, like a cow chewing the cud. He passes wind thunderously, which suddenly wakes him up. He thinks this is tremendously funny, so he cackles shamelessly. The stench of rotten cabbage drifts from the drunk, and hovers above Toloki' (Mda: 1995, 116).

colourful dancers with painted faces, dressed in silk suits. Their clownish antics and their funny songs always make the spectators on the pavements laugh (*Ibid*, 195).

Finally, the novel ends on the full sensorium dramatised by carnival — sight, sound and smell. There are glowing fluorescent lights and moonshine illuminates Toloki's and Noria's shack, the plastic colours of which become fluorescent. Attracted by the glow, crickets chirp and other insects buzz. The smell of burning tyres fills the air, but this smell is of life, not death.

'Laughing truth' and the speaking voice

Crucial to Bakhtin's notion of carnival is the idea of folk humour:

> *This folk humour … is a complex system of meaning existing alongside and in opposition to the 'authoritarian word' of dominant orthodoxy. Its most powerful mode of expression is laughter, but it stems from a comprehensive way of seeing human existence that cannot be isolated in any particular aesthetic form … Everybody participates in carnival* (Morris: 1994, 194).

In relation to apartheid and post-apartheid South Africa, laughter is politically subversive, destabilising authoritarian structures by introducing a comedy that proclaims equality. 'Medieval laughter,' Bakhtin writes, 'when it triumphed over the fear inspired by the mystery of the word and by power, boldly unveiled the truth about both. It resisted praise, flattery, hypocrisy. This laughing truth, expressed in curses and abusive words, degraded power' (*Ibid*, 210). Noria has, from her early childhood, possessed the gift of laughter, inspiring Jwara's creativity and drawing villagers into her ambit. Exposed to city life, where she works in a shebeen, Noria loses this gift until her life story intersects with Toloki's. When together they rebuild Noria's shack, Noria begins to laugh again as she and Toloki exchange stories of their past:

> *The stories of the past are painful. But when Toloki and Noria talk about them they laugh. Laughter is known to heal even the deepest of wounds. Noria's laughter has the power to heal troubled souls. This afternoon, as the two of them sit in front of the shanty, exhausted from building last night's creation, and refreshing themselves with stories of the past and soured porridge, Toloki lavishly bathes his soul in her laughter* (Mda: 1995, 95).

This laughter, 'the innocent laughter of a child' (*Ibid*, 152) reminds Toloki of Noria's famous peals of laughter when she was a little girl. It signals the end of the repression through which Noria has dealt, in her city life, with the death of her children. At the end of the novel, Toloki and Noria build a big shack to house Jwara's figurines, so that 'children could come and laugh whenever they felt like it'. Laughter in *Ways of Dying* is individually and collectively cathartic.

Noria cannot laugh, however, until she can speak, and she cannot speak freely until Toloki enables her to do so. Before Toloki asks Noria to speak of

Vutha's death, she has been pressured to keep silent: 'She should not condemn the perpetrators in any public forum, as this would give ammunition to the enemy' (*Ibid*, 178). Telling Toloki about her sense of betrayal, Noria speaks of her child's murder at the hands of the Young Tigers. Toloki weeps in sympathy, and the two begin a new phase of emotional closeness that fuels their creative collaboration and feeds back into the community.

This episode, which links laughter with free speech, highlights Bakhtin's proclamation of the novel's enactment of freedom: 'The human being in the novel is first, foremost and always a speaking human being; the novel requires speaking persons bringing with them their own unique ideological discourse, their own language' (Bakhtin in Holquist: 1981, 332). Bakhtin relates the motif of the speaking person to the realms of ethical and legal thought and discourse:

> *All fundamental categories of ethical and legal enquiry and evolution refer to speaking persons precisely as such: conscience (the 'voice of conscience', the 'inner word'), repentance (a free admission, a statement of wrongdoing by the person himself), truth and falsehood, being liable and not liable, the right to vote … and so on. An independent, responsible and active discourse is the fundamental indicator of an ethical, legal and political human being* (*Ibid*, 349).

This linking of free speech with ethical enquiry has particular cogency for the politics of a newly democratic South Africa.

Chapter Three

From 'the speaking voice' to intertextuality in *The Heart of Redness*

Introduction

From Bakhtin's notion of 'the speaking voice' in Chapter Two, we move here to the ways in which many voices dialogue to create intertextuality. Tobias Döring explains:

> *[A]ll literature partly continues and partly contests previous writing: continues because the very forms of language are inherited and taken over, contests because these forms are now used in a different context to establish different meanings ... texts are never closed, contained and clearly bounded by their authors, but principally open, limitless, accessible from many sides and for diverse influences* (Döring: 2008, 82–3).

The writing that intertextuality invites therefore contains 'repetition and resistance, or reliance on and reversal of ... given structures' (*Ibid*, 83). Particularly useful for the purposes of my argument is John Frow's definition: 'The concept of intertextuality requires that we understand the concept of text not as a self-contained structure but as differential and historical. Texts are shaped not by immanent time but by the play of divergent temporalities' (in Worton & Still: 1990, 45).

This chapter is made up of three sections. In the first, I compare and contrast Conrad's *Heart of Darkness* with Mda's *The Heart of Redness*. In the second, senior undergraduate students at the University of Cape Town explore the intertextual challenges that these two texts offer. In the last section, I explore issues of imitation and innovation in Mda's text as it builds on Peires' *The Dead Will Arise*.

Community and agency in *The Heart of Redness* and Joseph Conrad's *Heart of Darkness*

Zakes Mda has elicited strong critical response over the past decade. Rogier Courau, discussing 'literary and political historiography in the postcolony', draws attention to Mda's fusion of 'official history and community stories in the postcolonial context' (Courau: 2004, 7) through his use of 'the speaking voice of a communal consciousness' (*Ibid*, 8), his ability to draw on the past to invigorate the present, and his engagement in 'artistic and cultural translation' (*Ibid*, 12). Johan van Wyk speaks of what he takes to be a literature of transition marked by 'resurgence of the repressed, loss of the reality principle, dream and mysticism' (Van Wyk: 1997, 80), while Margaret Mervis sees Mda as incorporating orature and magic realism to move beyond anger at apartheid towards the reconstruction of individuals and their communities. David Lloyd discusses the 'polyphony of voices that allows Mda to present a richly complex and ironised debate about the issues facing contemporary South African society and its historical colonial antecedents' (Lloyd: 2001, 35), while J.U. Jacobs, writing of the new Constitution's refusal to define Africanness by race, colour, gender or historical origins, points out that unlike the stereotyped figures of liberationist writers, Mda's characters are 'allowed ... complex and (extra)ordinary individuality' (Jacobs: 2000, 68). He also draws on African music to show how 'Mda turns to traditional performance to mediate a culture in the process of transition and renewal', arguing that *The Heart of Redness* is a 'split-tone narrative' employing a 'palimpsest structure' (Jacobs: 2002, 227). Wendy Woodward shows how Mda as a postcolonial writer deconstructs Western dualisms in order to rehabilitate a traditional Xhosa world-view grounded in the 'contemporary issues of post-1994 South Africa' (Woodward: 2003, 173). She demonstrates the imbrication of place with identity in Mda's fiction and discusses his use of the Bakhtinian carnivalesque.

These writers insist on the importance for Mda of community,[1] history and memory in constituting postcolonial agency. Underlying their thinking is the concept, important from late 1996 onwards, of an 'African Renaissance'

1 Several critics dispute what I see as Mda's evocation of the ideal of community. Grant Farred remarks that in *Ways of Dying* 'Toloki the artist represents the benign face of post-apartheid society's preference for the upwardly mobile black individual rather than the demands of the township masses; he is a character obsessed with creative expression and spiritual self-improvement ... focused on the exceptionalism and singularity of the individual subject' (Farred: 2000, 192). For Farred, 'Mda's novel may be said to enunciate the death of radical politics, of the commitment to transforming and materially improving the lives of the black underclass' (*Ibid*, 196). Konstantin Sofianos sees *The Heart of Redness* as attempting to reconcile not just Believers and Unbelievers, 'but more importantly the contradictions within the discourse of African Renaissance' (Sofianos: 2004, 31). Sofianos remarks: 'It is a stark reality that the cumulative trickle-down prosperity prompted by the prophets of neo-liberalism and the free-market has remained as elusive in post-apartheid South Africa as the sight of fattened cattle rising from the waves was in 1856–1857' (*Ibid*, 35). He concludes: 'To speak with Benedict Anderson, the white middle-class is [...] invited to join the imagined community of the nation, but the price the text is willing to pay for this accommodation is the betrayal of those "co-operative" values it has invested with such redemptive possibilities' (*Ibid*, 38).

introduced in Chapter One, whose visionary language incorporates five crucial principles: 'The encouragement of cultural exchange; the emancipation of African women from patriarchy; the mobilisation of youth; the broadening, deepening and sustenance of democracy and the initiation of sustainable economic development' (Vale & Maseko: 1998, 274).[2] Equally important in the aesthetics of liberation post 1994 is the work of the black South African writer, Njabulo S. Ndebele. In *Rediscovery of the Ordinary*, Ndebele critiques the writing of politically engaged South African writers of the 1970s and 1980s as a literature of spectacle:[3] 'I came to the realisation ... that our literature ought to seek to move away from an early preoccupation with demonstrating the obvious existence of oppression. It exists. The task is to explore how and why people can survive under such harsh conditions. The mechanisms of survival and resistance are ... far from simple' (Ndebele: 1991, 158).

In this section I propose to juxtapose Mda's text of survival and resistance, *The Heart of Redness* (2000) — described by David Attwell as 'the most ambitious work of fiction by a black South African writer in well over a decade' — with Joseph Conrad's *Heart of Darkness*, written over a century ago (1898). My purpose is twofold: to demonstrate Mda's postcolonial deconstruction of the tropes of empire and his redeployment of history to create a transformed African reality, and to demonstrate Conrad's insight into the processes of colonial domination that his protagonist, Marlow, exposes and with which he simultaneously colludes. I want to draw attention to salient similarities between Mda and Conrad's texts: their rich intertextuality, their foregrounding of the importance of the reader's role in creating the meaning of the text, their interrogation of the binary thinking underlying Western thought and their exposure of colonial strategies of appropriation in mapping and naming. Then I move on to contrasts between the texts' depictions of landscape (Conrad's chiaroscuro settings versus Mda's vibrant, colourful Africa), discuss the divergent cultural significance of song and dance in both texts and end with a consideration of the dream-world, examining Conrad's departures from realism into surrealism and Mda's departures from realism into magic realism.

2 See also, on Thabo Mbeki and a 'people-centred society', J.U. Jacobs (2000).

3 'We can now summarise the characteristics of the spectacular in this context. The spectacular documents; it indicts implicitly; it is demonstrative, preferring exteriority to interiority; it keeps the larger issues of society in our minds, obliterating the details; it provides identification through recognition and feeling rather than through observation and analytic thought; it calls for emotion rather than conviction; it establishes a vast sense of presence without offering intimate knowledge; it confirms without necessarily offering a challenge. It is the literature of the powerless identifying the key factor responsible for their powerlessness. Nothing beyond this can be expected of it' (Ndebele: 1991, 46).

In the Dedication to *The Heart of Redness,* Mda acknowledges J.B. Peires's book, *The Dead Will Arise* (1989), as the main historical source for the story of the prophetess Nongqawuse and the Xhosa Cattle-Killing of 1856–1857. His indebtedness to *Heart of Darkness* is equally obvious. Kurtz's postscript 'exterminate the brutes' is transferred to the beheading of Xikixa, ancestor of the Believers and Unbelievers of Mda's novel, under British colonial rule. Marlow's appalled vision of heads on stakes as he approaches the Inner Station in the Congo is echoed by Mda's chief protagonist, Camagu, who recoils in horror when he sees five dried-out heads of Bushmen in London's Natural History Museum and is equally shocked to discover that '[i]n Paris, the private parts of a Khoikhoi woman called Saartjie Baartman are kept in a bottle' (Mda: 2000, 194). In these extracts, both Mda and Conrad interrogate the relationship between 'barbarism' and 'civilisation'. Other inter-texts suggested for *The Heart of Redness* include Zoe Wicomb's *David's Story* (also written in 2000), with its protagonist's Griqua ancestry reverberating with Mda's fusion of Xhosa and Khoi genealogies, and Gabriel Márquez's *One Hundred Years of Solitude,* with its magic realist narrative techniques.[4] Inter-texts for *Heart of Darkness* include works by Virgil, Dante, Goethe and Plato.[5] What the density of these intertextual connections foregrounds is a richness of figurative language, a juxtaposition of textual and cultural referents, and a deployment of irony and ambiguity that complicates the reader's response to both texts.

Shared terrain

Both Mda and Conrad challenge conventional Eurocentric ways of reading. The narrative structure of *Heart of Darkness* undermines teleological readings of history, for Marlow's journey, a travesty of the quest, is circular, ending where it began and recording a black hole at the centre of the story where — geographically and psychologically — Kurtz is situated. Where the frame narrator presents a version of history that is 'heroic, progressive, incontrovertible' (Fothergill: 1989, 15), Marlow's narrative is fissured by hesitations and contradictions as his story poses moral and epistemological challenges to the conventional binaries familiar to Western thought: 'Lightness/darkness … illumination/blindness, idea/idol, civilised/savage, conqueror/conquest, vital/dead, and dream/nightmare' (*Ibid,* 22). Mda's narrative transposes this binary structure into the specifically African world, undermining 'dualistic … thinking about differences

4 See Jacobs (2002, 228).

5 See Lothe, Jakob (2001) 'Cumulative intertextuality in *Heart of Darkness*: Virgil, Dante and Goethe's Faust'. In Fincham (ed) (177–196). See also Fincham, Gail (2003) '*Heart of Darkness* and Plato's *Republic*: A reverse parable' in *L'Epoque Conradienne,* 29, 95–109.

between the human and the nonhuman, as well as between the living and the dead, and the spirit world' (Woodward: 2003, 183).

Neither text allows the reader to reach a centre; in both ironies proliferate. Hillis Miller has remarked that 'Marlow promises to pass … illumination on to his hearers … the fulfilment of this promise to reveal … remains always future, something yet to come, eschatological or messianic rather than teleological' (Miller: 2002, 32–3). *Heart of Darkness* ends inconclusively, with Marlow unable to profit from his quest or to pass on comforting redemptive truths to the frame auditors or the reader. In fact, by the end of his story the frame narrator, whose earlier pronouncements were so full of jingoistic confidence, has taken on Marlow's bleak focalisation, seeing the Thames as continuous with the Congo River: 'The tranquil waterway leading to the uttermost ends of the earth flowed sombre under an overcast sky — seemed to lead into the heart of an immense darkness' (Conrad: 1946, 162). And what of Mda's central protagonist, Camagu? He has become, by the end of the novel, one of a 'little trinity' (Lloyd: 2001, 38). United with Qukezwa, the modern reincarnation of the prophetess Nongqawuse, and father to a baby named Heitsi in honour of his Khoi ancestor, Camagu appears to bring together Western know-how with African wisdom, 'the modernization of redness' (*Ibid*, 38). But this triumphant resolution is undercut by the novel's closing pages, in which the omniscient narrator records Camagu's pleasure at his integration into Qolorha, but issues a warning about the future:

> *[Camagu] feels fortunate that he lives in Qolorha. Those who want to preserve indigenous plants and birds have won the day there. At least for now. But for how long? The whole country is ruled by greed. Everyone wants to have his or her snout in the trough. Sooner or later the powers that be may decide, in the name of the people, that it is good for the people to have a gambling complex at Qolorha-by-Sea. And the gambling complex shall come into being* (Mda: 2000, 319).

For Mda, as for Conrad, the self-identification achieved by his protagonist is individual and provisional; it does not guarantee closure.

Both texts are striking in the dramatisation of the strategies of mapping and naming by which the coloniser controls the colonised. Early in his story Marlow recounts how

> *when I was a little chap I had a passion for maps. I could look at South America, or Africa, or Australia, and lose myself in all the glories of exploration. At that time there were many blank spaces on the earth, and when I saw one that looked particularly inviting on a map [...] I would put my finger on it and say, when I grow up I will go there* (Conrad: 1946, 52).

But by the time he is old enough to become an explorer himself, the enticing blank space of his childhood dream 'was not a blank space any more. It had got filled since my boyhood with rivers and lakes and names. It had ceased to be a blank space of delightful mystery — a white patch for a boy to dream gloriously over. It had become a place of darkness' (*Ibid*, 52). As David Spurr notes, 'The name of the principal blank space is repressed in Conrad's narrative, the name of Africa being everywhere displaced by the ambiguous and portentous phrase which serves as the title of the text. By means of this displacement of the referent, Africa is no longer bound in time and space, but becomes the *figure* of darkness and "nothingness"' (Spurr: 1993, 94). Marlow does not recognise this suppression of the referent in the 'blank space' of Africa because, as adventurer, he wants to insert himself there. He does, however, register the corruption of colonial appropriation that turns the 'blank space' into 'a place of darkness'. But this recognition is short-lived for in Brussels, visiting the Company offices prior to his departure for the Belgian Congo, he is once again stirred to excitement as he looks at the Company map and those places claimed by Britain in the Scramble for Africa: 'There was a vast amount of red — good to see at any time, because one knows that some real work is done in there, a deuce of a lot of blue, a little green, smears of orange and, on the East Coast, a purple patch, to show where the jolly pioneers of progress drink the jolly lager-beer' (Conrad: 1946, 55).

Of the map-as-logo in imperial cartography,[6] Benedict Anderson writes illuminatingly:

> *Its origins were reasonably innocent — the practice of the imperial states of colouring their colonies on maps an imperial dye. In London's imperial maps, British colonies were usually pink-red, French purple-blue, Dutch yellow-brown, and so on. As this 'jigsaw' effect became normal, each 'piece' could be wholly detached from its geographic context. In its final form all explanatory glosses could be summarily removed, lines of longitude and latitude, place names, signs for rivers, seas, and mountains, neighbours. Pure sign, no longer compass to the world. In this shape, the map entered an infinitely reproducible series, available for transfer to posters, official seals, letterheads, magazine and textbook covers, tablecloths, and hotel walls. Instantly recognizable, everywhere visible, the logo-map penetrated deep into the popular imagination* (Anderson: 1983, 175).

Colonial cartography, then, not only imposed an alien identity on indigenous territory; its purpose was equally to sever that territory from everything that

6 Elleke Boehmer emphasises the connections between colonial domination and the cartographic expertise on which it was built: 'From the European point of view ... colonialism was a metaphoric and cartographic — as well as a legalistic — undertaking. A country was "mapped" or spatially conceived using figures which harked back to home ground ... Classifications and codes imported from Europe were matched to peoples, cultures, and topographies that were entirely un-European' (Boehmer: 1995, 49).

constituted its social and geographical identity. Colonial cartography replaced indigenous names with names of its own devising: in *Heart of Darkness* Marlow's first sighting of the African coast is of places 'with names like Gran'Bassam, Little Popo, names that seemed to belong to some sordid farce acted in front of a sinister back-cloth' (Conrad: 1946, 61). Elsewhere I have argued for the intertextual significance of this portentous description, suggesting that Conrad intends us to recognise in it Plato's Cave and to understand his novella as a reverse parable, in which the coloniser is doomed to see only shadows on the wall, while the colonised may escape from entrapment and delusion.[7]

In Mda's novel, the nineteenth-century chronotope is dominated by the governor, Sir George Grey, 'The Man Who Named Ten Rivers'. This nickname is derisively given to him by the Xhosa, who are well aware that 'he is a thief' (Mda: 2000, 96). The omniscient narrator sarcastically remarks: 'Of course he had to take their land in return for civilisation. Civilisation is not cheap [...] It did not matter that the forebears of those natives had named those rivers and mountains from time immemorial' (Mda: 2000, 95). Grey's role in suppressing indigenous resistance becomes increasingly clear as the novel develops. Initially the trader Dalton had interpreted for Grey, claiming that he only wanted to spread British civilisation and bring peace to the area; but as the narrative progresses 'The Man Who Named Ten Rivers' is revealed as a systematic destroyer of Xhosa laws and customs, as he institutes a judicial system that suppresses them. Bringing to the area his experience in Australia and New Zealand, Grey offers the indigenous people not extermination but assimilation. But after the Cattle-Killing, when thousands are dying of starvation, many are forced to work as slaves in white settlements 'being paid only in food rations' (*Ibid*, 296). Grey's plan to turn the Xhosa into 'useful servants, consumers of our goods, contributors to our revenue' (*Ibid*, 291) appears to have succeeded triumphantly.

Mda gets his own back on Grey, however: his novel is studded with Xhosa names for people and places that the European reader does not understand. Where *Heart of Darkness* dramatises cultural and linguistic imperialism in the names the 'Pilgrims' give the indigenous population ('enemies', 'rebels', 'criminals'), Mda challenges his reader's historical understanding by using many of the same names in his novel's colonial and contemporary chronotopes. Where 'The Man Who Named Ten Rivers' is revealed to be a dangerous ideologue, Mda creates a powerful counter-voice in the prophet known by his people as 'The Man of the River'. Furthermore, Mda reappropriates the

7 See Fincham, Gail (2003) '*Heart of Darkness* and Plato's *Republic*: A Reverse Parable'. *L'Epoque Conradienne*. 29. 95–109.

African landscape by giving his chief protagonist, Camagu, mystical, erotic dreams about rivers. These play a crucial role in his achievement of identity and his eventual incorporation into the Qolorha community. In Mda's novel one is acutely aware of names as carriers of identity. The same is true for Conrad's novella. Its only named protagonists are Marlow and Kurtz; the rest of the characters are defined by their roles. In the frame narrative, we have the Lawyer, the Accountant, the Director of Companies; in the Congo narrative we have the Pilgrims, the Chief Accountant, the Manager of the Central Station, the Harlequin, Kurtz's Mistress, the Intended. What these nominations centrally foreground is loss of agency: *Heart of Darkness* is peopled by characters whose identity is conveyed entirely through their (public and instrumentalising) functions rather than through their individual voices.

Salient contrasts

I go on now to sketch some salient contrasts between Mda and Conrad's texts, starting with their depiction of gender relations. The first contrast I explore is between Conrad's marginal female characters in *Heart of Darkness* and the larger-than-life women who dominate Mda's *The Heart of Redness.* Here I deploy two recent contrasting perspectives on gender representation in Mda: those of Nokuthula Mazibuko and Meg Samuelson.[8]

Mazibuko sees Mda's women 'as being at the centre of reshaping and rebuilding a post-colonial, post-apartheid South Africa' (Mazibuko: 2007, 116). For Mazibuko, women are at the centre of the [African] Renaissance: 'in the community work they do and in how they uphold the spiritual and material well-being of their families' (*Ibid*, 116). She quotes feminists who insist that in the newly liberated South Africa, gender equality is at the heart of democratic debates. Mazibuko contends that Mda 'depicts women as the ones who bear the brunt of the poverty caused by intersecting racial and patriarchal and economic oppression ... [they are] colourful, transgressive characters' (*Ibid*, 118). Several of Mda's women she maintains 'have had to cross boundaries carrying the mountains of racism and patriarchy on their backs' (*Ibid*, 127). She concludes that Mda 'envisions a renaissance ... founded on the principles of love and compassion, a renaissance that puts ordinary people at the centre, led by women who are the custodians of spirituality as

8 The students whose voices are recorded in the next section, 'Mda in the Classroom', were also particularly interested in gender issues in this novel. See particularly De Jager's essay, 'African Renaissance and the Women of *The Heart of Redness*' and McGrath's essay, 'Women as Agents of Change'.

expressed through art and beauty' (*Ibid*, 130).[9] By contrast, Meg Samuelson sees Mda's retelling of the story of Nongqawuse's prophecy, which resulted in the Cattle-Killing, as an attempt to wrest authorship from the female prophetess in order to insist on his own authorial power: 'Women bear men's messages through their bodies and are firmly discouraged from seizing the tools of writing themselves' (Samuelson: 2009, 243). She argues that in his depiction of Nongqawuse, Mda is unwilling to acknowledge the power of the prophetess's female authorship. He therefore depicts her as 'an empty vessel for the words of others'.

For Samuelson Mda's handling of two opposing time schemes in the novel is designed to withhold modernity from the Xhosa so that they occupy a temporally prior position to the European colonists. The Xhosa can thus be made into a 'waged-labour underclass, servicing colonial capital' (*Ibid*, 234). The text, split between 'the romantic dream of a better world and the horrifying consequences of [the] act of female authorship' manages its contradictions by focusing on women's bodies.

It '[splits] aspects of Nongqawuse's legacy [into] Noma Russia and Qukezwa'. While Noma Russia's body 'figures authorial anxieties', Qukezwa's embodies 'claims of autochthony and dreams of redemption' (*Ibid*, 239). The novel thus 'offers anxious commentary on female assumptions to authorial power and women's entry into the public sphere' (*Ibid*, 243).

For Samuelson, it makes no sense 'to destabilise colonial and nationalist edifices while leaving intact the gendered representations that prop them up' (*Ibid*, 236). She maintains that Mda is unable to offer, in *The Heart of Redness*, a depiction of women protagonists that does not participate in colonial and patriarchal assumptions. My own response to Samuelson's challenging critique of the novel shifts to the narratological and applies to all of Mda's texts. In response to Samuelson's exposure of gender bias in *The Heart of*

9 Litzi Lombardozzi takes up a position close to that of Mazibuko in acknowledging Mda's sensitivity, in his plays, to gender issues: 'Mda's theatre is rich in offering perspectives of what it means to be a marginalised subject living in a male world. From these plays emanates a sense that to be female is to be faced with a special quality of violence and violation. His depictions of the cruelties against women will remain relevant in view of the still largely unchanged gender imbalances in the contemporary South African context. Mda therefore speaks as loudly to today's post-apartheid audiences as he did in the apartheid days, particularly when it comes to the portrayal of gender roles' (Lombardozzi: 2005, 225–6).

Redness,[10] and Mazibuko's celebration of the novel's female protagonists, I ask: why are Mda's most important female protagonists always voiced by male narrators? Not one tells her own story in her own voice. Mda appears here to inherit two powerful patriarchal traditions: that of the nineteenth-century European realist novel that privileges the (male) omniscient narrator and that of traditional African storytelling, which is similarly dependent on a dominant male voice.

I move now to a second contrast between Conrad's and Mda's texts, in their depiction of the African landscape. Mda's text is saturated with colour. There are the rocks around the sea at Qolorha-by-Sea where the women harvest oysters and mussels: 'Camagu is fascinated by the yellows, the brown, the greens and the red that have turned the rocks into works of abstract art' (Mda: 2000, 118); there is Zim's tree, in which red and green and yellow birds live (*Ibid*, 41), and there is the village itself, which seems to Camagu on first arrival to have been painted by a 'generous artist … using splashes of lush colour. It is a canvas where blue and green dominate. It is the blue of the skies and the distant hills, of the ocean and the rivers that flow into it. The green is of the meadows and the valleys, the tall grass and the *usundu* palms' (*Ibid*, 61). In a striking synaesthesia, Qukezwa 'sings in glaring colours. In vibrant colours. Dreamy colours. Colours that paint nightmares on barren landscapes. She haunts yesterday's reefs and ridges with redness' (*Ibid*, 312). Whereas *Heart of Darkness*, from its opening paragraph, generates only black, white and grey. The instances of this evoked chiaroscuro are too numerous to discuss. Suffice it to say that the same tension between darkness and light recurs on almost every page — in the frame narrative, in the central narrative, in Britain, Brussels, the Congo. Critics have made much of the systematic inversion of black/white stereotypes on which the story turns, but its lack of colour seems to me equally interesting. There are only two places where the text erupts into colour, and both instances are suspect: the multi-coloured map in Brussels that we have already discussed and the gaily bepatched Harlequin with his bright red and bright blue pockets, whom Marlow encounters as he approaches Kurtz's Inner Station. Neither of these epiphanies has any real connection with the African landscape. The map imposes falsely constructed identities on Africa; the Harlequin takes on an identity of shreds and patches that parallels

10 For a counter-reading to Samuelson's account of the significance of the past in this novel, see David Bell: '[In *The Heart of Redness*] … Mda uses traditional beliefs surrounding death and images of dying to explore the dynamic processes of belief-formation within the Xhosa people. In this respect, his representation questions a static concept of an African past and instead suggests a flexible African culture that absorbs, adapts and converts other beliefs into its own practices in a steady process of synthesis' (Bell: 2007, 105).

his cultural and psychic emptiness, his spirit of adventure that connects to no principles or value systems other than that of fervent discipleship.

But it is when we move to the cultural arena of song and dance and the unconscious arena of the dream that the differences between Mda's and Conrad's texts are most striking. Marlow, surrounded by what he experiences as primeval savagery, steels himself to resist 'going ashore for a howl and a dance' in the alien surroundings of 'an empty stream, a great silence, an impenetrable forest' (Conrad: 1946, 93). When he catches sight of black people on the shore, his vision of them is both fragmented and paranoid:

> *[T]here would be a glimpse of rush walls, of peaked grass-roofs, a burst of yells, a whirl of black limbs, a mass of hands clapping, of feet stamping, of bodies swaying, of eyes rolling, under the droop of heavy and motionless foliage. The steamer toiled along slowly on the edge of a black and incomprehensible frenzy. The prehistoric man was cursing us, praying to us, welcoming us — who could tell? We were cut off from the comprehension of our surroundings ... They howled and leaped, and spun, and made horrid faces; but what thrilled you was just the thought of their humanity — like yours — the thought of your remote kinship with this wild and passionate uproar* (*Ibid*, 96).

For Marlow, the antidote to regression to savagery is immersion in the conscious world of work — rivets, fixing the tinpot steamer, navigating among countless snags. He fears the unconscious world of dreams, fears libidinous atavistic excess once he succumbs to sleep. The dream is not a release. It partakes of the frightening isolation and solipsism that is man's condition: 'We live, as we dream, alone'.

In *The Heart of Redness*, by contrast, dance and dreams play a central role. Camagu returns to Africa after a thirty-year absence in America. But he has been out of the country when the toyi-toyi dance became fashionable at freedom rallies. Consequently, Camagu suffers from discrimination at job interviews, when potential employers enquire, 'Who is he? We didn't see him when we were dancing the freedom dance' (Mda: 2000, 31).[11] If the 'freedom dance' has become the exclusive property of the 'Aristocrats of the Revolution', dancing among the Xhosa at Qolorha fulfils an antithetical function, uniting the community in commemorative celebration of the ancestors. Here Mda achieves a remarkable crossover between the Believers — the traditionalists — and

11 'Liberation movements have always been attuned to the importance of their cultural expression in the power of manifestos, speeches, slogans, songs and insignia. In South Africa, during the states of emergency in the 1980s, the toyi-toyi dance — a combination of traditional African rhythms and military drill — added movement to the spectacle of the political funeral at which the praise poet, in defiance of the police ringing the cemetery, would eulogise the fallen comrade' (Chapman: 1998, 3).

the Unbelievers — those who want technological development. Both clans need to enact their connection to the past. Zim, patriarch of the Believers, sits under his wild fig tree, listening to the song of the birds. His tree is visited by the ancestors: 'there are four different kinds of ancestors: the ancestors of the sea, the ancestors of the forest, the ancestors of the veld, and the ancestors of the homestead. They are all regular visitors to the tree' (*Ibid*, 41). Similarly, Bhonco, patriarch of the Unbelievers, treasures the dance that has been taught to his followers by the original people of the area, the Bushmen or abaThwa, whose knowledge of local plants and animals is unequalled. The dance takes his people back to the land of the ancestors by inducing a trance. In this trance Bhonco's people experience a sadness that makes future happiness possible: 'Under the *umsintsi* tree the elders present a wonderful spectacle of suffering. They are invoking grief by engaging in a memory ritual' (*Ibid*, 83).

When towards the end of the novel the abaThwa threaten to take back the dance because the Unbelievers have become alienated from their traditions, Bhonco asks despairingly: 'How will the Cult of the Unbelievers survive without the dance?' The novel insists on the cathartic function of grief and the centrality of memory in creating a community's future. Memory and grief are embodied in dance, for (as David Coplan points out) dance, like orature, makes meaning visible (see Jacobs: 2000, 72). And as Mda himself points out, 'Among the marginalised and disadvantaged in the rural areas and in urban slums … art is still part of the common festival. We all sing and dance' (Mda: 1994, 145).

Equally, the world of dreams constantly intersects with the waking world, linking the present to the past. In the nineteenth-century chronotope, Qukezwa plays the *umrhubhe*, a musical instrument like the voice of mountain spirits that 'creates a world of dreams' (Mda: 2000, 177), particularly the vision of the new people who will arise from the waves and drive the colonists from the land. In the modern chronotope, the latterday Qukezwa is angry that Camagu '[o]f late … has been featuring in her dreams. And she tells him so. She does not like that. He has no business imposing himself on her dreams' (*Ibid*, 196). For Camagu — like Marlow — dreams are connected with the sexual drive; Qukezwa has the power to sing him to orgasm. But his connection with her is ultimately healing, for she teaches him to understand himself and his new environment. By the end of the novel they have married and borne (magically!) a son.

The importance of the dream-world for the characters in *The Heart of Redness* derives from Mda's indebtedness to an African oral tradition[12] that frequently converges with what has been called, in the South American context,

12 'Central themes in the oral traditions of southern Africa — in the tales, histories, heroic poetry and songs — have to do with tradition and freedom, and the implicit dilemma created in the conflict between the two concepts' (Scheub: 1996, xxi). *The Heart of Redness* centrally addresses this conflict.

'magic realism'. Mda, in interview, stresses that his preoccupation with magic realism predates his familiarity with Márquez and is specifically African — 'as Africans we always live with magic' (in Naidoo: 1997, 250) — just as his use of a communal narrator derives from African oral traditions: 'this is how African people tell stories' (*Ibid*, 254). Insisting that he was writing in a magic realist mode 'long before I heard of the Latin Americans', Mda declares:

> *[In African culture] the unreal happens as part of reality. The supernatural is presented without judgement. A lot of my work is set in the rural areas, because they retain that magic, whereas the urban areas have lost it to westernization* (Naidoo: 1997, 281).

It was not until I read Theo L D'Haen's 'Magical Realism and Postmodernism: Decentering Privileged Centres' that I saw connections between Conrad's use of surrealism in the colonial context of *Heart of Darkness*[13] and Mda's use of magic realism in the postcolonial context of *The Heart of Redness.* D'Haen expands Carlos Fuentes's insight that 'there [are] no privileged centers of culture, race, politics' (D'Haen: 1995, 194). He explains: 'It is precisely the notion of the ex-centric, in the sense of speaking from the margin, from a place other than "the" or "a" center, that seems to me an essential feature of that postmodernism we call magic realism' (*Ibid*, 194). D'Haen sees magic realism as continuing the tradition of its earlier progenitor, surrealism. He maintains that magic realism appropriates the techniques of the central line and then uses these 'to create an alternative world *correcting* so-called existing reality' (*Ibid*, 195). What magic realism does, then, is expose the fact that 'systems of generic classification are complicit with a centralising impulse in imperial culture' (Slemon: 1995, 408). It seeks to achieve 'psychic liberation from Old World domination and its cognitive codes' (*Ibid*, 413). Or as Brenda Cooper puts it: 'Magical realism at its best opposes fundamentalism and purity; it is at odds with racism, ethnicity and the quest for tap roots, origins and homogeneity; it is fiercely secular and revels in the body, the joker, laughter, liminality and the profane' (Cooper: 1998, 22).

What these theorists foreground is the literary technique of decentring, which is a key feature of both *Heart of Darkness* and *The Heart of Redness.* Where Conrad abandons realism to create surreal encounters — Marlow meeting the knitting women in Brussels, for example — it is precisely with this purpose of exposing the absurdity of colonial administration as dangerously self-absorbed and

13 Conrad's work, in its swings between realism and romance, anticipates the surrealist movement of the 1920s with its emphasis on dream-like sensations and the expression of the subconscious. In Conrad such distortions of reality verge on the grotesque and are consistently negative, whereas postcolonial writers employing 'magic realism' do so to create a positive, transfigured reality.

morally compromised. Mda uses magic realism to force the reader to suspend disbelief and to allow his characters — principally Camagu and Qukezwa — to transcend their physical limitations and access the visionary plenitude glimpsed in their dreams.

This essay has examined similarities and contrasts between Mda and Conrad's texts in terms of community and agency in *The Heart of Redness* and *Heart of Darkness.* I have argued that Conrad, a major metropolitan writer who remains always an 'outsider' in the country of his adoption, sees the coloniser in Africa as suffering from diminished agency and a loss of cultural community. Mda, as postcolonial writer, appropriates a profoundly colonial incident that he recontextualises. He creates agency by reconfiguring history and invoking memory, insisting on the possibility of meaningful community. His project is not unproblematic in that it risks androcentrism and essentialism[14] in the gender representation of the prophetess Nongqawuse in the nineteenth century and her reincarnation, Qukezwa, in the modern chronotope. Nevertheless Mda creates a richly layered, vivid narrative that effectively 'writes back' to Conrad's dense, disturbing interrogation of 'barbarism' and 'civilisation'.

Mda in the classroom: *The Heart of Redness*

This section is based on a third-year seminar I taught at the University of Cape Town in 2009. Entitled 'Reconfiguring the Canon', it considered intertextualities between three metropolitan and three postcolonial texts. *Heart of Darkness* was studied with Zakes Mda's *The Heart of Redness,* Charlotte Bronte's *Jane Eyre* with Jean Rhys's *Wide Sargasso Sea,* and Marina Warner's *Indigo* with Shakespeare's *The Tempest.* Students' responses to the first pair of texts are the subject of this section. When we met in the classroom initially I had no intention of incorporating their work into this book. But the excitement of their engagement with the texts under consideration, both in classroom discussions and in their essays, the range of topics their investigations opened up and the importance of their discoveries about the relationship between texts and contexts convinced me that such a section should be included in a study of Mda's novels.

14 On androcentrism, see Helen Bradford (1996); on essentialist depictions of women, see Dorothy Driver (1990 and 1992). I see Mda's presentation of Nongqawuse's story as problematic in two areas: she is 'voiced' by a male omniscient narrator and the elements of male sexual transgression contained in her narrative are, as in traditional accounts, simply omitted. In linking Qukezwa in the modern chronotope to the prophetess Nongwqawuse in the colonial chronotope and in attributing to both figures an essentialising identity that links women to nature rather than culture, Mda would seem to repeat uncritically 'the rigid categories passed down to us in different versions of patriarchy' (Driver: 1990, 253).

Intertextuality is a theoretically complex field, since it brings into play interpretation of both textual and contextual elements, or formalist/idealist and materialist/historical traditions of reading texts. I am indebted to Jeremy Hawthorn's *Cunning Passages: New Historicism, Cultural Materialism and Marxism in the Contemporary Literary Debate* (1996), which provides a theoretical anchor for this section since it counterpoints the textual against the contextual in the interpretation of literary works. In comparing Conrad's *Heart of Darkness* with Zakes Mda's *The Heart of Redness,* texts separated by over a century and deriving from divergent imperial and postcolonial contexts, my third-year students were involved in a Bakhtinian dialogism of remarkable sophistication. The writers of the extracts that follow were members of a particularly talented and engaging third-year class. As English majors at UCT they had benefited from three years' training in the textual analysis of novels, short stories, plays and poetry in the 'core' courses structuring their Majors. But their exposure to history and literary theory was far more variable, depending upon the elective courses they had chosen with members of staff from very different ideological traditions. Yet the writers of the extracts that follow, and the class as a whole in discussion of *The Heart of Redness,* demonstrated an awareness of cultural continuities across different periods. They were capable of sympathetic identification with texts while registering the differences between their life experiences and those of the writers studied. Hawthorn describes this flexible reader response as follows:

> *I think that we may have to confront the paradox that we can sometimes feel closest to the life of the past at just the point at which we sense its difference and alien nature most strongly — just as we experience intimacy with other individuals most strongly not, normally, when they seem most like us, but when their separateness, distinctness, difference — their independent identity — stand out in sharpest relief* (Hawthorn: 1996, 6).

My students were also aware of the *transactional* nature of reading texts from different periods. The argument put forward by cultural materialists is that 'all reality is situated, and is conducted from concrete and specific social, cultural and political positions ... because reading is an active and transactional process literary works investigate us while we investigate them' (*Ibid,* 7). My students saw that their investigations of Conrad and Mda's story-worlds were also an investigation of their own story-worlds as readers of literature in post-apartheid South Africa. Central to this recognition is the notion of storytelling: 'Both historians and novelists (and literary critics) tell stories, and the *way* in which they tell stories has been the starting point for attempts to demonstrate that the narratives of the historian have far more in common with those of the novelist than had previously been supposed — especially by historians themselves' (*Ibid,* 36). Crucial to all investigations of the comparative structure of texts is the distinction developed by Hayden White between a historical discourse that *narrates* and one that *narrativises*. A discourse that narrates 'openly adopts a perspective that looks out on the world and reports it' while one that narrativises 'feigns to make the world speak itself and speak itself as a *story*' (White: 1996, 2–3). Students' awareness of the multiply-mediated nature of Mda's *The Heart of Redness* — its narrative shifts between contrasting chronotopes, its deployment of African oral traditions, its Xhosa vocabulary naming events and characters — demonstrates their understanding of Mda's strategies of narrativisation in this novel. Conrad is also, of course, a narrativiser. His narrativisation is reflected, *inter alia*, in the novella's replacement of authorial with figural perspectives and in the collapsing structures of time and space that Marlow's story enacts.

Narratology, though historically related to structuralism, is always linked to an ideological perspective. Hawthorn remarks that 'techniques of emplotment are never ideologically neutral' (Hawthorn: 1996, 45). Looking at how texts are constructed therefore always brings cultural perspectives into play. Important here is the issue of referentiality, much contested by postmodernism. While recognising the *constructedness* of literary perspectives — seeing that interpretations alter with our historical positioning — students had to confront and reject the notion that there can be no true or false claims about the world. If, for instance, the Cattle-Killing episode at the heart of *The Heart of Redness* was merely a myth rather than a real event that resulted in the deaths of hundreds of thousands of indigenous peoples under British imperial rule in the Eastern Cape, or if the sufferings of the enslaved Congolese under Leopold's administration of the Belgian Congo, so hauntingly described in *Heart of Darkness*, were not based on fact, neither Conrad nor Mda would have written their novels in the first place.

Part of studying cultures in relation to political events is the recognition, insisted upon by Raymond Williams, that such study must concentrate on experiences and meanings that form no part of the effective dominant culture (*Ibid*, 55). So the challenge I put to my students was this: can one read *Heart of Darkness* in ways that highlight the disjunction between Joseph Conrad, an author writing in the heyday of imperialism but critical of it, from the values and attitudes of his fictional protagonist, Charlie Marlow? And how does Mda, an African humanist who always writes about ordinary people doing ordinary things, rewrite an imperial romance about European colonisers in such a way as to foreground the cultural and social richness of previously colonised Africans?

Reading both historical and contemporary texts is an open-ended process which impacts upon students' understanding of their own experiences. This phenomenon is eloquently explained by J. Hillis Miller:

> *Works of literature do not simply reflect or are not simply caused by their contexts. They have a productive effect in history. This can and should also be studied. To put this another way, the only thing that sometimes worries me about the turn to history now as an exploratory method is the implication that I can fully explain every text by its pre-existing historical context. But the publication of these works was itself a political or historical event that in some way or another changed history. I think that if you don't allow for this, then literature is not much worth bothering with* (Miller: 1996, 152–3).

Jeremy Hawthorn similarly writes of the connection between readers and texts, which makes for what he calls a *dialectically historicist* perspective:

> *To become dialectically historicist, [we] must also focus upon the interaction between our own historically situated selves and the art of the past; [we] must take full measure of the fact that as we read the literature of the past and the past in literature, we are also read by literature. As we seek to find out the hidden details of the work's historically situated identity, the work seeks out, finds and even in part produces our own. Such interaction does not diminish aesthetic value: it is its necessary precondition* (Hawthorn: 1996, 84).

The extracts that follow significantly reflect students' awareness of this dialectical historicism.

Narrative and ideology: Alice Meyer

Concentrating on how *The Heart of Redness* renarrativises *Heart of Darkness*, Alice Meyer sees the 'shared narrative' of *The Heart of Redness* as challenging the logic of Marlow's Congo story:

> *Shared narrative is potentially more at home in an African context, which has often been viewed as amenable to ideas of collectivity. Moving between different selfhoods, [Mda's] narrator complicates the concept of an independent Cartesian ego. Dualistic thinking is avoided through the coincidence of several view points. In opposition to the self/other binary logic [of Marlow's story], Mda's narrator crosses boundaries between people … the narrative style could then itself be argued to be an embodiment of community and communal vision.*

Expanding her essay to differentiate storytelling features in Europe and Africa, Meyer remarks:

> *Another stylistic feature of the novel is the manner in which it draws upon mythic and oral features of traditional African storytelling. For example stock epithets and phrases are sometimes used for different people and places. Mlanjeni is 'the Man of the River', a Christian is one who 'killed the son of his own god' and one hears repeatedly 'Bhonco, Son of Ximiya'. George Grey becomes 'the Man Who Named Ten Rivers'. Interestingly, this last process of naming is also a manner of deflecting colonial practices back upon the empire. Colonialism typically sought to deprive African people of agency through presuming authority to name their practises, environments and identities.*

A major tension between the texts resides, Meyer suggests, in Mda's appropriation of a European language and novel-writing tradition to present African experience:

> *African manners are inserted into an English heritage that would not usually employ certain discourses. A reader accustomed to English tradition will inevitably find oral conventions absurd ... One might suggest that this element of the bizarre calls into question the viability of seriously presenting Africa, its traditions and people from within the English language. The novel might stylistically enact some of the problems of dramatising community and agency in an African context.*

Focusing upon the temporal aspects of Mda's use of different chronotopes to present the colonial and modern stories, Meyer remarks:

> *One of the most striking features of the style is the alternation between the present and the past. This might suggest the continuity of communal identity and heritage. In the last chapter the narrative alternates between Qukezwa and Heitsi in the nineteenth century and their namesakes of the present. For example: 'Qukezwa sings in soft pastel colours and looks at Heitsi. Qukezwa swallows a mouthful of fresh oysters and looks at Heitsi'. The first sentence is meant to pertain to the present whilst the second presumably relates to the past. Yet it is hard to starkly divorce one temporal plane from another. This is because disparate time zones are closely juxtaposed in the present tense. One effect is to view time as non-linear. This would accord with a project that aims to deconstruct colonial history and that envisages the past as a gradation from barbarity to civilisation.*

Perceptive as this commentary is on Mda's frequently overlapping chronotopes in the historical and contemporary sections of the novel, it does not take into account Conrad's dismantling of teleology in *Heart of Darkness*. Marlow's first remark — 'And this too has been one of the dark places of the earth' — forces the reader to see that the 'barbarity' of Roman times cannot be separated from the 'civilisation' of Victorian times. Both Conrad and Mda's texts participate in this cultural deconstruction.

Meyer clearly sees, however, that *The Heart of Redness* refuses conventional categories just as *Heart of Darkness* reverses colonial binaries:

> *It is fascinating that the inversion of binaries in Conrad is matched by the dismantling of polarities in many parts of Mda's text. This is because the hybrid, divided and multifaceted nature of communities and identities prevents a clean separation between ideas of civilised and savage, moral and immoral, humane and brutal. For instance Camagu seems to embody and embrace both Western and traditional forms of knowledge. Pondering Camagu's situation, the man in the village 'did not expect a man with such education, a man who has lived in the lands of the white people for thirty years, to have such respect for the customs of his people'.*

Concluding her investigation into the role of community to enable agency, Meyer remarks:

> *Community is seen as far from unifying. Multiplicity emerges within individual identities, between individuals and amongst disparate groups.*

While Meyer rejects the idea of 'a single, unified "community" within the novel', she tellingly relates the idea of a complex, dynamic agency amongst the inhabitants of Qolorha to the novel's use of storytelling: 'the possibility of an African portrayal of community is actually forged and expressed through the process of storytelling. Mda transforms the novel itself into an act of agency'.

This is a strong argument and underlines a crucial disjunction between Conrad and Mda's texts. Both concentrate on the verbal telling of stories and the effect of storytelling on auditors. But where storytelling in Mda's text enables communal response, in Conrad's text Marlow's story is not understood by his auditors and ends in the darkness in which it began. Meyer's essay is remarkable for its understanding of how social context shapes formal, stylistic features of language and narration.

Imagination and landscape: Katie Gumbley

Forging a vital connection between imagination, identity and landscape in *The Heart of Redness*, Katie Gumbley points out:

> *The narrative form itself ... transcends the boundaries of realist representation and presents memory, dreams and imagination as legitimate forms of both knowledge and creation ... The imagination in* The Heart of Redness *is presented as the central 'enabling praxis' for both individual and community agency ... imagination is shown to be central in breaking the binaries of realist representation, emancipating the narrative from essentialised categories and metanarratives, and supplanting dualisms with dialectics. In this way, the imagination and the aesthetic become a means of resisting and overcoming oppression.*

Mda's novel undermines the constructions of voice and gaze dramatised in *Heart of Darkness*:

> *It is necessary to identify the practices of colonial domination and appropriation that* The Heart of Redness *demonstrates, parodies and transcends. Effectively 'writing back' to Conrad's* Heart of Darkness, *Mda's text inverts 'the gaze' onto the coloniser himself. As David Spurr comments ... the colonial subject has no voice in imperial discourse and as such is denied the power to shape his or her own narrative: 'Gazed upon, they are denied the power of the gaze; spoken to, they are denied the power to speak freely'. In this sense, it is clear that Conrad's text, despite its criticism of colonial practices, is implicated within a discourse that, in the very act of representation, denies agency to the colonised African subject.* The Heart of Redness*'s depiction of the Man Who Named Ten Rivers is ... an embodiment of colonial practices of appropriation; like the Western author, he imposes a set of binaries upon the landscape, fixing it in terms of 'savage' versus 'civilised'.*

Just as *The Heart of Redness* restores voice and gaze to the African protagonists, so Mda's depictions of the African landscape remove it from the falsifying stereotypes imposed upon it by the Western explorer:

> *The contrast between Mda and Conrad is their protagonists' strikingly opposed relationships to the African setting. In* Heart of Darkness, *the landscape is a 'silent wilderness' which undermines Marlow's sense of self, transforms his memories into surreal dreams and severs his ties to both community and reality: 'The broadening waters flowed through a mob of wooded islands; you lost your way on that river as you would in a desert, and butted all day long against shoals, trying to find the channel, till you thought yourself bewitched and cast off forever from everything you had known once — somewhere — far away — in another world perhaps. There were moments when one's past came back to one, as it will sometimes when you have not a moment to spare for yourself; but it came in the shape of an unrestful and noisy dream, remembered with wonder amongst the overwhelming realities of this strange world of plants, and water, and silence. And this stillness did not remotely reassemble peace. It was the stillness of an implacable force brooding over an inscrutable intention. It looked at you with a vengeful aspect.'*

In stark contrast to the demoralisation that the African landscape imposes on the Western explorer,

> *Qolorha, as a deeply symbolic and contested landscape, is a place that both evokes memory and inspires imagination. In this sense, identity is inextricably tied to the natural setting, which is shown to have a restorative power.*

This landscape embodies the living heritage that the people of Qolorha must protect:

> *It is clear then that Qolorha is a symbolic place of encounter between past and present, living and dead, coloniser and colonised; all of which is mediated through the landscape as a dialogic space. The landscape then should be understood as the very embodiment of heritage, linking both chronotopes together and constituting a visual representation of a past that is still essentially present.*

Gumbley concludes that *The Heart of Redness* illustrates that Mda's depiction of African landscape is integral to community identity and creative agency:

> *A symbolic reappropriation of lost agency, enacted through creative performance, memory and dreams, is therefore coupled with the physical reclamation of the landscape and resources of Qolorha. Such a process dramatises issues of community and agency in a uniquely African context, in order to illustrate the integral part that imagination and aesthetics play in achieving a true 'African Renaissance'.*

Gumbley's investigation of Qolorha as 'symbolic place of encounter between past and present' skilfully interweaves the spatial and temporal dimensions of Mda's use of Qolorha as chronotope. Frequently concerned with rehistoricising colonial perspectives so as to enable postcolonial agency, Mda is always interested in the role of place. This role is given central emphasis in Gumbley's explorations of African Renaissance.

Landscape and identity: Joanna Mostert

Like Katie Gumbley, Joanna Mostert links the achievement of identity in *The Heart of Redness* to the protagonists' understanding of their environment:

> *Somehow, the physicality of the village and its surroundings interacts with its historical rootedness to bring healing to Camagu's state. Qolorha becomes not just a place, but rather 'a ground of being'* (Koyana: 2003). *It is no accident that 'it is among people who have a history of belonging in a place that [Camagu] finds a new home'* (Vital: 2005). *Mda's suggestion is that 'place and identity are mutually imbricated'* (Woodward: 2003).

Qolorha links the past of the colonial world with the present and future of the contemporary world:

> *It is crucial to note that the two conflicts around which the novel is structured ... are both fundamentally linked to the physical place of Qolorha. The past is constantly wound in and about the present — in the very fabric of the landscape. Qolorha is 'a palimpsest, constantly revealing traces of the past'* (Graham: 2009). *Zim and Bhonco, opposed as they are, both rely deeply on the past and on the landscape for their self-definition.*

Writing of protagonists' involvement in both their history and their environment, Mostert notes:

> *The Believers, mostly embodied in Zim, are openly involved with their own history and with how their history interacts with their environment. Zim 'talks passionately about this valley. When he began to walk, he walked in this valley. He looked after cattle in this valley. He was circumcised here. His grandfather's fields were here. His whole life is centred in this valley. He is one with* Intlambo-ka-Nongqawuse *— Nongqawuse's Valley'* (Mda: 2000, 50–1). *This is perhaps one of the most explicit links between the space and time of Qolorha — both of which (if they can be thought of as separate) lie at the centre of Zim's identity. Another crucial passage shows the wild fig in Zim's compound, under which 'he finds solace, for it is directly linked to the ancestors ... [the ancestors] are all regular visitors to this tree'* (*Ibid*: 41). *Zim's connection with the ancestors, his history, an essential part of his communal and individual identity, is perforce bound up with the fig tree.*

Mostert concludes:

> *Camagu's journey of self-discovery clearly dramatises the issues of community and agency in Zakes Mda's* The Heart of Redness. *His process of self-reconstruction interacts with the various ways in which other characters build their communal and individual identities around the landscape and history of Qolorha. Of course, this process is not without ambiguity, doubled and halved meanings. In the end, it is the hybridity of past and present, tradition and modernity that enables Camagu to belong in the hybrid landscape and history of Qolorha. Paradoxically, or perhaps appropriately, he uses this new communal agency to protect and nurture the community and landscape that has contributed to his healing.*

Mostert's acute analysis of Camagu's 'journey of self-discovery' throws into focus the relation of place to history to selfhood at Qolorha-by-Sea. Nowhere has Mda created a more powerful chronotope to dramatise the process of the search for identity than Qolorha in *The Heart of Redness.*

African Renaissance and the women of The Heart of Redness: *Justine de Jager*

Justine de Jager links the concept of African Renaissance with the agency of the women protagonists in *The Heart of Redness.* These women are forceful and proactive in their community, as opposed to the marginalised, passive and disempowered women of *Heart of Darkness.*

> *Mda juxtaposes the past with the present in this novel to show the influence of history in determining current culture. Mazibuko suggests that Mda's texts optimise an African Renaissance in post-apartheid South Africa, and that he takes into consideration the development of peripheral areas of South Africa that many scholars dealing with this Renaissance tend to miss. One of the main portrayals Mda focuses on when emphasising the historical change in Africa is the strength of females in our society.*

De Jager continues:

> *The novel is based on the Xhosa tradition in the Eastern Cape. The fact that it is constantly vacillating between the past and the present shows the importance of history in shaping a community. The present-day community of Qolorha constantly struggles to incorporate their past traditions with the modern world of post-apartheid South Africa. In terms of African Renaissance, the novel highlights the importance of creating a hybrid between the old African traditions and the modern world (which is seen in the development of Qolorha).*

Crucial to the concept of African Renaissance are forceful, creative women protagonists:

> *Throughout the present-day depiction of Qolorha, there are female characters that play a vital role in the text. All the female characters that exert agency are clearly depicted as everyday women and are mostly placed in a rural context. This highlights Mda's belief that citizens on the periphery of society have to become agents of change in order to see a successful, multi-cultural South Africa.*

De Jager concludes that:

> *Mda illustrates the females in this text as complex, paradoxical characters — much like the post-apartheid context in which he writes. He also allows the everyday woman to play a monumental role in development and progress. This representation suggests that peripheral groups in South Africa, such as rural women, need to take a stand and improve their living conditions and their community as a whole. His depiction also emphasises the importance of the African Renaissance, in which Africa preserves its cultural heritage and combines it with elements from the West.*

De Jager's essay, modulating between Europe and Africa, the past and the future, is a fine example of what Hawthorn has called a dialectical historical consciousness. She concentrates on the interaction between us as historically situated readers and the art of the past, suggesting ways forward for African women to become powerful actors in the post-apartheid community — a desideratum far from achieved yet in rural South Africa.

Women as agents of change: Chloe McGrath

Chloe McGrath's essay on Mda's women protagonists starts off with an interesting ambiguity: though Mda's feisty women in *The Heart of Redness* enjoy considerable autonomy (unlike their counterparts in *Heart of Darkness*), their power is more limited than that accorded to Camagu. The novel revolves around this male figure:

> *The agency of women in Mda's* The Heart of Redness *is especially significant when contrasted with that of the women in* Heart of Darkness. *While Conrad's women are pivotal to his narrative, they stand as static canvases on which Conrad paints the roles that they play in Marlow's Congolese endeavour. Mda's women in* The Heart of Redness *are dynamic, insightful characters driven by their individual ideologies and places in the community as a whole. Mda's female characters are given an agency that is distinctly lacking in Conrad's female characters; however, I observe that Mda's female characters are still used as tools to create the necessary literary context for Camagu to execute his full agency. Thus the female characters, although able to execute their agency, are not as free to navigate their way through life as is Camagu.*

McGrath argues that Mda sets up a feminist discourse in the contemporary chronotope dominated by Xoliswa Ximiya and Qukezwa, in order to suggest that patriarchal societies must alter their gender roles if they are to come to terms with modernity. The climax of women's agency and its link with the community is illustrated by Camagu's cooperative:

> *It is here that the unity of the women of Qolorha is exemplified, where women who were previously bound to their respective 'cults' are united in the common purpose of celebrating and showcasing their community and traditions to the world.*

McGrath celebrates the operation of this cooperative:

> *Ultimately, the working cooperative of the women of Qolorha supersedes the boundaries that have separated them and together they unify for a common purpose.*

Powerful as this example of cooperation and achievement is, *The Heart of Redness* contains contradictions in relation to gender roles. These contradictions McGrath suggests earlier, but does not pursue. They imply an area of authorial coercion: women are granted some freedoms but the authorial voice reserves the main areas of public decision-making for males. These contradictions have troubled several critics[15] and are worth developing in considering Mda's perspective on gender equality in the 'new' South Africa.

History and prophecy in The Heart of Redness*: Megan Lyons*

The final essay chosen for discussion brings into play the notion of prophecy as the link between the alternating chronotopes on which the novel is constructed:

> The Heart of Redness *is a culturally rich novel permeated by amaXhosa history and prophecy. It is through these important elements that the generation of the past is connected to the present.*

This connection is reflected in the family tree by which Mda illustrates the relations between Believers and Unbelievers:

> *An important factor in the way that history itself is recorded is that of the family tree, which is present at the very beginning of the novel. There is a definite beginning marked by the headless ancestor, Xikixa, which progresses into the generations of the twin brothers, Twin and Twin-Twin. The generations are then intercepted en route to the present by the Middle Generations, a seemingly unplaced time frame with no recorded names or ancestral paths. The middle section is seen as unnatural to both the past and present generations because there was a complete absence of divided belief, that is, no disputes between the Believers and the Unbelievers.*

Bhonco emphasises the unnatural nature of the Middle Generations by comparing them to both a dream and a nightmare:

> *The primary link between the past and the present, which is different to their existence under the Middle Generations, is the ability of the Xhosa living at Qolorha-by-Sea to control their own destiny* (Jacobs: 2005, 23). *For example, in Nongqawuse's time (the past) destiny is centred on the decision of whether or not to kill the cattle, while in the present day destiny and positive future direction seem to find their orientation around the bringing of developers into the village.*

Throughout her essay, Lyons connects prophecy and history:

> *Prophecy in* The Heart of Redness *plays a pivotal role in dramatising the issues of community and agency within an African context because it serves as a shaping force in history. This concept of prophecy shapes history through determining the course and outcome of events depicted throughout the novel.*

Remarking that prophecy is not restricted to the Xhosa culture, but 'impacts on the lives of all people', Lyons concludes:

> *Mda introduces people's beliefs in prophecies and prophets, in saviours and redeemers, as ways to understand what drives people and what contributes to decisions that people make. Prophecy in this regard is a powerful force within the novel because it*

15 See, for instance, Meg Samuelson (2009) and Helen Bradford (1996).

> *influences the choices people make in both the past and present generations … History and prophecy relate to and dramatise issues of community, affecting the characters in different ways and influencing their future.*

Lyons' essay clearly shows how prophecy links the past with the future in Qolorha and how it foregrounds the issue of choice or agency in the Believers and the Unbelievers of both chronotopes. But her argument could usefully be expanded into an investigation of the theological registers present in, and linking, *The Heart of Redness* with *Heart of Darkness.* Of these, J. Hillis Miller writes: '*Heart of Darkness* is a secular version of what are … intertwined religious or sacred genres: apocalypse, parable, allegory' (Miller: 2002, 31). What, Miller asks, is the revelation promised by Conrad's tale? When we look at Mda's novel, can we see any relation between the failure of the original prophecy that led to the Cattle-Killing and the failure of revelation in *Heart of Darkness*? Was Nongqawuse's doomed prophecy of colonial times a false promise that now haunts our postcolonial history? How does Mda's novel reread 'the promise of universal prosperity' (*Ibid,* 38) that marks the thinking of both the political left and the political right in our technologically advanced civilisation?

Finally…

The suite of essays from which I have quoted demonstrates students' insightful readings of Mda's *The Heart of Redness* in relation to Conrad's *Heart of Darkness.* Balancing textual with contextual elements in considering narrative structure, their analyses exhibit what Hawthorn has called 'dialectical historicism' — the ability to see oneself as a historically situated individual in relation to texts both of the colonial past and the postcolonial present. The life experiences of South African students in their early twenties at the University of Cape Town are at some distance from those of Zakes Mda, a Xhosa-mother-tongue novelist in his 60s who has spent many years in political exile from apartheid South Africa and who is now Professor of Creative Writing at the University of Ohio. Yet the story-worlds invoked by Mda — geographically, historically and culturally — speak to students' perceptions of a complex South African reality. Possibly this groundedness in a known world enables them to respond sympathetically to Conrad's imperial romance, despite the difficulties of its linguistic and narrative layerings and its presentation of a colonial Congo long since vanished. In order to look at these texts together, students need sophisticated textual and contextual skills. Perhaps their successes in deploying these skills points to the pedagogic truth that human intelligence is always multi-faceted, and that the nature of intertextuality can result in insights into wholes that are greater than the sum of their parts.

Duplicity, plagiarism or transformation? Zakes Mda's *The Heart of Redness* and Jeff Peires' *The Dead Will Arise*

Offenburger's 2008 article on Mda's dependence on Peires[16] has elicited many pages of response, as any Internet search on the topic will confirm. What Offenburger's research demonstrates is the extent to which parts of Mda's novel are built on the historical edifice of Peires' book. This is acknowledged by Mda in his Dedication to *The Heart of Redness* and by Peires himself, who in an afterword (written in 2003) to *The Dead Will Arise* refers to 'Zakes Mda's

16 The notion of 'appropriation' central to this section draws the reader's attention to issues of intertextual borrowing in Mda's work. There has been an international controversy over Mda's incorporation in *The Heart of Redness* of verbatim quotations derived from Jeff Peires' historical account of the Great Xhosa Cattle-Killing of 1856–1857 from his book *The Dead Will Arise.* The controversy was sparked by the publication of an essay by a Yale PhD student, Andrew Offenburger, who accused Mda of lifting dozens of quotations from Peires' book without acknowledgement. Online book newspaper BOOK Southern Africa (www.book.co.za) ran a series of commentaries from South African and international scholars, including the South African writer Stephen Gray (who alleged plagiarism), American academic Byron Caminero-Santangelo (who denied plagiarism) and Mda himself. Mda argued that the Xhosa language is full of proverbs based on the Cattle-Killing episode, just as Xhosa culture is full of songs about the Prophetess: 'It is our story. Jeff Peires does not own that story. So I can't steal it from him' (Mda: 2008b, online). Mda also quoted South African philosopher, Aryan Kaganof, who argued that nobody objects to the intertextual borrowings of James Joyce, T. S. Eliot or William Shakespeare. Kaganof pointed out that 'the greatest philosopher of all, Nietzsche, rarely, almost never, used footnotes. And indeed, he also lifted sentences wholesale from Schopenhauer, and from the New Testament, and from Kant, without mentioning where he lifted them from' (Mda: 2008b, online). I close with the conclusions of the editor of BOOK SA. He maintained that Peires' acceptance of Mda's acknowledgement made the accusation of plagiarism untenable:

> Peires is a top South African scholar. Call him a dissident scholar, in contrast to Offenburger's orthodoxy, because, by accepting Mda's acknowledgement as sufficient, he accepts the possibility of a world of greys. The thoughts of a top scholar are not nothing: indeed, they are oppositional to the thoughts of other scholars; they are potentially standard-setting. This means that in a top scholar's opinion, the question of the book's literary merit is the central one in relation to the value of the work. It follows that Offenburger has only succeeded in rejuvenating this question with his accusations: he has not displaced it, not succeeded in crystallising *The Heart of Redness* as 'that work with plagiarism at its heart', not transported the book to a world of blacks and white. We remain in grey territory, where art rules.

Readers may wish to consult Andrew Offenburger's 'Duplicity and plagiarism in Zakes Mda's *The Heart of Redness*'. *Research in African Literatures*, Vol. 39, No. 3 (Fall 2008), 164–79, and Mda's 'Response to "Duplicty and plagiarism in Zakes Mda's *The Heart of Redness*"'. *Research in African Literatures*, Vol. 39, No. 3 (Fall 2008), 200–03.

acclaimed *The Heart of Redness*' (Peires: 1989, 388) and remarks, '[W]orks of creative fiction inhabit a different order of reality to mine, and I do not think it at all appropriate to comment on their contents. I am sincerely honoured by the notice that Zakes Mda has taken of *The Dead Will Arise*, but for me to engage with *The Heart of Redness*, however delightful it might be to post-modernists, would be fair neither to Zakes nor myself' (Peires: 1989, 389).

This engagement with the intertextuality between Peires and Mda's texts is precisely what I address in this chapter. Enough water has flowed under enough bridges on the ethical problems of Mda's use of Peires' work. I concentrate instead on the features that make both books remarkable, looking first at what Mda's text derives from Peires and then at how it reshapes that legacy. In this project, I am greatly indebted to Derek Attridge's *The Singularity of Literature*, which addresses the uniqueness of individual artworks. I attempt to apply the terms Attridge explores — 'invention', 'singularity' and 'alterity' — to both books. Essential to the reader's understanding of these terms is his or her performance of the act of reading. This involves recognising the 'shaped' or 'authored' 'event' of a text: what constitutes its particular linguistic power and enables both writers' and readers' 'creative welcoming of the Other'.

The Dead Will Arise

One way to illustrate the singularity invention and alterity of both texts is to look closely at the opening chapter of Peires' text. How does Mda's text build his story-world on this story-world? I turn now to Chapter One, 'Riverman's War' of *The Dead Will Arise*. The literary qualities of this book must be apparent to any careful reader. Its accessibility is reflected in this reader's letter: 'I loved *The Dead Will Arise*, it's the kind of non-fiction that's written with a ferocious passion and impeccable research that tosses you headlong into the story. No dry history this. Brilliant in-depth insight into the context of the cattle killings; strong personalities, stupidity on both sides … It's a marvellous, marvellous book' (Beukes: 2008, 3). Written with a remarkable combination of narrative immediacy and historical scholarship, Peires' account of the Cattle-Killing and its context in nineteenth-century colonial British Kaffraria fuses a vivid storyline with the veracity of historical voices. The Mlanjeni of the opening chapter is both a striking, idiosyncratic character and the spokesman of a cosmology that appeals to the dreams and visions of a people pushed to the brink by an oppressive colonial regime. Mlanjeni communicates 'revelations concerning Mdalidephu the god of the black man, Thixo the god of the whites, and Thixo's son Tayi, whom the whites had murdered' (Peires: 1989, 24). The Riverman's powers thus draw on the combined authority of both Xhosa and Christian beliefs to achieve near-mythical status: 'He lights his pipe on the sun ... he heals the sick, makes the blind see, the lame walk, and the dumb speak' (*Ibid*, 26).

To involve the reader in the story-world that the teachings of Mlanjeni initiate, Peires graphically describes the landscapes with which characters interact. His techniques of focalisation make the reader *see* the physical surroundings of British Kaffraria — the Amathole Mountains, the Waterkloof, the Fish River bush and the flat plains of North Victoria. Sometimes the narrating voice is Peires' own:

> *The Waterkloof itself was a deep valley a little over ten kilometres long, enclosed by almost perpendicular hills crowned with masses of stone and intersected by a succession of precipices and kloofs. The deeper one entered the Waterkloof, the denser the vegetation became. Gigantic yellow-wood, assagaaiwood and sneezewood trees blotted out the sky, suspending tangled masses of creepers and monkey-ropes from branches 50 or 60 metres high to merge with the dense under-growth of acacias and other thorny bushes* (*Ibid*, 38).

This description of the Fish River bush is again narrated by Peires:

> *Unlike the Waterkloof, the Fish River bush consisted of thorny acacia bushes, pelargonium creepers and stunted euphorbia trees. Nevertheless, these grew so thickly upon each other that the bush was passable only by old tracks made by elephants in former years ... For those who knew the paths ... these elephant tracks provided rapid access from one part of the bush to another and linked up with similar bush along the Keiskamma, Kat and Bushman rivers* (*Ibid*, 40).

Sometimes the narrating voice describing the landscape is that of a local newspaper, like this description of the Amathole Mountains from an entry from the *Grahamstown Journal* of 1846: 'Its sides are bald and precipitous; it is split and intersected with ravines; it is broken by masses of rock, and it is clothed with noble forest trees'. Throughout the opening chapter the description of location and setting is botanically, geographically and topographically accurate.

Combined with vivid depiction of the flora and fauna of the landscape in this opening chapter is both historical specificity — the protagonists are the Xhosa of the Ndlambe district of British Kaffraria — and metaphorical richness, for Mlanjeni teaches his followers in a slow, elliptical style full of 'obscure and incomprehensible hints and metaphors'. What is particularly striking to the reader beginning *The Dead Will Arise* is the oral character of this tale, carried by the many Xhosa words and their translations in the text. Mlanjeni, we learn early in the chapter, is preoccupied with eradicating the *ubuthi* — evil substances — poisoning his people and so exhorts them to abandon witchcraft. Peires is illuminating on his recreation of the Xhosa-language vocabulary used by the believers in the Cattle-Killing, pointing out that '[m]any of the most relevant concepts of the Cattle-Killing movement either do not translate directly into English, or are translated by English words which lack the weight and connotations of their Xhosa equivalents and thus hide from the English reader associations and connections which would be immediately apparent to a Xhosa' (*Ibid*, 146). Equally striking to a reader beginning this book is Peires' incorporation of detailed archival sources. Either introduced as quotations in the text or referenced through footnotes in a manner that never interrupts the flow of the narrative are excerpts from letters, church records, local journals, missionary accounts, interviews, Imperial Blue Books, biographies and diaries, county records, regimental museum excerpts and registers of baptisms and marriages.

Throughout *The Dead Will Arise* Peires makes it clear that he considers the Cattle-Killing 'the greatest of all Xhosa disasters' (*Ibid*, 336) since it resulted in the deaths of the majority of the Xhosa population and the suppression and instrumentalisation of the surviving minority. Yet his ideological stance towards the Xhosa people as he records their history 'in the spirit of theoretical practice ... [where] ... my theoretical knowledge shaped my understanding and my interpretation of the primary sources' (*Ibid*, 364) is always sympathetic, based on his familiarity with their language and customs. Steeped in Xhosa belief systems, Peires draws the reader's attention to 'something missing in Xhosa religion, a gap through which some of the central ideas of Christianity were able to infiltrate' (*Ibid*, 57). The deep ambivalence about death and the afterlife in Xhosa religion contributed to this gap, since on the one hand death was considered merely 'a transition between the state of being human and the state of being an ancestor' (*Ibid*, 57), but on the other, death was feared as both evil and unnatural (*Ibid*, 58). The Christian message of the resurrection therefore had strong appeal.

The first chapter of *The Dead Will Arise* chronicles the beliefs, teachings and charisma of the believer Mlanjeni, whose visions were a prelude to the visions of the prophetesses Nongqawuse and Nomkosi and therefore a preparation for the Cattle-Killing disaster. This introduces the question discussed in Peres' Chapter 10: '"Everything you always wanted to know about the Xhosa Cattle-Killing": why some Xhosa believed and others did not'. This question introduces complex issues of social ethos and economic structure in relation to the 'soft' believers (*amathamba)* and the 'hard' unbelievers (*amagogotya*):

> *The believers described themselves as 'soft' because they submitted themselves and their private interests entirely to the requirements of the national community as defined by Nongqawuse. By and large, they stood committed to the social ethos and the economic structure of the old, precolonial social function which depended on reciprocal generosity and communal endeavour. The unbelievers were thought of as 'hard' because they stuck by their own conceptions of what was right and stingily exalted their private economic interests above the national well-being of the community at large. In as far as the personal lives of the leading unbelievers are known to us, it would seem that the*

> *backbone of the 'hard'* gogotya *party was made up of prosperous and wealthy men who were in a position to profit from the new economic opportunities created by the expansion of the colonial market* (*Ibid*, 334–5).

For Peires, the division between believers and unbelievers was not simply a response to the crisis of the prophecies 'but a reflection of the deeper communal tensions generated by the breakup of Xhosa society under colonial pressure' (*Ibid*, 335).

Another striking feature of 'Riverman's War' are the words of Sir Harry Smith, who called himself *Inkosi Inkhulu* (Great Chief) (*Ibid*, 27), but who commanded European settlers to 'rise en masse ... to destroy and exterminate these most barbarous and treacherous savages' (*Ibid*, 37). Hence the bitter fighting of the War of Mlanjeni, which opens *The Dead Will Arise.* But succeeding chapters describing succeeding governors of the Cape Colony chronicle continuing intransigence — as in the cases of Sir George Cathcart and Sir George Grey who imposed 'harsh and brutal measures' on the Xhosa. Peires remarks that 'Grey's distinguishing feature as a colonial governor was not his liberalism, but his extraordinary opportunism and ruthlessness' (*Ibid*, 339): 'Inspired perhaps by Carlyle's vision of the hero, he aspired to an absolute dictatorship which he viewed as the just entitlement of his superior abilities' (*Ibid*, 330). The reverberations of Smith's extermination campaign resound throughout *The Dead* and are chillingly reminiscent of Conrad's protagonist Kurtz, who appends to his tract on the civilising mission the phrase '[e]xterminate the brutes'.

Connecting again with Conrad's novella and with the nineteenth-century 'scientific' interest in phrenology, Peires' opening chapter describes the boiling off of human skulls by colonists:

> *Doctor A — of the 60th had asked my men to procure for him a few native skulls of both sexes. This was a task easily accomplished. One morning they brought back to camp about two dozen heads of various ages. As these were not supposed to be in a presentable state for the doctor's acceptance, the next night they turned my vat into a cauldron for the removal of superfluous flesh. And there these men sat, gravely smoking their pipes during the live-long night, and stirring round and round the heads in that seething boiler, as though they were cooking black-apple dumplings* (*Ibid*, 49).

A similar account is given by a soldier whose account is recorded in the Greenjackets Regimental Museum:

> *As we ascended the evidences of the fight became more frequent; rolling skulls, dislodged by those in front, came bounding down between our legs; the bones lay thick among the loose stones in the sluits and gulleys, and the bush on either side showed many a bleaching skeleton. A fine specimen of a [Xhosa] head, I took the liberty of putting into my saddle-bag, and afterwards brought it home with me to Scotland, where it has been much admired by phrenologists for its fine development* (*Ibid*, 52).

The motivation behind these ghoulish practices was nothing more than 'private amusement' (*Ibid*, 49), providing British soldiers with souvenirs from Xhosaland. By contrast, the Xhosa practice of disembowelling the enemy was driven by fear and the need for self-preservation:

> *The Xhosa believed that war medicines generated supernatural forces (*iqungu*) within the stomach of a soldier. If he was killed, the* iqungu *attacked his slayer, bloating and swelling up his body until he too died. To dissipate the* iqungu *of the British soldiers they killed, the Xhosa ripped open the stomachs of their dead enemies (Ibid, 48).*

Peires' factual account of the War of Mlanjeni demonstrates that British soldiers slaughtered Xhosas without compunction, as though they were cattle or vermin, demonstrating 'the generalised incapacity of the white soldier to regard his Xhosa enemy as a "human being"' (*Ibid*, 49) and thus emphasising the ironic reversal of 'barbarism' with 'civilisation' on which Conrad's novella turns.

Finally, 'Riverman's War' brings home to the reader an occluded area of colonial history: the collaboration of the Khoikhoi people (or 'Bushmen') with the embattled Xhosa in the Eastern Cape: 'For more than 18 months the small Xhosa-Khoi force, estimated by some colonists to number no more than 200 fighting men at any one time, defied more than 4,000 of the British Army's finest troops' (*Ibid*, 39). The Khoi rebels introduced to the Xhosa 'a new and revolutionary brand of Christianity'. Products of mission education, 'the Khoi read their Bibles regularly and they prepared themselves for battle by the devout singing of hymns' (*Ibid*, 160). The influence of the small number of Khoi rebels fighting with the Xhosa against the British was thus considerable. Adding to the power and the millenarian appeal of Christian teaching was the work of Wilhelm Goliath, a Xhosa who spoke fluent Dutch, was a baptised member of the Methodist Church in Grahamstown and preached with the missionary Nathaniel James Merriman. Peires' opening chapter prepares the ground for the coming-together of several forces that culminated in the Cattle-Killing disaster: the ruthless administration of the colonial government at the Cape, the strength of traditional Xhosa beliefs and the Christian promise of resurrection after death.

The Heart of Redness

> *History … determines writing, but it is the task of writing to exceed that determination, to differ, to imagine something other than what the historical present has articulated* (Helgesson: 2004, 18).

> *The most innovative artists … have usually had an exceptionally great capacity to incorporate cultural materials, and have therefore been able … to make the strongest impact upon their cultures. Nor is this merely a question of the richness and range of the stuff which the mind has to work on: what the original creator finds in the*

> *cultural field ... is not just material but gaps in the material, strains and tensions that suggest the pressure of the other, of the hitherto unthinkable, of that which is necessarily excluded* (Attridge: 2004, 36).

The task of this section is to assess whether *The Heart of Redness* succeeds in that exploration of the 'gaps, strains and tensions' in Peires' story-world on which Mda builds his novel. I begin with continuities with Peires and then go on to develop divergences.

Continuities: oral storytelling

The most obvious continuity between Mda's novel and Peires' historical account is the character of oral storytelling introduced by Peires' use of scores of Xhosa names and terms for which he provides translations. Mda adopts Peires' use of Xhosa words and his translations of these words for that part of the novel set in the nineteenth century. For the contemporary story, however, that unfolds at Qolorha-by-Sea, Mda produces a large new repertoire of Xhosa words that he also translates for the reader. So at Vulindlela Trading Store, we have *ityala* (credit) and *nkamkan* (pension). Connected to Zim's extramarital affair, we have *igqirha* (a diviner) and *ukukrexeza* (having lovers outside marriage). A host of terms describe Xhosa fashions in clothes and jewellery for the *amahomba* (those who take pride in their traditional appearance): the wearing of *amatiki, icangci* and *uphalaza* beads, and the statuesque *iqhiya* (turban), which Xoliswa Ximiya the Unbeliever sees as evidence of *ubuqubqa* (backwardness and heathenism), when she admires *qgobkoka* (enlightenment). Describing Qolorha's flora and fauna, we have *usunda* palms, the *Nomyayi* bird, the *umsintsi* tree and the wild banana or *ikhamanga*. Birds that laugh (*wak-wak-kiririri*) are identified as *uthekwane*, the hamerkop, and *uxomoyi*, the giant kingfisher. There is also *uthekwane*, the brown hammerhead bird, and *ing'ang'ane*, the hadeda ibis, as well as the *amahobobo* weaverbirds that fill Zim's homestead with their swirling song. Around the harvesting of seafoods by the cooperative, we have *imbhaza* (mussels), *imbhatyisa* (oysters) and *amaqonju* and *amangquba* (perlemoen). On the cultural front we have *izibiri* songs popular at concerts, the *umrubhe* musical instrument on which Qukezwa performs her split-tone singing, while Bhonco and NoPetticoat sing *umshotso* songs and perform *tyityimba* dances. Finally, on death and the spirit world, we have the *igqirha* who explains that Zim is lingering because he is torn between the ancestors (the *amaGqunukhwebe*) and his living daughter, Qukezwa. Since the living must always be in connection with the dead, Qukezwa can only join her husband Camagu after the special ceremony of the *umxhentso* dance, which men and women perform together to commemorate the dead. As in Peires' book, Mda's use of an extensive Xhosa lexicon vividly creates an oral storytelling context, giving the reader access to Xhosa beliefs and customs: to the food, clothes and ornaments of Qolorha's inhabitants, to its plants, birds, sights, sounds and smells. This creation of an oral storytelling narrative framework connects with, and continues, Peires' story-world, providing the dramatic infrastructure on which Mda builds the new features of his novel.

Reversing 'barbarism' and 'civilisation'

Peires' focus on the barbarism of the colonial administration of the Eastern Cape is clear in the evidence he marshalls of their inhumanity towards indigenous people. The quoted passages from his book detail British soldiers' collection of enemy skulls as souvenirs; this collecting activity overlapped with the nineteenth-century interest in phrenology. In Conrad's text Marlow has his head measured at the Company headquarters in Brussels where the doctor, speaking of Europeans in Africa, remarks cryptically: 'The changes take place inside'.

In Mda's text, Dalton explains to Twin-Twin that the head of his father Xihixa was boiled 'to remove the flesh from the skull' and comments 'these heads are either going to be souvenirs, or will be used for scientific enquiry'. Mda's narrator comments: 'Souvenirs. Scientific enquiry. It did not make sense. It was nothing but the witchcraft of the white man' (Mda: 2000, 21). The witchcraft of the white man, Twin-Twin believes, extends to cannibalism, for why would anybody cook anything not intended to be eaten? Peires' book establishes that amongst the Xhosa the practice of cannibalism, even amongst those starving after the Cattle-Killing, was very rare and that 'the majority of believers, though starving themselves … hunted down and killed any who were suspected of cannibalism' (Peires: 1989, 263).

The inhumanity documented in Peires' book in relation to the colonial administration at the Cape in the nineteenth century is not, Mda insists, a thing of the past. He has his protagonist Camagu report to the people of Qolorha that on his travels abroad he visited the Natural History Museum in London and there 'was shocked to discover … five dried-out heads of the so-called Bushmen stored in boxes in some back room of the museum'. Camagu is bewildered: 'He has never understood this barbaric habit of the British of shrinking heads of the vanquished people and displaying them in these impressive buildings where ladies and gentlemen go to gloat and celebrate their superior civilisation' (Mda: 2000, 193). When Camagu makes this announcement, Believers and Unbelievers alike 'stare in disbelief'. Camagu goes on to insist: 'Not only heads. In Paris the private parts of a Khoikhoi woman called Saartjie Baartmen are kept in a bottle!' (*Ibid*, 194). What Mda takes from Peires' book therefore, and extends to the contemporary story the role reversal of European 'civilisation' with African 'barbarism' — the reversal on which Conrad's novella turns: 'For this also has been one of the dark places of the earth'. Mda extends Peires' exposure of European barbarism towards indigenous African people in the nineteenth century to the greed and xenophobia of the corporate business world in the contemporary world of the 'new' South Africa.

New directions

While *The Heart of Redness* connects strongly with *The Dead Will Arise* in its peopling of its story-world with Xhosa words and its ironic reversals of the concepts of barbarism and civilisation, it is in Mda's focalisation of the Eastern Cape and his reconceptualising of the central divide between the 'soft' believers *(amathamba)* and the 'hard' unbelievers *(amagogotya)* that *The Heart of Redness* makes its strongest claims to the 'singularity' 'alterity' and 'invention' that Attridge describes.

Focalisation

Mda's novels are all richly invested with the sense of place on which the development of his characters depends. Readers are shown township life among the shack-dwellers of *Ways of Dying*, the sunflower fields of *The Madonna of Excelsior*, the divergent marine ecology of the seas off Hermanus in *The Whale Caller*, the wild beauty of Nongqawuse's Valley in *The Heart of Redness*; the Appalachian countryside of Kilvert, Ohio, as well as the cotton plantations of the South in *Cion*, and the rich white suburbs of *Black Diamond* from which BEE executives flee to the social and cultural resources of Soweto. Mda's ability to focalise the places of his novels — to make the reader *see* the geographical and psychological story-worlds in which his characters interact — parallels Peires' in his descriptions of the Eastern Cape. From the beginning of *The Heart of Redness* we are shown the unspoilt natural surroundings of Qolorha-by-Sea that will so captivate Camagu: 'Godforsaken? I think it is the most beautiful place on earth' (*Ibid*, 69). Bhonco, walking up the hillock to the Trading Store, has his arduous climb rewarded by the view from the top:

> *Down below, on his right, he can see the wild sea smashing gigantic waves against the rocks, creating mountains of snow-white surf. On his left his eyes feast on the green valleys and the patches of villages with beautiful houses painted pink, powder-blue, yellow and white* (*Ibid*, 5).

Zim's fig tree becomes a world full of birds and birdsong. Apart from connecting with the ancestors of the sea, forest, veld and homestead, it is home to many varieties of birds:

> *Today the spring weather is particularly beautiful. Green leaves are shyly beginning to appear on the tree. The green pigeons, with their red legs and red beaks, are flying around. Soon they will be feeding on the wild figs that will be ready even before summer. The* amahobobo *weaverbirds are adding more nests to the city that is already dangling and would be weighing the tree down if it had not gathered so much strength over the generations* (*Ibid*, 41).

Nongqawuse's Pool is shown to retain the magic that it had in the days of the prophetesses, although the aloes and reeds that Zim remembers no longer grow there:

> *[Qukezwa and Zim] are walking past* usunda *palms among the wild irises that grow in the valley. It is a cool afternoon, and the Namaqualand dove is cooing softly. In Nongqawuse's Pool a variety of eels, springer fish and river otters are engaged in various antics, showing off to the visitors. 'There used to be aloes around the pool. In the days of Nongqawuse there were aloes', says Zim, talking in whistles* (*Ibid*, 50).

Again, it is Qukezwa, defender of all that is indigenous, who mediates Camagu's focalisation of the many-coloured rocks at the seashore:

> *They walk silently among tall grasses that are used for thatching houses. Then they get to the rocks that are covered with mosses of various colours. Camagu is fascinated by the yellows, the browns, the greens and the reds that have turned the rocks into works of abstract art* (*Ibid*, 118–19).

Qolorha is surrounded by ecological variety, and this will become part of Dalton's plan for the future. First, however, the reader must be shown — as the Water Project Committee must be shown — the divergence of species on Bhonco's land:

> *Bhonco showed the committee a small piece of land surrounded by wild irises, orchids and* usunda *palms. On it grew protea flowers, which was strange since they are found nowhere else in the Eastern Cape. He told his colleagues that it was his land that had been left for him by his father. Dalton suggested that they develop the land into a botanical garden where they would cultivate rare indigenous plants, especially those that were endangered* (*Ibid*, 171).

Perhaps the most remarkably focalised sequence in the novel is Mda's description of the synaesthesia of Qukezwa's split-tone singing:

> *Qukezwa sings in such beautiful colours. Soft colours like the ochre of yellow gullies. Reassuring colours of the earth. Red. Hot colours like blazing fire. Deep blue. Deep green. Colours of the valleys and the ocean. Cool colours like the rain of summer sliding down a pair of naked bodies. She sings in soft pastel colours, this Qukezwa. In crude and glaring colours. And in bright glossy colours. In subdued colours of the newly turned fields. All at the same time* (*Ibid*, 223).

Mda's depictions of Qolorha are striking and memorable, perhaps because he himself grew up in the Eastern Cape. This landscape is vividly described in his autobiography, *Sometimes there is a Void* (Mda: 2011).

Reconceptualising Believers and Unbelievers

Where Peires' Believers and Unbelievers are ideologically distinct and internally consistent, Mda's Believers and Unbelievers — both in the nineteenth-century story and the contemporary story — embody contradiction. The family tree that opens the novel, facing the first page, is a case in point. It shows the descendants of the 'headless ancestor' Xikiya, with the Believers on the left and the Unbelievers on the right, descended respectively from Twin and Twin-Twin. Here Mda's creation of a divided lineage originating in twins creates an ontological and epistemological separation that is immediately suggestive and that connects with his fiction as a whole. From the novel's opening lines we are confronted with paradox: Bhonco the Unbeliever is close to tears because he is thinking of beautiful things. And he is 'different from the other Unbelievers in his family' (Mda: 2000, 1) because he *does* believe — as does his wife NoPetticoat — in the importance of the songs and dances in which they participate and in the pleasures of each other's company: 'The custom is that men walk in front and women follow. But Bhonco and NoPetticoat walk side by side. Sometimes holding hands!' Bhonco and NoPetticoat discuss the promotion to school principal of their daughter, Xoliswa Ximiya, fearing that the Believers will reject her headship. But the fact that Xoliswa has already achieved her promotion demonstrates that the power structures governing gender and status in Qolorha are changeable. The opening chapter foregrounds the competition between Believers and Unbelievers — when first Bhonco buys a dining-table with four chairs and then his rival Zim, leader of the Believers, outdoes him by buying one with six chairs. This small-scale domestic drama brings home to the reader the everyday absurdities with which ordinary people can be preoccupied because they are *not* fighting for survival — unlike the Believers and Unbelievers of Peires' book who are exterminated en masse by an intransigent colonial power.

Present-day Qolorha is full of characters who reflect the ethnic and cultural heterogeneity of South Africa post-apartheid — for example Dalton, the white owner of the Vulindlela Trading Store, and Camagu, the recently returned black intellectual who has spent many years in America. Although Dalton's Xhosa is excellent, his 'Missis' is a Free State Afrikaner who knows no African language. A former Cherry Queen in the all-white Cherry Festival in Ficksburg, she 'finds it difficult to understand her husband's cosy relationship with these rustics' (*Ibid*, 9). Camagu's story is also marked by the unexpected.

That he should find, on returning to the 'new' South Africa after many years' exile overseas, that there is no place for him within the corporate values of a black economic empowerment elite because he never learned the freedom dance, is hardly surprising. But the narrator makes much of Camagu's sexual drive, particularly in relation to social inferiors: 'There is something about servitude that seems to set the crotches of Camagu's ilk on fire. It must have been the same urge that drove the slave-master, normally a level-headed, loving family man with a rosy-cheeked wife and bouncing babies, from his mansion to a night of wild passion with the slave girl in the slave quarters or in the fields' (*Ibid*, 30). Camagu's involvement in the Qolorha community — particularly his attraction first to Xoliswa Ximiya and then to Qukezwa, two women who are his equals and who are both spirited and independent — will change this need for male sexual domination.

Both Dalton and Camagu declare their independence of the Believer/Unbeliever battles. Camagu insists: 'I am not an Unbeliever. I am not a Believer either. I don't want to be dragged into your quarrels' (*Ibid*, 135), while Dalton protests: 'I am not fickle. And I am not on the side of the Believers. Neither is Camagu. We just happen to agree with you, or you with us, on this matter of development ... We are not Nongqawuse's people' (*Ibid*, 281). But both Dalton and Camagu become crucial to the future of Qolorha. Dalton, determined to 'win his people back' from 'the clutches of the over-eager stranger from the city of Johannesburg' (*Ibid*, 311), defeats the developers by producing the court order that declares Qolorha a national heritage site, while Camagu's union with Qukezwa allies him with 'those who want to preserve indigenous plants and birds' (*Ibid*, 319). The end of the novel sees a rapprochement between these two leaders of the community. Camagu reassures Dalton that '[t]his rivalry of ours is bad. Our feud has lasted for too many years. Five. Almost six. And for what? Nothing! There is room for both the holiday camp and the cultural village at Qolorha. We must all work together' (*Ibid*, 319).

Believers and Unbelievers in Mda's novel cannot be differentiated employing the tools of rationality. Camagu, despite his Western education, declares his loyalty to the ancestors (*Ibid*, 119) and to Majola, the brown mole snake who is the totem of his tribe, the amaMpondomise (*Ibid*, 110). Bhonco the Unbeliever, despite his enthusiasm for technological development, depends for his psychic equilibrium on the Dance that the Khoikhoi taught his people, a dance that induces trance and connects back to the past and the world of the ancestors. As we might expect from the leader of the Believers, Zim, around whom fly green pigeons with red legs and beaks and the nesting *amahobohobo* weaverbirds, is powerfully connected with the flora and fauna of his surroundings. His fig tree connects him with the 'four different kinds of ancestors: the ancestors of the sea, the ancestors of the forest, the ancestors of the veld, and the ancestors of the homestead'. But his rival Bhonco is equally embedded in this community. At the end of the novel he grieves that because of the work of Dalton and Camagu 'he has nothing more to lose ... he lost the abaThwa dance, he lost his wife, he lost his daughter, and he lost the respect and prestige that he enjoyed in his village' (*Ibid*, 314). No less than Zim, Bhonco is rooted in his attachment to tradition (the Dance and the Ancestors) and in his connection to his kin. Fundamentally it is Belief that defines him: in his family, in his community and in the importance of remembering the past. Unlike others in Qolorha who have forgotten the past, Bhonco remembers and celebrates the conflicts of generations before. He holds to them, for 'they have shaped his present, and the present of the nation' (*Ibid*, 4).

What unites Zim and Bhonco is precisely the memory of the past. This memory is denied by the collective amnesia of Believers and Unbelievers alike:

> *The sufferings of the Middle Generations are only whispered. It is because of the insistence: Forget the past. Don't only forgive it. Forget it as well. The past did not happen. You only dreamt it. It is a figment of your rich collective imagination. It did not happen. Banish your memory. It is a sin to have a memory. There is virtue in amnesia. The past. It did not happen. It did not happen. It did not happen* (*Ibid*, 157).

Without memory, there can be no forgiveness and no moving on to the future. Those who refuse to remember the past have no stake in the present, as the emigrants to Australia and New Zealand who are selling up their property in Qolorha demonstrate in their discussions with Dalton:

> *'You are the only one who will remain in this mess, John ... Everyone is leaving.' 'Not everyone,' says Dalton ... 'I am staying here ... I am not joining your chicken run. This is my land. I belong here. It is the land of my forefathers.'* (*Ibid*, 160).

Dalton, defending the Afrikaner, accuses the would-be emigrants of racism and xenophobia:

> *You call the Afrikaner racist when he wants a homeland for his people. You laugh at his pie-in-the-sky Orania homeland as a joke — which it is — but you are not aware that you yourselves have a homeland mentality. Your homelands are in Australia and in New Zealand. That is why you emigrate in droves to those countries where you can spend a blissful life without blacks ... with people of your culture and your language ... just like the Orania Afrikaners* (*Ibid*, 160).

Dalton is not intimidated, however: 'He has his community of Qolorha-by-Sea. And his wife's people' (*Ibid*, 162). The new dispensation that Mda's novel suggests may be possible in a newly created South Africa depends on remembering the past, not denying its factions and divisions, but working together to heal them. Believers and Unbelievers can collaborate, as the stories of Dalton and Camagu illustrate. But Believers and Unbelievers can no longer be contained within the conceptual categories described by Peires. Bhonco wants to encourage development at Qolorha, but this is because he thinks the community will benefit. Peires explains that 'the unbelievers were thought of as "hard" because they stuck by their own conceptions of what was right and stingily exalted their private economic interests above the national well-being of the community at large', but this description does not explain Bhonco's motivations, for he is centrally concerned with the welfare of the community. Nor does he fit into the cohort of 'prosperous and wealthy men who were in a position to profit from the new economic opportunities created by the expansion of the colonial market' (Peires: 1989, 334–5). Rather, the Bhonco we meet early in the novel at Vulindlela Trading Store has to plead for *ityala* because he has no *nkamkan*; his greatest luxuries are to indulge in tobacco and corned beef. Nor does his wife NoPetticoat fit into the traditions and belief systems that Bhonco and Xoliswa Ximiya advocate. Towards the end of the novel NoPetticoat defects to Camagu's cooperative, less because she wants to make money than because she wants to express her own creativity by making traditional jewellery and costumes of the *amahomba*, like NoManage and NoGiant. In her defection NoPetticoat is simply expressing her own needs, which don't correspond with those of her husband or daughter; she is not choosing to neglect her family.

In Camagu and Dalton's view the way forward for the communities of Qolorha requires people from different backgrounds and traditions to collaborate in creating a Qolorha that will be equitable and democratic. This collaboration entails a bridging of former divisions. Qukezwa in the original story, facing starvation after the Cattle-Killing, bridges the gap between ancestors and descendants when she takes on the cultural identity of the Khoikhoi:

> *Indeed Qukezwa went back to the god of her people. She begged his forgiveness for abandoning him. Qukezwa, daughter of the stars, returned to worshipping the seven daughters of Tsiqwa, the one who told his stories in heaven, the one who created the world and all humanity. The prodigal daughter communed once more with the bright stars that were also known as the Seven Sisters* (*Ibid*, 294).

The link forged between the original Qukezwa and her Khoikhoi ancestors at the time of the Cattle-Killing is used by Mda to link the past to the present, in the split-tone singing of both Qukezwas: '[I]n *The Heart of Redness* the traditional *umngqokolo* singing is described in performance by the ancestral Qukezwa and her great-great-granddaughter Qukezwa, in prose that attempts to evoke the colours of its unique blend of overtones and undertones as a way of understanding the narrative blending of past and present, history and fiction, and the mundane and the fantastic' (Jacobs: 2009, 279).

Reading *The Dead Will Arise* and *The Heart of Redness* through Attridge's *The Singularity of Literature*

The chief concepts discussed in Attridge's book are *invention*, *singularity* and *alterity*. *Singularity* he defines as follows:

> *The singularity of a cultural object consists in its difference from all other such objects, not simply as a particular manifestation of general rules but as a peculiar nexus within the culture that is perceived as resisting or exceeding all pre-existing general determinations* (Attridge: 2004, 63).

Invention he explains as follows:

> *The act of invention is a mental feat, a step into the unknown, which makes possible both the manufacture of the new entity and, perhaps even more importantly, new histories of inventiveness in the culture at large* (*Ibid*, 42).

Alterity is conceptualised as follows:

> *To respond to the demand of the literary work as the demand of the other is to attend to it as a unique event whose happening is a call, a challenge, an obligation* (*Ibid*, 131).

Linked to these terms are the concepts of *authoredness*, 'the presupposition that the words we are reading are the product of a mental event or a number of such events, whereby the processes of linguistic meaning are engaged' (*Ibid*, 101), *event*, 'an act, an event of reading, never entirely separable from the act-event of writing that brought it into being' (*Ibid*, 59), and *performance*, 'reading is a performance of the singularity and otherness of the writing that constitutes the work as it comes into being for a particular reader in a particular context' (*Ibid*, 87). Attridge's conceptual framework fits into reader response theory, in that readers collaborate with writers to apprehend the ethical dimension that underlies all singular texts. Essential to the text's performativity is the writer's *shaping of language*, which reconfigures a familiar cultural repertoire so as to expose the 'gaps, strains and tensions' in the material being worked:

> *The most innovative artists ... have usually had an exceptionally great capacity to incorporate cultural materials, and have therefore been able ... to make the strongest impact upon their cultures. Nor is this merely a question of the richness and range of the stuff which the mind has to work on: what the original creator finds in the cultural field ... is not just material, but gaps in the material, strains and tensions that suggest the pressure of the other, of the previously unthinkable, of that which is necessarily excluded* (*Ibid*, 36).

This passage speaks directly both to Peires' and Mda's achievements. Peires' *The Dead Will Arise* is singular in every sense of the word: it is a unique intervention in South African history, the only impartial and fully documented record of the greatest catastrophe in Xhosa history, as the Preface makes clear:

Despite the widespread interest in Nongwaquse's prophecies, the full history of that terrible period has never been written. There has never been a book on the Cattle-Killing, not even a bad one. Several histories have commented on the topic, but none has completed it. The reason for this is that the primary sources, the evidence on which the historical account is based, are riddled with lies, both deliberate lies and self-delusions (Peires: 1989, 11).

Researching his book over a period of several years, Peires came to the conclusion that both conspiracy theories — 'Grey's Plot' and 'The Chiefs' Plot' — were equally suspect:

I am more than ever convinced that there was no plot on either side. Moreover, I am convinced that we do not need a plot or a conspiracy to explain the Cattle-Killing movement. I believe ... that the Cattle-Killing was a logical and rational response, perhaps even an inevitable response, by a nation driven to desperation by pressures that people today can barely imagine. I further believe ... that the Cattle-Killing would not have been so fatal an error had it not been for the measures of Governor Grey, which first encouraged and then capitalised on the movement. In this sense, though not in the one related by the old men of Xhosaland, Grey was the true perpetrator of the isihelegu sikaNongqawuse, *the catastrophe of Nongqawuse. That is why I nowhere use the well-known term, 'The National Suicide of the Xhosa'. The Nongqawuse catastrophe was as much a murder as it was a suicide* (*Ibid*, 12).

Contributing to the singularity of Peires' historical account is its marriage of inventiveness with historical accuracy. It is inventive in its shaping of language, its performance of the oral contexts through which its protagonists understand their world and which make for what Attridge describes as event-ness. Peires' text is an ethical justification of the people with whose history, language and belief systems he is preoccupied. Its documented evidence exposes the gaps, strains and tensions in both the colonial accounts of the Cattle-Killing — which blamed the Xhosa chiefs and people for the tragedy — and the Xhosa accounts, which blamed the colonialists for the tragedy. But looking back to *The Dead Will Arise* in the Afterword written in 2003, Peires draws the reader's attention to the 'gaps, strains and tensions' created by an historical account that is now closed:

It is not that there is no value in writing the most detailed history possible of Nongqawuse. Nor should we allow our interpretation of historical events to be influenced by fluctuating political circumstances. But we do perhaps need to define our priorities more in terms of the needs of the moment. South Africa ... cannot afford the luxury of an irrelevant history (*Ibid*, 390).

Finally...

The singularity of Mda's text builds on the singularity of Peires' because he allows the people of Qolorha-by-Sea to work towards constructing a new future, thus avoiding 'the luxury of an irrelevant history'. The future to which they look is both precarious and uncertain, but it fundamentally involves an agency denied to Peires' Believers and Unbelievers. Mda's novel, no less than Peires' historical account, is the result of his *shaping of language.* He shows us the quirkiness and unpredictability of human behaviour, documenting its comedy, allowing us to respond to the singular otherness of his characters with the mix of significant and trivial motives that drive their stories. Singularity, Attridge argues, is inseparable from inventiveness. And this inventiveness 'blends familiarity and surprise' (Attridge: 2004, 84), so that our creative reading of the text 'displaces the opposition of inside and outside, before and after' (*Ibid,* 91) as we respond to the ways in which our present in contemporary South Africa has been shaped by our past. This dialectic is demonstrated by the linguistic power and the *singularity* of *The Heart of Redness,* which builds on the linguistic power and *singularity* of *The Dead Will Arise.* The happening together of these two remarkable texts is 'a call, a challenge, an obligation' to us as readers.

Chapter Four

Towards a new ontology of postcolonial vision: *The Madonna of Excelsior*

Introduction

This chapter moves from a consideration of intertextuality in *The Heart of Redness* to Mda's use of the visual and perceptual in *The Madonna of Excelsior.* Chapter Five extends this emphasis on the visual by considering the relationship between art works and landscapes in three of Mda's novels.

Mda's third novel, *The Madonna of Excelsior,* is centrally concerned with 'examining the lives and experiences of ordinary people' as they move between apartheid and democracy. *The Madonna* achieves this dramatisation of a culture in transition by drawing extensively both on popular media representations (the newspaper coverage of the notorious Miscegenation Trial in the small town of Excelsior in the Orange Free State) and the expressionist/symbolist paintings of the Jesuit priest, Frans Claerhout. In this chapter, I concentrate on Mda's remarkable relationship as a writer of fiction to the visual. I argue that he inducts the reader into processes of vision or focalisation[1] that radically destabilise conventional patriarchal perspectives. Creating these altered ways of seeing has the potential, I believe, to construct a new ontology of postcolonial vision, one that challenges our contemporary sense that vision always implies surveillance or coercion.

The phrase in my title, 'Towards a new ontology of postcolonial vision', derives from David Levin's discussion, in *Modernity and the Hegemony of Vision,* of the way in which Western culture 'has been dominated by an ocularcentric paradigm, a vision-generated, vision-centred interpretation of knowledge, truth and reality' (Levin: 1993, 2). This paradigm of vision has been associated with domination. Levin asks, '[w]hat is left, today, of the rational vision of the Enlightenment? Has its institutionalisation in the course of modernity given it historically distinctive forms of incorporation, power and normativity? How has the paradigm of vision ruled, and with what effects?' He remarks

1 Mieke Bal defines focalisation as 'the relationship between the "vision", the agent that sees, and that which is seen' (Bal: 1997, 146).

that these questions are complex since they involve 'historical connections between vision and knowledge, vision and ontology, vision and power, vision and ethics'. Where Levin asks whether there is 'a postmodern future beyond the governance of ocularcentrism' (*Ibid*, 3) and wonders what such a postmodern vision would look like, I ask to what extent a postcolonial writer like Mda can shift the boundaries of the visual in his readers' apprehension so as to create an entirely altered political reality. Of course this subversion of dominant culture has been undertaken by artists and critics throughout the centuries. The contemporary theorist, Mieke Bal, shows how Rembrandt's painting *Danae* (1636) '[constructs] a masculine viewer whose visual potency is extremely problematic' (Bal in Levin: 1993, 387). She further argues that in *Olympia* (1863), Édouard Manet makes the gaze of the black woman looking at the white woman deeply ambiguous. Is her glance 'of desire, of engagement, of friendship, or is it one of curiosity, of jealousy, of contempt?' (*Ibid*: 401). In Bal's readings of these paintings 'vision can be pluralised so as to deprive the colonising, patriarchal gaze of its authority' (*Ibid*, 401). In this challenge to patriarchy issues of race, class and gender become central.

Claerhout's symbolist/expressionist paintings similarly foreground issues of race, class and gender, and Mda appropriates these perspectives for *The Madonna of Excelsior*. Where the discussion of art as subversion of dominant culture is for Bal centred on European artists, my investigation of Mda's use of the paintings of Frans Claerhout brings into play a specifically African context: the political, social and cultural environment of a small town in the Orange Free State as South Africa moves from the oppressions of apartheid to a multiracial, multicultural context post-apartheid. Mda appropriates Claerhout's vision by creating a story-world drenched in the colours and forms of Claerhout's paintings. The design of *The Madonna* is distinctively African, both in its geographical settings and in its narrative structure, which incorporates such oral storytelling devices as the voice of a communal narrator who speaks for the whole community.

In the Trinity's studio

Frans Claerhout is referred to as 'The Trinity' because he is 'man, priest and artist' in Mda's story-world. Jacobs points out that the actual Frans Claerhout was born in Pittem, West Flanders, in 1919 and came to South Africa in 1946 to work as a Catholic missionary, eventually settling at Thaba 'Nchu in the eastern Free State (Jacobs: 2009, 284). Claerhout was a leading exponent of South African expressionism and his work is both locally and internationally recognised. Jacobs divides the history of South African expressionism into three waves. The first, based on German expressionism, is represented by Irma Stern and Maggie Laubscher, the second by the Flemish immigrants Maurice van Essche, Hermann van Nazareth and Claerhout himself, and the third by a number of black artists of the 1960s 'such as Gerard Sekoto, Sydney Kumalo, Julian Motau, Tshidiso Motjuoadi, Louis Maqhubela, Lucky Sibiya, Cyprian Shilakoe and Dan Rakgoathe'. Later waves include 'André van Vuuren, Phillip Badenhorst and Marnus Havenga' (Jacobs: 286).

Claerhout drew his models from the very poor local people on his mission station, who earned money by sitting for him. Plate I shows him sketching two women seated next to a table on which paint tins and brushes are arrayed. Mda creates his fictional characters from these non-fictional models of Excelsior visible in Claerhout's studio.

The most important fictional protagonists in *The Madonna of Excelsior* are Niki and Popi, the mother and daughter whose story dominates the novel. Niki works as a domestic servant for the white, Afrikaans-speaking, middle-class burghers of Excelsior and ekes out her meagre wages by modelling with her child for the Trinity at the Roman Catholic mission at Thaba 'Nchu, 30 kilometres away from Mahlatswetsa Township where she lives. The first chapter of the novel introduces Niki and Popi, who are visiting the Trinity. Popi, a child of five, is both excited and distressed by the lack of realism of the Trinity's paintings. She is moved by his striking elongated people amid skewed houses, but distressed by their distortion, since she feels she can draw more accurate people and houses. Niki and Popi do not, of course, figure in this photo of the paintings in Claerhout's studio, because they are Mda's fictional characters rather than the real-life villagers on whom Claerhout based his paintings. Mda appropriates Claerhout's paintings for the story-world he creates around Niki and Popi.

On Plate II the artist can be seen to the side of a painting of a brown-skinned girl with dark eyes, long dark hair and a white dress. Mda uses this painting to describe Popi at 14: a mixed-race or 'Hotnot' girl born of the liaison between an Afrikaner farmer and his black servant. Such liaisons give rise to the Miscegenation Trial at the heart of the novel. Popi is introduced here by a question: 'Who is this little girl standing against a powder-blue sky with pink flowers for stars? Big sky and pink cosmos down to her bare feet like wallpaper. Who is this little girl in a snow-white long-sleeved frock?' (Mda: 2002, 113). The questions framing Popi's identity are central to her adolescent consciousness, for she is in search of herself and longs to be more like the other black children of Mahlatswetsa Township. Her slow journey towards self-acceptance is to become a feature of her *Bildungsroman*. The celebration of difference at the heart of Popi's story is evident everywhere, both in Claerhout's paintings and in Mda's fictionalisation of these paintings.

For instance, in Plate I a brown Madonna can be seen on the wall at the back of the studio. She is described by Mda as having a 'gaping mouth' and 'naked breast'. She is cradling a baby on her lap. The Madonna of this painting bears little resemblance to her Western Renaissance counterparts. She is secular, embodied, sculptural and somatic, wrapped up in the nurturing of her infant. Mda is attracted to this visceral closeness of mother and child, which Claerhout constantly explores. What in Mda's novel distinguishes the gaze of the Trinity from the gaze of the white farmers who lust after black women is his calm, non-erotic attention to the subjects of his paintings.

Two paintings away from the Brown Madonna, the photo shows Claerhout sketching at his easel. Beside the figure of the sketching artist is a striking, full-scale painting (see Plate III, *A Sunburnt Christ*). This Christ is brown-skinned. The heavy lines and blood-stained colouring of his face bespeak his agony. Yet he is surrounded by vibrant colour and growth: huge yellow sunflowers and pink and white cosmos against a turquoise background. Behind the crucified Christ, a shadowy, nun-like figure in a blue veil takes the place of the grieving Mary. Four figures in blue with blue and red hats pass a round green and blue sun. The sky is swirling with cloud effects, suggesting a gathering storm. This powerful painting is appropriated by Mda for the depiction of his protagonist Niki, victim of the cruelty of apartheid laws. No less a figure than the crucified Christ is appropriated by Mda to figure Niki's suffering. Unlike that of Christ, Niki's face has been ravaged not by the sun but by the skin-lightening chemicals she has applied over the years to change her racial categorisation from black to white. These chemicals have now caused her skin to cake and crack. Her trauma, as a victim of racial prejudice, is to be taken seriously, no less seriously than the suffering of the incarnate Christ — despised, rejected, and tortured on the cross. Here, truly crossing gender and race boundaries, are Claerhout's and Mda's visions of the Mater Dolorosa. Once again, there seems little connection between Claerhout's painting, Mda's story-world and the conventional religious paintings of the Renaissance. Where paintings of the Mater Dolorosa in Renaissance iconography convey the Madonna's premonitions of the tragic fate of her child, this shadowy Madonna figure behind the Christ figure is enigmatic.

Ecphrasis: turning paintings into fiction

Explaining the process of *ecphrasis*, J.U. Jacobs writes:

> *To appreciate fully how in* The Madonna of Excelsior *Mda narratively further indigenises a Western European art form that has already been indigenised by*

> *Claerhout, one needs to understand his fictional discourse in this novel in terms of* ecphrasis, *'the literary description of a work of art'* (Hollander: 1998, 86) ... The Madonna of Excelsior *is ... an example of actual* ecphrasis, *where a literary work incorporates actual, particular works of art that pre-exist it, as opposed to notional* ecphrasis *where a literary text incorporates descriptions of purely fictive works of art* (Jacobs: 2009, 288, 289).

I argue that Mda's explorations of refigured identity are rooted in his strong painterly imagination. This teaches the reader how to see anew by creating changed spaces in memory and culture that redress the negativity of the colonial experience. Mda uses authorial and figural points of view, perspective and focalisation to alter the reader's understanding. Both the novelist Zakes Mda and the painter Frans Claerhout create, for 'ordinary people', the social and psychological conditions that may result in freedom.[2] Through the narrator's graphic depiction of the paintings, the reader is shown the art of Frans Claerhout. Claerhout's style is a blend of expressionism and symbolism, transposing into an African context the bright colours, bold impasto brush strokes and deviation from realism that connects back to his European past: to Van Gogh, Gauguin, Munch and Cézanne, right back to Breughel. Like Breughel, Claerhout's subjects are 'ordinary folk doing ordinary things'. Yet, the novel insists, 'God radiates from them' (Mda: 2002, 131).

Why does Mda build his story-world on Claerhout's art? According to Leon Strydom, Claerhout's expressionism foregrounds emotion, using contrast, dynamic movement and distortion to convince the viewer in a direct and empathetic way of the artist's interpretation of reality: 'The expressionist painting suggests involvement (wonder, compassion, humour) rather than detachment (contrast, judgement, caricature). It implies a view of reality rather than a mere representation of reality, one which is felt rather than seen' (Strydom: 1983, 10). In addition to his involvement of the viewer, Mda is attracted to the painter's capacity to reconcile oppositions and to place individuals in dynamic, creative interaction with their communities.

From the opening of the novel the reader is inducted into a visual and epistemological world of startling complexity. Real paintings by a real painter

2 Drawing on the concept of *ecphrasis*, Susan Rogers writes about the ways in which A. S. Byatt and Zakes Mda 'mix media, incorporating the works of established artists in their fiction as tools to investigate the process of healing after an experience of suffering and grief' (Rogers: 2008, 42). Rogers quotes Claerhout's own description of his symbolist/expressionist world-view, which inspires Mda in *The Madonna*: 'I am *expressionisties.* If you paint a horse, you cannot make it funny or long tail or ear, *maar* a donkey ... you can make it long ear, you can make them blue or yellow. It's like a *boerebok*, you can give him a long beard and its tail up ... but everyone wants a donkey. Maybe I'm a kind of donkey' (*Ibid*, 51–2).

illuminate the lives of fictional characters. These real paintings are seen and interpreted by Mda's authorial narrator, who not only describes Claerhout's expressionist and symbolist techniques, but also suggests that Claerhout's 'threeness' as 'man, priest and artist' captures the 'threeness' of the 'open skies, the vastness and the loneliness of the Free State' (Mda: 2002, 2). The Claerhout paintings at the centre of Mda's story-world are vividly described by the narrator's words. For instance, the *Brown Madonna* who appears on the back wall of Claerhout's studio in the photo is depicted as

> *[e]xuding tenderness. Burnt umber mother in a blue shirt, squatting in a field of yellow ochre wheat. Burnt sienna baby wrapped in white lace resting between her thighs. Mother with a gaping mouth. Big oval eyes. Naked breast dangling above the baby's head. Flaky blue suggesting a halo. Unhampered bonding of mother and child and wheat* (*Ibid*, 11).

But the reader has to imagine and focalise this portrait without the assistance of any visual material in the novel itself, for the text contains no traces of the Claerhout paintings. The only exceptions are an enlarged black and white Madonna and child on the inside front cover, against which is juxtaposed a photo of a smiling Zakes Mda, and part of a black and white painting showing a donkey, a sunflower and some skewed houses on the inside back cover. No acknowledgement is made of either of these visual extracts, although the full-colour photo of sunflower fields near Bethlehem, in the Free State, used on the front cover, is acknowledged. My chapter reproduces and discusses several of the Claerhout paintings that are important for *The Madonna of Excelsior*. These are taken from the book entitled *Claerhout: Artist and Priest* by Dirk and Dominique Schwager (1994). The paintings are easily recognised from the narrator's descriptions of them, but the only visual 'quotations' from Claerhout's paintings used by Mda are postage-stamp-sized images extracted from the paintings. These small, sepia fragments preface each chapter, occurring as tiny images on the left next to each chapter heading. Their relationship to the paintings from which they are extracted is virtually unrecognisable. Mda's verbal and textual appropriation of Claerhout's images is total. He adopts only those painterly depictions that fit his fictional world, leaving the reader in no doubt that it is not Claerhout but Mda who controls the novel's story-world. This supremacy of textual authority over painterly authority is made clear on the last page, where the authorial narrator comments on the healing begun in Niki and Popi by the creations of the Trinity. Yet, the authorial narrator insists, 'the trinity never knew all these things. His work was to paint the subjects, and not to poke his nose into their lives beyond the canvas' (Mda: 2002, 268). This fact brings me back to my title, 'Towards a new ontology of postcolonial vision', and the question of how a postcolonial writer may wish to adopt focalising strategies that enable readers to perceive cultural and political perspectives not endorsed by a dominant culture. When Bal writes about artists' subversions of European culture, she does so from a feminist perspective. But both Mda and Claerhout are males, very much in the 'God business' of authoring fictional or painterly worlds. Can their mediation enable the escape from patriarchal values that my title implies?

Mda's selection and ordering of Claerhout's paintings makes use of two principles derived from multi-panelled altarpieces in Claerhout's native Belgium that date back to the eleventh century: the principle of the *cycle*, which depicts a theme in a time-space continuum showing consecutive episodes or phases in a history such as the Stations of the Cross; and the 'principle of a *series*, which is the repetition of a theme discontinuous in time and space' (Strydom: 1983, 16). These alternating principles of cycle and series allow the viewer or reader to understand continuity and change, development and variety: 'the viewer recognises time and again the old in the new in a different guise' (*Ibid*, 17).

A further complication with which the reader is confronted from the very beginning of the novel is that of narrative levels. Mda makes use of two complementary but very different narrators. The first is the authorial narrator, responsible for delivering the author's overall design. Through the authorial narrator may be glimpsed the implied author. Seymour Chatman explains this term: 'The implied author is the agency within the narrative fiction itself which guides any reading of it. Every fiction contains such an agency. It is the source — on each reading — of the work's intent [and refers to] a work's "whole" or "overall" meaning, including its connotations, implications, unspoken messages' (Chatman: 1990, 174). In addition to the authorial narrator, Mda uses the communal narrator, a resident of Mahlatswetsa Township who knows all the protagonists and is involved in the novel's action. As a member of Mda's story-world, the communal narrator is what Chatman calls a 'fallible filter', a term that he prefers to that of 'unreliable narrator'. As Chatman explains, '"fallible" seems a good term for a filter character's inaccurate, misled or self-serving perceptions of events, situations and other characters, for it attributes less culpability to the character than does "unreliable"' (*Ibid*, 150). Thinking of the communal narrator in this novel as a 'fallible filter' of the experiences of his community allows the reader to register his remarkable insight and compassion as he recounts the lives of his fellow township-dwellers. It also explains his occasional lapses into racism and sexism. These are the inevitable result of his social conditioning under the oppressive and distorting ideology of apartheid. He is, after all, historically as much a victim of apartheid as any other character in the novel.

Women, donkeys, sunflowers

From the first page of the first chapter of *The Madonna of Excelsior*, the reader is drawn into the landscape of the Free State and the paintings of Frans Claerhout, whose chief subjects are women, donkeys and sunflowers. (See Plate IV, *Women Harvesting*, and Plate V, *Boy Riding Donkey Backwards*). These subjects are imbricated throughout the novel and woven into Mda's story-world:

> *Colour explodes. Green, yellow, red and blue. Sleepy-eyed women are walking among sunflowers. Naked women are chasing white doves among sunflowers ... A boy is riding a donkey backwards among sunflowers. The ground is red. The sky is blue. The boy is red. The faces of the women are blue. Their hats are yellow and their dresses are blue. Women are harvesting wheat* (Mda: 2002, 1).

The novel begins with the voice of the authorial narrator who remarks 'all these things flow from the sins of our mothers' (*Ibid*). His is also the novel's closing statement: 'From the sins of our mothers all these things flow' (*Ibid*, 268). The cycle begun in the first sentence — where the narrator ironically registers patriarchy's simultaneous demonisation and instrumentalisation of women — will be closed by Mda's choice of the concluding painting of four women described in the last chapter. This description begins:

> *The real new millennium has dawned. Four women with painted breasts walk in single file. Their long necks carry their multicoloured heads with studied grace. Their hair is white with age, but their faces glow with youth. They do not lose their way, even though they undertake their journey with closed eyes* (*Ibid*, 265).

The cycle of exploitation and humiliation that started with the Afrikaner farmers' rape of young black women in the sunflower fields and reached its climax in the notorious Excelsior Miscegenation Trial has ended with the same women. They now access a new identity as they choose their own way forward — just as Niki and Popi have moved from victimhood to agency by the end of the novel.

This section is entitled 'Women, donkeys, sunflowers'. What of the donkeys? (See Plate V, *Boy Riding Donkey Backwards*; Plate VI, *Donkey and Cock*, and Plate VII, *Profound Nostalgia*). Here I think Mda is again making use of the idea of the cycle, relying on the reader to perceive the connections between the donkey paintings and the characters and events of his story-world. The donkey paintings can be understood as constituting another cycle. The first initiates us into Claerhout's vibrant use of colour and expressionist distortion. Why is the boy riding backwards? For the same reason, presumably, that

Claerhout sometimes places signposts in the middle of sunflower fields or depicts people 'without feet or toes' (*Ibid*, 1). The reader has to suspend disbelief and enter the characters' own imaginative worlds, however unlike the real world these imaginative worlds may be. That is to say, he or she has to relate to the intensity of the yellow sun, the yellow sunflowers and the yellow donkey. Together these represent the joyful union of man, animal and landscape against the blue sky.

There are dozens of women, donkeys and sunflowers in the Claerhout paintings; but the donkey that starts the chapter titled 'The Cherry Festival' is quite unlike the other donkeys described in this chapter. It records festivity with gaily decorated processions of floats, people and animals in the main street on a Saturday morning. The donkey in this painting is not part of a landscape or a procession; rather, it is enormous and takes up the whole painting. The authorial narrator comments: 'There is no room for anything else, except the red cock that the ass carries in a transparent bag strapped on its back and hanging from its side. The donkey and the cock own the world' (*Ibid*, 43). This donkey is obsessive, excessive, exaggerated. Why?

In Mda's accompanying story-world, Niki and the Afrikaner, Johannes Smit, are at the Ficksburg Cherry Festival selling their wares at wooden tables under umbrellas. The white farmers, Johannes Smit and Stephanus Cronje, fight for Niki's favours. Cronje wins and triumphantly drives Niki to a field on the outskirts of town for a night of passion, while the disconsolate Smit mopes alone at the Cherry Ball back in town. Now Niki has the husband of her enemy, Cornelia Cronje — who has previously humiliated her by forcing her to strip naked in front of the workers at the Excelsior Butchery — completely at her mercy. Niki's focalisation changes in this moment:

> *[Stephanus Cronje] was deep inside her. Under the stars. She looked into his eyes in the light of the moon. She did not see Stephanus Cronje, owner of Excelsior Slaghuis. She did not see a boss or a lover. She saw Madam Cornelia's husband with the emphasis on Madam. And she had him entirely in her power* (Mda: 2002, 50).

Now Niki can see the stars that she could not see in the previous chapter. Like the cock and the donkey who preface this chapter, she feels that she owns the world. So the magisterial donkey and red cock are chosen by Mda as objective correlatives for Niki's moment of triumph. But the donkey is blinkered. Niki's 'triumph' will prove short-lived in that it will lead to Cronje's suicide and Niki's and Popi's ostracisation by the community. Niki will be shunned because of her liaison with the white farmers and Popi will be shunned because she is 'coloured'. This trajectory of suffering and bitterness on the women's part will only be resolved at the end of the novel. Unlike the first donkey, which celebrates creative freedom, Mda chooses this blinkered donkey because it communicates foreboding.

Finally, the third donkey painting introduces a new era. It occurs in a late chapter called 'Profound Nostalgia', which begins, 'All things are bright and beautiful' (*Ibid*, 239) and tells of the changed fortunes of Niki and Viliki, the Pule Siblings, after the arrival of democracy in South Africa. Now the communal narrator enters, recording a major change that affects many of the township residents: they have 'gradually moved from cow-dung to coal' (*Ibid*, 239). The authorial narrator, though, records a much deeper and more pervasive change. Despite the new political freedom, neither Popi nor Viliki is contented. They long for the past: 'A profound nostalgia for the romantic days of the struggle attacked them. Days of sacrifice and death. Days of selfless service and hope' (*Ibid*, 240). In this painting of the donkey with the candle, Mda seems to challenge the reader to imagine a new time of transformation and hope where — the evils of apartheid now over — people of all races will be able to create a better future together. But as the following chapter, 'Betrayed by the Elders', makes clear, the way forward is full of pitfalls and disappointments. The candle-bearing donkey fuses the ordinary with the visionary. This fusion recalls the photographs in Schwager's book, which show Claerhout's simple, usually illiterate congregation attending services in the mission church they built themselves. Their eyes are bright and they hold candles in their hands. In the spirit that J.U. Jacobs has called 'evenhanded' for its ability to show corruption amongst blacks currently in power as well as amongst their white predecessors (Jacobs: 2009, 5), Mda signals that change must be social as well as political.[3] The candle must be kept burning to ensure that one cycle of oppression does not end only to be followed by another.

'Women, donkeys, sunflowers' — and what of sunflowers? Yellow sunflowers and pink, red and white cosmos appear abundantly in Claerhout's paintings as constant accompaniments to individual depictions. In this respect, the flowers are woven into the painter's chronotopes, part of the recurring space-time continua of his paintings. They also mark significant cycles. It is in the sunflower fields at the beginning of the novel that the histories of Mda's instrumentalised women begin, and in the sunflower fields at the end of the novel that these same women come to experience creative community.

3 For a discussion of the contrast between political revolution (following the removal of colonial political control) and social revolution (promoting equity and justice) see Mike Kissack & Michael Titlestad in Bell, David & Jacobs, J. U. (2009) *Ways of Writing*, 149–67.

Appropriating the Madonna motif

Frans Claerhout was a Belgian artist and must have been thoroughly familiar with the depictions of the Madonna in Western painting, which have so complicated a relation to the legacy of Eve. Marina Warner writes: '[t]he emphasis on Mary's body, on her miraculous virginity and motherhood, concentrates attention on female physicality and biological processes; it carnalises her figure, *grounding her character in the flesh even as it makes her an exception to all mankind*' (Warner: 2000, xviii. Author's emphasis). Derived from tenth-century Byzantine icons that survived the Roman Empire, early Madonnas were stylised and formalised rather than realistic. However, later artists such as Cimabue, Giotto and Duce in the thirteenth century moved away from symbolism to a much more humanistic approach in their depictions of the Madonna. Raphael portrayed ordinary women in his Madonna paintings, which reflected a new secularisation through robust, sculptural qualities, while the Florentine painter, Masaccio, broke away from the conventions of European Gothic art and depicted realistically observed people in convincing situations. He was interested particularly in the way people see each other. In the high Renaissance paintings of Piero della Francesca, the Madonna is surrounded by panoplies of saints and angels. In this 'Sacre Conversazione' mode between Madonna, saints and angels, della Francesca may be seen to convey a balance between humanism and scientific enquiry by depicting the changes in the world in which he was living, exploring particularly the new relationship of Man to God.

The Madonna motif that recurs in both Claerhout's paintings and Mda's text is a good example of what Strydom has called the series as opposed to the cycle: 'the repetition of a theme discontinuous in time and space' (Strydom: 1983, 16). *The Blue Madonn*a who frames Chapter 17 is described by the authorial narrator as 'different from the other madonnas. No cosmos blooms surround her. She is not sitting in a brown field of wheat. No sunflowers flourish in her shadow. Yet she exudes tenderness like all the others' (Mda: 2002, 107). (See Plate VIII, *The Blue Madonna*.) This tender and youthful Madonna embodies, in Mda's overall design, the creative interactions between the Trinity and the people he paints. In this chapter the Trinity transforms his models, Popi and Niki of the flesh. He gives his Madonna the features of her child — or rather, the features Popi will have as she grows older. Though initially neither woman perceives the extent of the Trinity's influence on their lives, both Niki and Popi come to recognise the importance of his vision and of his values to their sense of themselves. Initially indignant at his creative licence, his 'right to change things at the dictates of his whims … [T]o invent his own truths' (*Ibid*, 108), Niki will come to value the Trinity's humorous interventions. She wonders, '[f]rom where did he get all that power, to re-create what had already been created' (*Ibid*, 108). Niki also comes to treasure the priest's near-miraculous ability to heal discord. He dissolves an argument between mother and daughter through the gift of laughter when his impersonations of the braying of a donkey convulse Popi and completely melt her anger against Niki. Vision and the laughter that leads to self-acceptance: these are the Trinity's gifts. The gift of laughter will later be celebrated in the novel when the daughter makes the mother laugh. Popi alludes to her identity as a coloured or mixed-race person and Niki laughs 'for the first time in many years'. She exclaims: 'I am so happy that at last you are so free of shame about being coloured that you can even make a joke about it' (*Ibid*, 260). On one of her visits to the Trinity's mission station, Niki prays for the continuing creativity of the priest who is also a comforter: 'for his hands that must stay strong. For his vision that must continue to find joy in cosmos, donkeys, women and sunflowers. For his passion for colour that must never fade. And for his muse that occasionally flung him into a mother-and-child mode' (*Ibid*, 112).

The final painting I want to touch on is from Chapter 11. (See Plate IX, *Eyes in the Sky*.) Here we are shown an unusual Nativity. The Holy Family is bottom centre but most of the painting is given over to the 'big eyes in the sky' that observe the trio. Here surely Claerhout — and Mda — are responding to the 'Sacre Conversazione' mode of della Francesca's Madonnas, surrounded as they are by saints and angels who help the viewer to understand the relationship between man and God. Discussing 'Sacre Conversazione' Charles Hope remarks: 'It has been suggested … that the saints gathered around the Virgin are celebrating the celestial liturgy, or that the child is held up like the Eucharistic host … more generally, altarpieces are said to be "about aspects of doctrine, such as the Incarnation"' (Hope in Verdon & Henderson: 1990, 536). Unlike della Francesca's saints and angels, the voices and gazes of the citizens of Mahlatswetsa Township who are Niki's neighbours are far from unambiguously affirmative. Their mockery has, over the years, ostracised Niki for her miscegenation, and Popi as the product of that miscegenation. The communal narrator confesses his own involvement in the community's media-fuelled accusations:

> *'We fear that even in your Johannesburg, people will see us as the bad women of Excelsior,' added Susanna.*
> *We jeered and cheered. The women were both heroes and villains to various sections of the crowd.*
> *We mocked Maria: 'Hello, Mrs Lombard'.*
> *We taunted Mmampe: 'Hello, Mrs Smit'.*
> *We leered at Niki: 'Hello Mrs Cronje'.*

> *We called each of the women by the name of the lover with whom she had been charged* (Mda: 2002, 98).

Equally, the communal narrator enters into the community's contempt of the black women's white Afrikaner lovers: '[w]e cheered and jeered even louder when Johannes Smit and Groot-Jan Lombard emerged from the courtroom' (*Ibid*, 98).

By contrast with the communal narrator, the authorial narrator is not judgemental. In this his world-view resembles that of the Trinity, whose paintings celebrate and immortalise the previously instrumentalised. Although both Mda and Claerhout are male, their verbal and visual strategies may be argued to destabilise the will to domination of the male gaze. Bal, writing about the way in which the paintings of Rembrandt and Manet problematise the voyeuristic gaze, remarks:

> *The mode of vision I am trying to describe is ... a different way of getting to know. The epistemology that is being tested here is based on relationality, or more precisely, on the model of friendship. Friendship requires getting to know other people in a dialogic mode. In the visual domain, this means a seeing radically different from the voyeuristic, asymmetrical mode that has for too long been hegemonic ... it calls for a suspension of what we think we see, for a recognition of historical positionality, and for an appreciation of relations of reciprocity* (Bal: 1997, 400).

Claerhout's distorted, impassioned expressionist-symbolist paintings refuse voyeuristic hegemonic ways of knowing and seeing. This is why Mda appropriates them for *The Madonna of Excelsior.*

Chapter Five

Art, Landscape and Identity in *She Plays with the Darkness*, *The Madonna of Excelsior* and *Cion*

Introduction

This chapter continues to investigate the imbrication of Mda's texts with the visual arts. In Chapter Four I traced the relationship between the story-worlds of *The Madonna of Excelsior* and the story-worlds depicted in Frans Claerhout's paintings, arguing that Claerhout and Mda's refusal of hegemonic ways of seeing induct the postcolonial reader into new understandings of class, race and gender issues. In this chapter, I extend the examination of visual arts into the arena of landscape, looking at the ways in which *She Plays with the Darkness*, *The Madonna of Excelsior* and *Cion* link the visual in paintings and quilts with a particular understanding of the environment. As Robert Layton and Peter J. Ucko point out, 'Landscapes are ... ways of expressing conceptions of the world and they are also a means of referring to physical entities. The same physical landscape can be seen in many different ways by different people, often at the same time ... the term may refer both to an environment, generally one shaped by human action, and to a representation (particularly a painting) which signifies the meanings attributed to such a setting' (Ucko & Layton: 1990, 1).

Denis Cosgrove has linked the concept of landscape in the evolution of European societies to 'a way of seeing — a way in which some Europeans have represented ... the world about them and their relationships with it' (Cosgrove: 1988, 1). This concept of landscape implies 'an attempt to sustain the moral order [of] pre-capitalist conceptions of human relations with the land and nature against the economic order of industrial capitalism' (*Ibid*, 252). After the nineteenth century, this concept of landscape was unsustainable, squeezed out by economic and technological forces.

But Mda's landscapes depict an indigenous or pre-capitalist conception of individuals in concord with their environments. This is portrayed in the healing rituals celebrated by the Bushmen in The Cave of Barwa in *She*

Plays,[1] in the ecological balance between the human and the natural world emblematised by the Free State's sunflower fields in *The Madonna* and in the farming economies of poor Appalachian communities in *Cion*. These novels connect non-commodifying environments with non-commodifying art forms,[2] whether in paintings or quilts, and foreground the role of community. Bateson's remarks on the connection between artworks and the environment are apposite here:

> *The role of art in technological culture is to act as a corrective to our too-purposive view of the world and consciousness. Art calls attention to a systemic view of life. This means that the wisdom of art is humility: the knowledge that the human is only part of a larger system and that the part can never ultimately control the whole* (Bateson, quoted in Frielick: 1992, 71).[3]

1 Thomas Dowson writes about the cultural and political importance of representing Bushman art in non-commodifying ways. He is speaking about rock-art imagery as it appears in the South African landscape, but his argument applies equally to the fictional representation of Bushman art undertaken by Mda in *She Plays*:

> Just as rock art had a power for the original producers and scores of subsequent and diverse consumers, so too these images have a power to transform and re-negotiate popular perceptions, not only about so-called 'primitive art', but also the past, which itself is constituted in the present. Rock art need not be seen as an early stage in the origins of Western art, as it is often presented in the grand evolutionary histories of art from earliest times to the present. In its reproduction and consumption today, rock art imagery can be used to challenge the prejudices of the past. The power of the images that resulted from the working of art in times past can continue to be harnessed by generations to come (Dowson: 1996, 321).

2 Mda's linking of environmental awareness with graphic and performative arts, and the idea that art can enable psychic growth in the poorest circumstances, recalls Alice Walker's *The Color Purple*. There Celie's development is shaped by her interactions with Shug Avery, 'singer and magic-maker — a woman who has taken charge of her own destiny' (dust-jacket blurb). Living with Shug in Memphis, Celie is charmed with a house and garden full of monuments and fountains, and with Shug's bringing together of America with Africa in the 'turtles and elephants … in the fountain … under the trees. And all over the house' (Walker: 1983, 188). Together, Celie and Shug draw extensions to the interior and exterior of the house — flower-beds, geraniums, stone elephants, turtles and ducks — so that the whole environment is imaginatively transformed: 'By the time we finish, our house look like it can swim or fly' (*Ibid*, 189). This creativity is figured in Mda's fiction by the three novels discussed in this chapter and prefigured in the imaginative collaborations of Toloki and Noria in *Ways of Dying*.

3 Marita Wenzel similarly remarks:

> Zakes Mda perceives art as a form of self-expression which induces self-knowledge, acts as a survival technique … and enables insight and transcendence through the imagination (125). … For Mda, all forms of art provide the necessary distance, the … space that induces change and new ways of 'seeing' life as well as an alternative perspective on and interpretation of reality (Wenzel: 2009, 125–126).

An asymmetrical progression emerges when we compare *She Plays with the Darkness*, *The Madonna of Excelsior* and *Cion*. At the centre of *She Plays* is a destroyed or extinguished imagined /Xam cave painting. *The Madonna* is dominated by an array of the real paintings of Frans Claerhout and *Cion* invites the reader to imagine an art world quite different from the traditional quilt patterns it describes in relation to escaping slaves on the Underground Railroad. So we move from a destroyed art world that inspires the creativity of the artist/dreamer Dikosha, to the real paintings on which Mda builds the story-worlds of his characters Niki and Popi, to an art-world in *Cion* that, although related to traditional quilting patterns, must be created by the reader's imagination. What links all three novels is the relationship they create between their protagonists' performative activities and the landscapes that surround them and enable their creativity.

She Plays with the Darkness

Set in Lesotho and published in the same year as *Ways of Dying*, the opening of *She Plays* is a tour de force. We are shown a vividly portrayed mountain setting and witness the singing and dancing of the young girls who perform the songs of the pumpkin. Yet from the opening page this vibrant performance exists within a context of death and loss, for the girls fear that 'one day the great mist will rise and suffocate them all to death' and the young girls' songs are full of 'lost loves and unfulfilled desires. Of husbands who have been devoured by the city of gold, never to return to their families again' (Mda: 1995b, 1). The main protagonist, Dikosha, refuses to submit to domestic patriarchal pressures; instead of preparing and cooking the staple dish of maize porridge she chooses to dance and sing, and instead of agreeing to marriage she chooses her own path. Dikosha is thus a precursor both for the free spirits who will challenge traditional roles and for the figure of the artist capable of transforming her society — as Niki and Popi do in *The Madonna*. This female artist figure, T. Spreelin MacDonald writes, '[provides] a vision of the role of the marginal creator in bridging the dichotomies of post-colonial existence. Asserting the vitality of the creator of non-instrumental art, Mda's Dikosha is the figure of the post-colonial cultural innovator, isolated yet vital' (MacDonald: 2009, 114). Dikosha's creativity is stimulated by the *dikema* patterns painted by villagers on the walls of their homesteads, and finds its most powerful inspiration in The Cave of Barwa, which had been home to the ancient Barwa people hundreds of years before:

> *The Barwa, or Bushmen as the white people called them, were the original inhabitants of the land. They lived here happily for centuries, hunting animals and gathering wild fruits and roots, until* [*Dikosha's*] *ancestors came and drove them away, and killed some, and married others. They left a legacy of caves with wonderful paintings on the walls, and the Cave of Barwa was the most famous of*

> *them all. It had red and black paintings of big-buttocked people chasing deer with bows and arrows, or dancing in a trancelike state. Dikosha was spellbound by one painting especially, which showed a dancer with the body of a woman and the head of a beast. It was a fierce-looking beast that no one had ever seen before. Dikosha saw herself as the monster-woman-dancer, ready to devour all the dancers of the world, imbuing herself with their strength and stamina, and then dancing for ever and ever, until the end of time* (Mda: 1995b, 16).

The Cave of Barwa painting teaches Dikosha not only about dancing, but about healing in the trance-states enacted by the San dancers, for whom the ancestors are all-important. From the people of the Cave she learns 'the power to see songs'. But in Chapter 10, 'The Great Snow', the monster-woman-dancer of the Cave of Barwa is finally extinguished by the graffiti painted by tourists on the Cave walls; with her go also the other /Xam dancers. For Dikosha this is the end of 'the healing dances of the night with the people of the cave. It was not only the death of the dance, but the death of a lifestyle as well' (*Ibid*, 128).

From this point, halfway through the novel, Mda's attempts to render justice to the political events that keep overwhelming Lesotho causes a falling-off of intensity in the characterisation of the protagonists whom we have met in an ecologically rich and challenging environment. Dikosha's twin, Radisene, now becomes involved in fraudulent business practices in the Lowlands, while Dikosha is reduced, after losing her connection with the Cave of Barwa, to hearing the confessions of the village men — an ambiguous role at best. Has she now become merely an instrument of patriarchy, or does her prophetic role allow her some autonomy?

In 'Twinship and Humanism in *She Plays with the Darkness*', T. Spreelin MacDonald argues that the novel, through its creation of the twin protagonists Dikosha and Radisene, undermines social binaries and '[asserts] the role of the marginalised artist' (MacDonald: 2009, 173). Discussing the destructive paternalism that robs Dikosha of her creative potential, Macdonald maintains that 'the realm of privacy most closely achieved in the Cave of Barwa is the "darkness" of the novel's title … In her quest for the self-contained aesthetic transcendence of her life station, Dikosha risks becoming fully enveloped by the darkness of isolation' (*Ibid*, 139). As ingenious as this reading is, it leaves, in my opinion, certain questions unanswered. The first has to do with the power of art as a non-instrumental agent of change — which Mda demonstrates in *Ways of Dying, The Madonna of Excelsior* and *Cion*. Why is the desire to create art — whether it be dancing, singing, painting or storytelling — necessarily destructive of community? What is even more disturbing however, is why Mda allows the real power of the Bushman painting, which inspires Dikosha, to be extinguished, given his insistence throughout his fiction on the vitality of /Xam traditions.

In their remarkable book *My Heart Stands in the Hill* (2005), Janette Deacon and Craig Foster superimpose the images of the original Bushman interlocutors — /A!Kunta, //Kabbo, /Han ≠Kass/O, Dia!kwain, ≠Kasin and !Kweitan-ta (who served as interlocutors to Lucy Lloyd and Wilhelm Bleek in the correspondence recorded in the 1870s called the Bleek and Lloyd Collection)[4] on the landscapes that make up their ancestral homes. Their images appear on the cracked mud around the waterhole at the Bitterpits; on grasslands stretching as far as the eye can see; on the *kokerboom*, or tree aloe, whose hollowed-out branches were used to store Bushman arrows; on the carapace of a tortoise; on the water falling over an upstream weir; on the rocks on which the /Xam painted lizards, buck, elephants and elephant-shrews; onto a hillside in the flat Bushman heartland; onto the heart of the eland that the /Xam held sacred; on the leaves and branches of a tree by the waterhole; on engraved rocks; on the lichen of a dolerite boulder and the white reeds of grasslands. Accompanying these striking images is a text that records 'the rich complexity and depth of understanding of /Xam concepts and beliefs about their spirituality in relation to the land that sustained them both physically and emotionally' (*Ibid*, 16). The authors comment:

> *'The /Xam who lived in /Xam-Ka! are still there in spirit, if not in person. This was the firm belief of the /Xam people themselves who relied on their ancestral spirits for help ... Our words and photographs layer past and present experiences to celebrate the intangible beliefs that sustained this landscape for millennia. In the theatre of our minds, the /Xam's words and images can still give life to the land'* (*Ibid*, 36).

Connections between individuals and their surroundings are reflected in the section headings designed by the authors. Part I, 'A Landscape Full of Memories', is subtitled 'Landscapes are like theatres accumulating memories of performances over many years'. Part II, 'Earth', is subtitled 'The /Xam lived with the land, not simply on it'. Part V, 'My Heart Stands in the Hill', is subtitled 'When a Bushman dies he goes to this place'. The authors comment:

4 In his recent study of the Bleek and Lloyd manuscripts, entitled *Bushman Letters*, Michael Wessels demonstrates the textual complexity of these tales. He rescues them from the essentialising tendencies of Western theorists who have read them as representing a stable world-view like that described by Derrida's discussion of the myth of origins. Wessels comments: 'It has been my contention that much of the interpretation of the stories reflects the intellectual tradition from which it has emerged rather than the /Xam narratives themselves. I have followed Derrida in characterising this tradition as predicated on the myth of the lost origin and a metaphysics of presence ... the lack of attention to the detail of individual stories points to a hermeneutic practice that is more interested in overarching or underlying patterns and structures than it is in the signifying practices of the /Xam discursive tradition itself' (Wessels: 2010, 309).

> *The landscape was integral to /Xam beliefs. The land itself and the things it had to offer were personified. People were buried in it. Spirits of the dead inhabited it. Breaking through, or simply transcending the imaginary barrier between the natural and the supernatural worlds, is what the /Xam beliefs were all about. Their environment provided the sensory stimuli the /Xam chose to humanise through mythology* (*Ibid*, 54).

In novel after novel, Mda has recorded his sense of this abiding legacy. Toloki, protagonist of *Ways of Dying* and *Cion*, explains to Ruth Quigley in Ohio that '[t]here are strong possibilities that my ancestry is a Khoikhoi one, which is the case for many Southern Sotho and Nguni people in South Africa' (Mda: 2007, 25). In *The Heart of Redness*, Twin's marriage to Quxu, a Khoikhoi woman called Qukezwa by the Xhosa, is repeated several generations later in the contemporary marriage between Twin, son of Zim, and Qukezwa, whose son is once again given the hybridised Xhosa/Khoikhoi name Heitsi Ebib, after the son of Tsiqwa, bearer of ancient traditions. In *The Whale Caller*, the protagonist imagines seeing 'before there were boats and fishermen and whalers, the Khoikhoi of old dancing around a beached whale' (Mda: 2005, 2). And in *The Madonna of Excelsior*, many of the people in Claerhout's paintings resemble the mixed-race 'coloured' people around whom the Miscegenation Trial revolves; they are descended from slave labourers from the East as well as from the nomadic Bushman or Hottentot people and from the indigenous African people. The Khoikhoi legacy is thus remembered and celebrated everywhere in Mda's South African fiction, in ways that marry creativity with sensitivity to the environment.

For me, therefore, *She Plays with the Darkness* takes the first steps in a direction that is developed further in *The Madonna* and *Cion*. But the novel fails to sustain the momentum created by the now-vanished /Xam inhabitants of the Cave of Barwa, and the story-worlds of Dikosha and her twin brother collapse into incoherence. Mda, as his memoirs attest, spent many formative years in Lesotho, where the language and culture were not the same as his own — he is a Xhosa-speaking South African. Perhaps this is why it is not until Mda wrote his first South African novel — *Ways of Dying* — that he was able to bring his insights into the transformative potential of art into full relationship with the landscape.

The Madonna of Excelsior

I start with a few remarks about the relationship between landscape and 'the Western gaze', since these concepts are so central to *The Madonna's* setting in the sunflower fields of the Orange Free State and its use of the story-world of Claerhout's expressionist/symbolist paintings. Landscape has been described as 'situated on the interface between the physical and the cognitive',[5] and as encompassing both 'an object external to perception' and 'the expression of an idea'.[6] The eye seeing this landscape has, in the Western tradition deriving from the Cartesian 'I', embodied surveillance. In the Enlightenment paradigm, Western knowledge is considered globally to be more valid and superior to the local knowledge of indigenous cultures. Barbara Bender writes:

> *'The Western Gaze' succinctly expresses a particular, historically constituted, way of perceiving and experiencing the world. It is a gaze that skims the surface; surveys the land from an ego-centred viewpoint; and invokes an active viewer (the subject) and a passive land (object). This active viewer is equated with 'culture' and the land with 'nature', and viewer/culture are gendered male, land/nature ... female. Finally, the Western Gaze is about control* (Bender: 1999, 31).

I move now to the first chapter of *The Madonna of Excelsior*: a short chapter of just over three pages that describe women, donkeys and sunflowers in the landscape of the Orange Free State. It is the time of the wheat harvest. As in many of the chapter openings, we start with a description of Claerhout's paintings: the vibrant, surreal world of exploding colour — green, yellow, red and blue — and the characteristic distortions of Claerhout's symbolist/expressionist vision: the boy riding the donkey backwards, people without feet or toes, skewed houses. The world of Claerhout's paintings — that is the story of the Catholic priest whom Mda calls the Trinity (because he is, man, priest and artist, and because he paints the 'threeness' of the Free State's open skies, vastness and loneliness) — is immediately linked to, and appropriated by, Mda's story-world. This is the story of Niki and Popi, the mother and daughter Madonnas of Excelsior who will both figure in the Trinity's paintings and be at the centre of the town's notorious Miscegenation Trial.

In the opening chapter, we see the Trinity's paintings and the landscape of the Free State through the child Popi's eyes. Twenty-five years of the Mda story-world are juxtaposed against the present in a scene that fuses past and present, drawing our attention to the continuity of people living in, and working with, the landscape.[7] What, then, attracts Mda to the Claerhout paintings

5 Ucko, Peter J. & Layton, Robert (1999) *The Archaeology and Anthropology of Landscape: Shaping Your Landscape*, 7.

6 *Ibid*, 1.

7 As Marita Wenzel notes, there is a close association in *The Madonna* between art and nature:

> [Mda] pays attention to the ... patterns of life that emulate seasonal cycles and find resonance in the depiction of human lives and their representation in art ... The natural world is depicted in shades of vibrant colours that assume unnatural connotations when juxtaposed with violent human actions that disrupt the natural harmony ... the emphasis on colour in *The Madonna of Excelsior* results in vivid verbal images that accentuate the vibrancy of the African landscape, its inhabitants and their lack of self-consciousness and affinity to nature (Wenzel: 2009, 128–129).

around which he constructs *The Madonna*? To begin with, the visual analogies that feed Mda's fictional world demonstrate an ecological symbiosis, a living in harmony with the universe, which links back to Claerhout's European ancestor, Breughel. Like Claerhout, Breughel depicted simple people doing ordinary things, often in contexts of community celebration. This context is very different from the controlling, patriarchal, technological, exploitative and instrumentalising relationship to nature implied by 'the Western Gaze'.

The landscape of the Free State — its hills, wheat fields, sunflower fields and cosmos — falls outside the nature/culture binary created within the 'Western Gaze'. Flowers of course are natural, although sunflowers, being a cash crop, are also linked to the cultivated agricultural world. As a landscape, sunflower fields escape the negative associations of, let's say, sugar-cane plantations in the Caribbean or cotton plantations in the American South, which destroyed indigenous vegetation and relied on slave labour to produce profit. Sunflower seeds are eaten, sunflower oil is used for cooking or to produce margarine. *Wikipedia* tells us, in addition, that sunflowers may be used to extract toxic ingredients — such as lead, arsenic and uranium — from soil. (They were apparently used to remove uranium, cosium-137 and strontium-90 from the ground after the Chernobyl disaster.) Heliotropic in their budding stage, sunflowers turn towards the east at sunrise and follow the sun over the course of the day, inclining from east to west. Indigenous to the Americas, the sunflower has been 'domesticated' since around 2000 BC. The Aztecs, Otomis of Mexico and Incas of South America venerated the sunflower as the symbol of the sun deity. Incorporating in its life-cycle a particular closeness to sun and earth, the sunflower is often depicted as a symbol of green ideology, just as the red rose is a symbol of socialism or social democracy. Van Gogh, of course, immortalised sunflowers in painting after painting. In the Claerhout story-world, sunflowers are everywhere.

From the first paragraph of the opening chapter, Mda interrogates the 'Western Gaze': 'All these things flow from the sins of our mothers. The land that lies flat on its back for kilometre after restless kilometre … the sunflower fields that stretch as far as the eye can see — the land that is awash with yellowness. And the brownness of the *qokwa* grass' (Mda: 2002, 1). Here immediately we encounter Mda's deconstruction of the 'Western Gaze'. When the Bible speaks of 'the sins of our fathers' the reader links these back to the story of the Fall — the expulsion from Eden, the story of the travails of Adam and Eve, now forced to labour by the sweat of their brows and bear children in pain. In this story, Eve is the main culprit because she eats the forbidden fruit and tempts Adam to do so too. The misogyny of the Western tradition, which demonises Eve and her daughters for their transgressive sexuality, is satirised by Mda. As is the trope of the land as feminised, passively awaiting the penetration of the active male explorer. Here the 'explorers' are Afrikaans farmers who rape helpless black women in the sunflower fields where they work.

Throughout the novel, Mda's imbrication of his characters' story-worlds with those of Frans Claerhout's paintings challenges the 'Western Gaze'. For instance, Chapter 6 is titled 'She is holding the Sun' and describes Claerhout's painting *Catcher of the Sun.* (See Plate X) Here the sun is explicitly a feminine principle of life and death — although in the Western canon the sun is usually depicted as masculine, and the moon as feminine. (Similarly, Francis of Assisi's canticle says: 'Brother Sun and Sister Moon'.) Probably the attribution of male deity to the sun goes back to Europe's indebtedness to Roman and Hellenic mythology — for in numerous non-European cultures, sun goddesses are venerated. Certainly, the sun is all-powerful, for in this chapter the drought 'incinerating parts of the Free State' is so severe that it makes the Afrikaans farmers forget their lust for black women in the crisis created for their crops by the scorching weather.

Another Claerhout painting that challenges the Western gaze by disrupting chronology is one that 'conveys our yesterdays in the continuing present' (*Ibid,* 38). In *Giant With Star* (Plate XI), the villagers are sad because the sky is 'bereft of stars' (though a lonely full moon is present). Suddenly they see 'a giant with a boyish face', dressed in 'red hat and red boots and yellow overalls', who carries over his shoulder 'a big star attached to a stick', which he brings to illuminate the village: 'The friendly giant transformed the blues and yellows into a scintillating light-filled land of promise. A world conceived of beautiful madness' (*Ibid,* 39). Here Mda, shifting into the magical realist mode that occasionally interrupts his realistic depiction of individuals and communities, uses Claerhout's painterly vision to suggest the ways in which past and present, factual and fictional, individual and communal memory, fuse in the oral storytelling world of non-literate people, whose view of their own history falls outside of the Western discourse of rationality but has strong resonances within oral cultures.

In the chapter titled 'The Pan' we are shown the Claerhout painting of the church in which, in Mda's story-world, Niki worships (see Plate XII):

> *People walk out of the skewed houses that form a circle. A blue church completes the circle. The houses are pink with cobalt blue doors. People are floating to the church. People with black faces, each holding a giant white flower … A woman in a long white dress and white veil leads the procession into the church. The procession glides augustly on the raw sienna path. Blazing light surrounds the solemn procession. Absorbing the devout into a halo of yellowness.*

This, the narrator assures us, is 'our church … Niki's church. She belongs here' (*Ibid,* 28). Its congregation is very poor. The minister speaks consolingly

> *of how the meek would inherit the earth and the poor in spirit would see the kingdom of heaven. How those who were oppressed and persecuted would get their reward in heaven. They were the salt of the earth and the light of the world. But in the meantime, he would plead, while they were still on earth preparing for their inheritance in heaven, it was necessary that the leaking roof of the house of the Lord*

> *be repaired. How did the congregation think the Lord felt about being praised in a dilapidated building with a leaking roof and cracked walls with peeling paint? The congregation would respond with amens. But only small brown coins would find their way into the collection plate* (*Ibid*, 29).

From the affectionate, humorous focalisation of the narrator we move to Niki's focalisation. On this Sunday she is not going to her own church, but to the 'whites only' church. She will be looking after Tjaart Cronje, whose parents, after the church service, will be going on to a people's congress in nearby Clocolan. Niki and Viliki, who may not enter the church, listen to the service outside the gates. Staring up at the Reverend Francois Bornman's 'beautiful church built of sandstone and roofed with black slate', Niki fails to see how the shape resembles hands in prayer: 'Often she had tried to work out how exactly the strange architecture translated into hands in anything, let alone prayer' (*Ibid*, 29). The reader shares in her alienated perception of this Calvinist monument to racial prejudice — so different to the vivid, scruffy, community-inspired church in which the townspeople of Mahlatswetsa worship. Claerhout's painting evokes the simple church of his mission station, built by hand by fervent non-literate practitioners. This is the church we see through the narrator's description of the painting: Bornman's affluent whites-only church is not made visible to the reader, who shares Niki's disaffection with it.

Popi's focalisation, as she moves from childhood into adolescence and then early adulthood, is a striking example of rejection of the metaphysical straitjacket of the Western gaze. Initially Popi the child is ambivalent about the Trinity's paintings. Excited by their vibrancy, she is also distressed by their refusal to render physical reality recognisably:

> *At five, she was precocious enough to wonder why the houses were all so skewed. And crowded together. She thought she could draw better houses. Her people, those she sketched in the sand in the backyard of her township home, were not distorted like the priest's* (*Ibid*, 2).

But as a young adult, Popi's most treasured postcard is titled 'Jesus among the flowers': 'Its celestial blue calmed her when she had had a particularly bad day' (*Ibid*, 139). She turns to Claerhout's paintings when overwhelmed with nostalgia. But Niki herself — not yet over the bitterness of her treatment during the racist and sexist Miscegenation Trial — rejects Claerhout's vision as mendacious: 'Jesus was not black. You have seen his photos in church … And which of these women is Mary? If it's this black woman, how come she is wearing a purple hat and a red dress like the women of today? Jesus didn't live today. And if it's this white woman, how come she is a nun, and how come she is white and her child is black?' (*Ibid*, 140). Popi, unlike Niki, loves her three postcards of the Trinity's pictures because she unconditionally accepts their contradictions, acknowledging an emotional power with which she challenges her mother: 'How come you remember every detail of [the painting] even when you are not looking at it ... Admit it, Niki ... it has got into you too' (*Ibid*, 140). The story of Popi's *Bildungsroman* — her learning to accept her coloured identity and to be at peace with herself — has enabled her to accept the Trinity's imaginative transpositions as far richer and truer than realistic depictions of a socially unjust society.

The Madonna of Excelsior ends with Niki, who has come much further in her journey towards self-acceptance, under the bluegum trees and evergreen melliodora and the black ironbark beloved of honeybees. She is arranging coloured hives for the bees, placing the wooden hives randomly because she realises that hives in straight rows would have confused the bees who would not have known to which hive they belonged. She has learned, on a beekeeping course, that 'unlike American bees, South African bees did not know how to count' (*Ibid*, 228). But she assumes that they can distinguish colours — red, blue, yellow, and green — and arranges her hives in clusters, back to back and facing in different directions. Niki, who has taught Popi that 'anger eats the owner' (*Ibid*, 231), tells the community that rather than looking after the bees, the bees look after her, for they communicate 'calming messages to her through their airborne hormones. It was as if she shared the same pheromones with the bees' (*Ibid*, 229). But Niki's healing is far from passive acceptance of the injustices she has suffered: to Johannes Smit's plea for 'a truce' she replies: 'I do not understand all this nonsense about a truce. I don't remember any war between us. You, Johannes Smit, wronged me. You stole my girlhood. And now you talk of a truce?' (*Ibid*, 261).

On the last page of the novel, we hear the songs of Viliki and the Seller of Songs, who are making music and love in the distant sunflower fields (See Plates XIII, XIV and XV: Musicians). These fields have now come to represent the symbiotic, unexploitative relationship between human beings, non-human beings and the environment that Claerhout's paintings have depicted throughout. This celebration of the performance activities of singing and dancing demonstrates community values like those celebrated in Claerhout's paintings, a mutuality between the physical and the social environment. Mda's achievement in *The Madonna* is to appropriate this non-racial, non-gendered vision for his novel, showing us how, out of the sins of the mothers, beautiful people flow.[8]

8 Of the relationship between Claerhout and Mda's story-worlds, Marita Wenzel remarks:

> Both [Claerhout and Mda] celebrate nature and the role of human nature. This correspondence becomes clear in an extract taken from an interview with Claerhout. Asked whether he was 'a priest who paints, or a painter who is a priest', he replied: 'I am one, a human being created to grow — the rural environment, the seasons, the human being, a smile, a curse, a prayer, love, nudity, fertility, humour; from the soil, of the soil, Christian mysticism, nature, God, the question why, are all composites of my painting and drawing' (Wenzel: 2009, 144).

Cion

Cion (2007) is a novel about the importance of ancestors and the centrality of the past in shaping the future. In its Acknowledgements, Mda pays tribute to 'Sello K. Duiker, Phaswane Mpe and Yvonne Vera, who continue to transmit to me buckets of inspiration from the world of the ancestors'. The novel imbricates the story of the development of Mda's first protagonist, Toloki the Professional Mourner from *Ways of Dying*, with the quilt-making tradition and skills of a poor rural community in Appalachian America, where Toloki comes to live with the Quigley family. The Quigleys are of mixed white, Indian and Negro ancestry and are descended from the plantation slaves of the South, whose escapes on the Underground Railroad were inspired by a matriarchal quilt-making tradition that pointed their way to freedom. Now in present-day Kilvert, Ohio, Ruth Quigley continues to produce traditional quilt patterns, while her rebellious daughter Orpah plays the sitar, reads Gothic novels and draws amazing quilt designs that she refuses to constrain within traditional forms since she wants to 'tell her own story'. Along comes Toloki the Professional Mourner, who is in the process of individuating himself from his creator the Sciolist and will learn in America new and more powerful ways of mourning, inspired by other times and other cultures. The stories of Toloki and of the quilt-makers, past and present, of Ohio and the deep South coexist and jointly demonstrate values of tradition, community and non-commercialism against the consumerist, violent and militarily aggressive values of George Bush's Republican America.

I will illustrate this section by referring to some quilt designs of rural America in the nineteenth century. Some of the original quilt designs — the North Star, the Drunkard's Path, the Log Cabin, the Monkey Wrench, Flying Geese — have given rise to a fascinating but apocryphal body of research and writing. This links a secret system of symbols contained in the quilt designs with the Northward escape routes taken by fugitive slaves. But the overwhelming consensus amongst historians today is that the quilt code should be understood as a mnemonic device rather than an actual code. As *Cion* puts it, 'Quilt designs did not map out the actual route to the Promised Land but helped the seekers to remember those things that were important in their lives' (*Ibid*, 109). We may conclude, and Mda's novel corroborates this, that early quilt designs, although they had great cultural and symbolic value — as had freedom songs in apartheid South Africa, or Negro spirituals in slave-owning America — were never intended to provide secret maps to enable escape to the North.

I therefore move away from the traditional designs described in the novel. These were made by the slave matriarch named the 'Abyssinian Queen' for her sons, the escaping slaves Abednego and Nicodemus. Instead, I move to the more futuristic quilt designs to which Toloki refers when he remarks that 'many modern quilt-makers create works of art that are inspired by traditional designs but that venture into new directions' — exactly what he is trying to encourage Orpah to do. Quilt-making in this novel therefore encompasses not only the traditions of the past but also the future potentialities of quilting as an art form. In the same way, Toloki's Professional Mourning moves into newly individuated creative and eclectic forms that are far more sophisticated than his original practice of Professional Mourning in South Africa. Quilt-making and Professional Mourning have many similarities: they celebrate memory and the past, have strong ecological or environmental connections and affirm community values in a non-consumerist, non-capitalist ethos.

Like several of Mda's novels, *Cion* alternates two time-scales in its story-worlds: the past of the plantation slaves in the South and the present of their ancestors in Kilvert, Ohio. There are numerous crossovers between these story-worlds: for instance, Toloki, newly arrived in Ohio, memorises the landmarks of his route 'in case I have to return this way on my own', just as earlier Abednego and Nicodemus were taught by their mother to notice their surroundings because their survival depended on having 'sharp ears for every sound of escape'. They had to listen for, and understand, the noises made by 'birds, frogs and crickets' because '[a]ll these spoke the language of flight' (Mda: 2007, 49). Similarly, the remarkable performances of the Abyssinian Queen — quilter, singer, dancer, storyteller — are recaptured in the contemporary memory rituals enacted by the 'medium man' Mahlon Quigley and his daughter Orpah, the 'spirit child'. From the beginning of the story, the reader is made aware of living history, unfolding in an ecological context that has strong continuities with the past. Obed Quigley talks about the sycamore trees as 'carriers of memories' and tells Toloki about 'the pull of the ancestors', which keep his people 'in poor villages like Stewart, Kilvert and Cutler'. This talk of ancestors resonates strongly with Toloki, since he is aware 'that there are strong possibilities that my ancestry is a Khoikhoi one, which is the case for many Southern Sotho and Nguni people in South Africa' (*Ibid*, 35). Ruth Quigley, making pickles, tending her vegetable garden and quilting, is a figure who connects with the women of the past. The worn fabric on her table is another 'carrier of memories', and the ensuing story will be told 'by the earthy scent of the quilts'. Quilts, Ruth tells Toloki, 'embody the life of the family' because 'people were born on them, people got sick on them, people died on them' (*Ibid*, 30).

Moving back into the past story-world we meet the remarkable 'Abyssinian Queen', a slave in the Fairfield slave-breeding farms. A gifted storyteller, she sews and mends for the slave community, initially in a purely functional capacity — creating shirts and dresses from feed sacks — then in the decorative idiom of 'crazy' patchwork, in which she becomes expert decades before 'crazy' quilts became fashionable in Virginia. Although the Abyssinian Queen next learns 'the language of the quilts' — that is, traditional designs — she includes in the 'seemingly haphazard arrangements' [of her 'crazy' quilt designs] certain elements that teach her children 'to identify some landmarks. A hill here ... A forest there. A creek. A river. She had painstakingly stitched and knotted the map of the plantation and beyond, using information she had gathered from those who had seen these places. Patches of different colours represented actual landmarks' (*Ibid*, 44). The Abyssinian Queen's tapestries serve her boys in their escape by teaching them certain principles: how to follow the North Star, to take note of the Drunkard Path lesson 'never to take a straight line in all your journeys' and to recall the Monkey Wrench's reminder that before setting off one must be equipped with essential tools and provisions to facilitate flight.

'Crazy' quilt designs like those in which the Abyssinian Queen encrypts topographical clues for her sons' escape reflect a transition between the realistic and the symbolic.[9] They incorporate many asymmetrically arranged elements — some natural (deer, butterfly, stork, flowers, moon and stars) and some geometrical, in which each block exemplifies minute detail. These details are more important than overall design harmony. Similarly, 'Crazy' designs may replicate features of local scenery. The editor of *The Pieced Quilt*, a history of quilting in America, remarks that '[q]uilts of this type often look like aerial landscapes' (Holstein: 1973). 'Crazies' may also incorporate futuristic designs in which no two blocks are alike. 'Crazy' quilts, which the Abyssinian Queen has perfected, anticipate the originality and unpredictability possible in drawing and painting. 'Crazy' patterns have elements of both reality and fantasy; what the Abyssinian Queen perceives as 'rudimentary maps', for her boys represent 'a world of dreams out there ... an attainable world' (Mda: 2007, 44). The Abyssinian Queen's storytelling magic draws on matriarchal African folklore. She performs the stories of 'Ananse the wily spider who came

9 Commenting on the transgressive potential of quilting for the marginalised women of nineteenth-century North America, Jill Gribble remarks, 'The slaves of the south were taught quilting so that they could make quilts for their mistresses. Oral historian Jacqueline Tobin points out that West African handicrafts would often be embedded with mnemonics to assist the keepers of oral history, and that these traditions could easily have been adapted as the slaves appropriated the quilting craft to their own ends. Slave women who had no voice would tell their own stories in the making of a quilt, while for others a quilt draped over a fence to air was possibly embedded with intricate codes to guide fugitive slaves to safe houses, or to people who would help them to pass from the slave states of the south to the freedom of the north' (Gribble: 2000, 213). Although Gribble is writing about quilt-making in Margaret Atwood's *Alias Grace*, her comments are equally applicable to quilt-making in *Cion*.

Plate I: Frans Claerhout sketching two models

Plate II: Frans Claerhout with a painting that Mda appropriated for Popi at 14 (left)

Plate III: *A Sunburnt Christ*

Plate IV: *Women Harvesting*

Plate V: *Boy Riding Donkey Backwards*

Plate VI: *Donkey and Cock*

Plate VII: *Profound Nostalgia*

Plate VIII: *The Blue Madonna*

Plate IX: *Eyes in the Sky*

Plate X: *Catcher of the Sun*

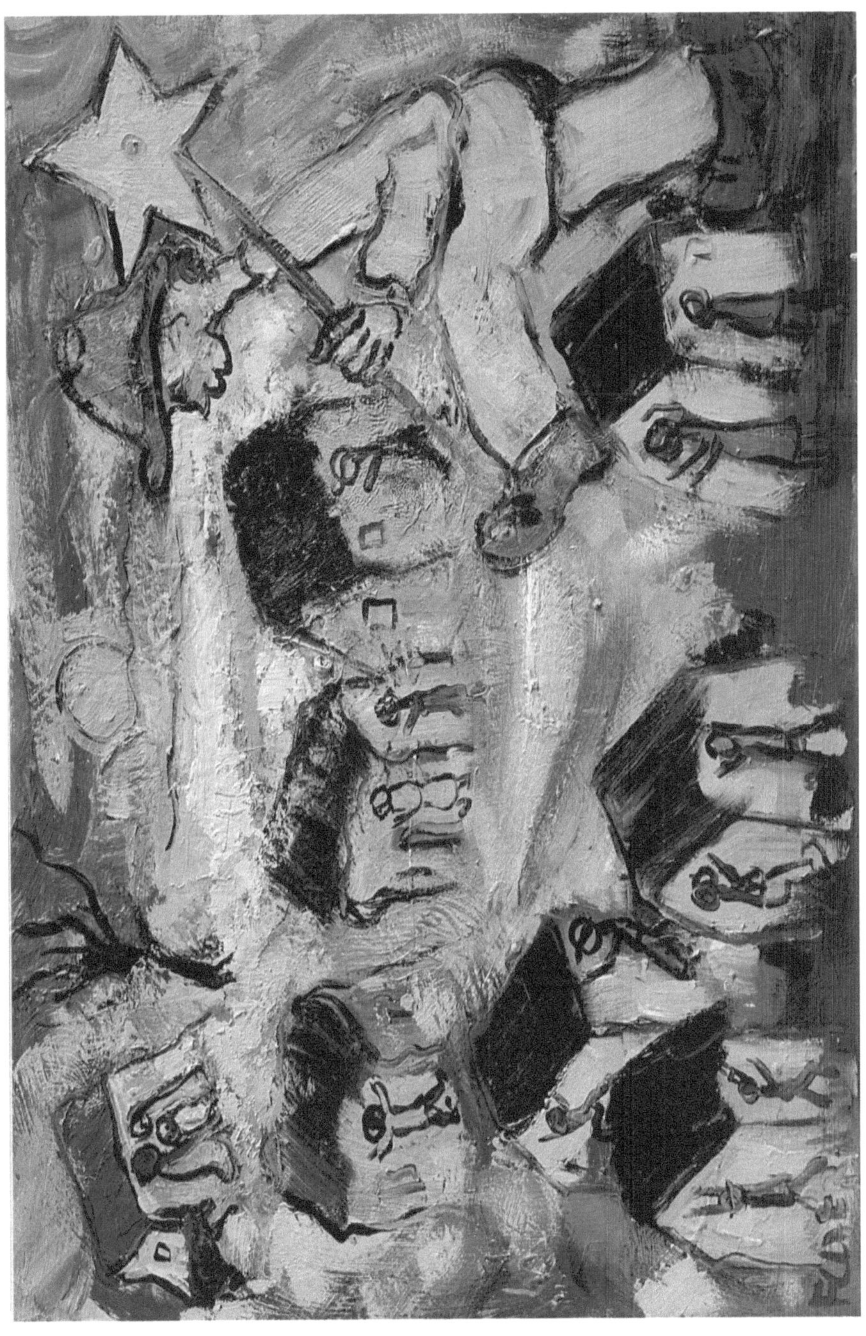

Plate XI: *Giant with Star*

Plate XII: *Niki's Church*

Plate XIII: Musician

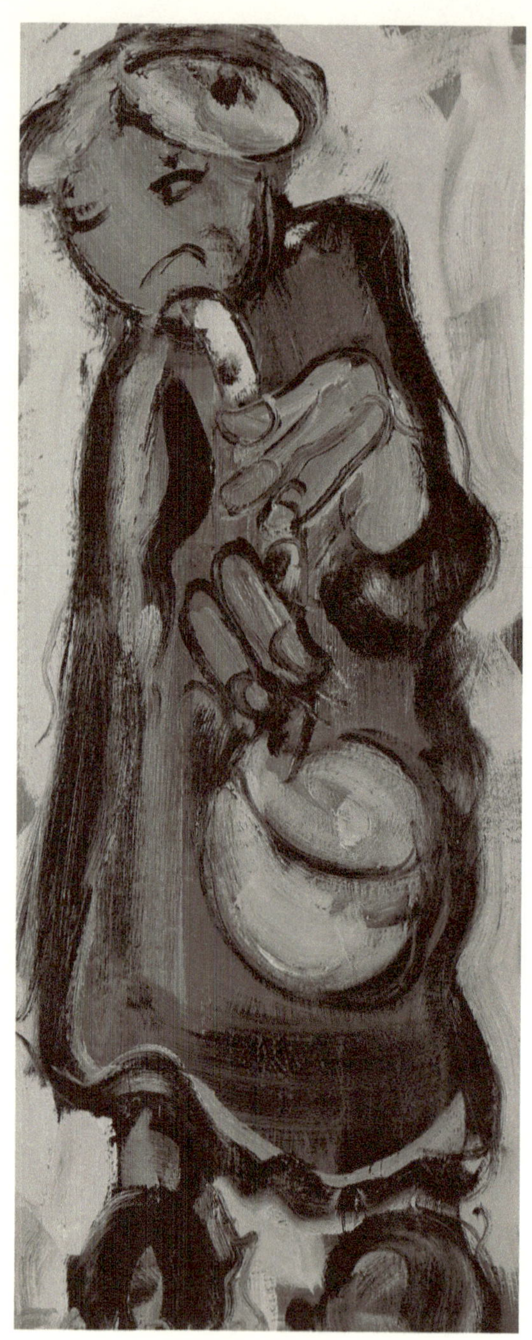

Plate XIV: Musician

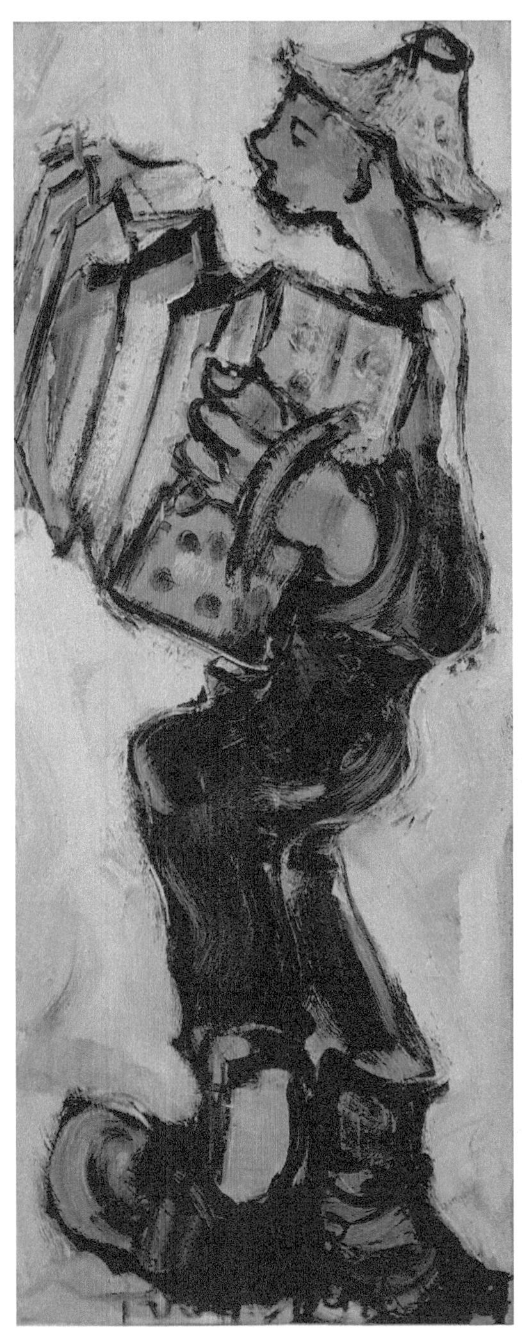

Plate XV: Musician

Plate XVI: The intertwined figures in this painting by Mda could be seen as dancers; in their deliberate distortion they also bear a relationship to the symbolist/expressionist paintings of Frans Claerhout on which Mda builds *The Madonna of Excelsior* (shown on earlier plates).

with the ancestors from the old continent' and who is capable of assuming protean forms. Quilts can also capture the intricate delicacy of gossamer and the geometrical complexity of spider-web patterns, exemplifying the transgressive power of the female artist (spinning, painting, weaving) as an endlessly inventive antidote to marginalisation under patriarchy. This spider-like activity engenders creativity across generations. As the Abyssinian Queen tells of Ananse's exploits, the listening children become involved in her tales and create their own stories. These African-derived stories, inspired by the originary myth of a female sun, create a cosmology and an ontology that is ecologically far richer (although the Slave Owner's wife describes them as 'voodoo') than the Bible stories of the Western tradition.

Through descriptions of orality and communal performance we move to the next stage of the story, which is told by 'ghost trees', or sycamores. Still growing in Kilvert, they were used in slave-owning times to provide refuge for runaway slaves; now Orpah deposits her transgressive drawings in them to protect them from her mother. Ruth, driven by a fundamentalist Old Testament censure of representation, demonises and destroys Orpah's patterns. Unlike Ruth's, the worldview of the other Quigley family members — Obed, Mahlon — closely resembles the worldview of the Shawnees, Pochattans and Cherokee Indian tribes of Abednego's story, to whom the Quigleys are related. This worldview is matriarchal — the Creator is a woman. It strongly celebrates memories of the ancestors and escapes the nature/culture binary characteristic of Western patriarchy. Transcending the Christian Chain of Being, it embodies an ecological mutuality that extends to all creation.

Defending Orpah's unconventionality, Toloki draws attention to the fact that quilt-making is not just an important link with the past, but a generative art form undergoing constant transition: '[M]any modern quilt-makers create works of art that are inspired by traditional designs but that venture into new directions' (*Ibid*, 145). Deploring the lack of inventiveness that keeps the Kilvert Community Centre quilters working within traditional historical American parameters Toloki, as he masters the art of quilt-making, wishes to create 'art quilts'. If we searched in a book like *The Pieced Quilt* for stylised optical effects that make quilts resemble modern paintings, we could find quilt-makers contrasting inner with outer space in a manner that recalls the experimental art of the Cubists. Cézanne formulated the theory that everything in nature is modelled on the *sphere*, the *cone* and the *cylinder*, claiming that if one could paint these one could paint anything. These three shapes frequently figure in art quilts, extending the challenge of creating the illusion of three-dimensionality in paint to fabric.

In the preceding sections, I have sketched the ethos of quilt-making as an art form that is constantly evolving and that has strong community ties. The editor of *The Pieced Quilt* remarks: 'Most [quilt] designs were given names meaningful to the makers and drawn from the whole realm of American experience: *nature*: Bear's Paw, Pineapple, Spider's Web; *religion*: Tree Everlasting, Jacob's Ladder, Star of Bethlehem, Job's Tears; *politics*: Whig's Defeat, Kansas Troubles, Lincoln's Platform, Jackson Star; *historical events*: Nelson's Victory, Free Trade Patch, Underground Railroad, Kentucky Crossroads; *games*: Johnny-Round-the-Corner, Leap Frog, Puss-in-the-Corner; *places:* Philadelphia Pavement, New York Beauty, Indiana Puzzle; *common objects*: Monkey Wrench, Fan, Indian Hatchet' (Holstein: 1973, 59). The quilt-makers' repertoire, then, fuses realistic with imaginative elements, recording but transforming real events, places and objects.

Toloki, as chief protagonist of *Cion* mounting a metafictional tour de force in which he supplants his author, is equally involved in dynamic aesthetic and performance practices as he brings his Professional Mourning to new heights. Where in South Africa he relied on the Nurse to provide the biographical information about the deceased that he required for the funeral ceremony, in America he has to find or invent individuals' life stories before he can mourn them. With his American family, the Quigleys, he learns the importance of the past not just as nostalgia but as a psychological condition that enables engagement with the present. By finding the grave of Mahlon's mother and so facilitating the mourning that celebrates her life, Toloki releases Mahlon into a new state of being that is ecologically renewing. He now plants living things in his garden instead of garden gnomes. Similarly, Toloki gets Ruth to reconcile her quilt-making talents with her fundamentalist religious obsessions; she is determined now to find a book that will teach her to make Bible quilts. At the end of the novel Toloki declares: 'Before I came to Kilvert I lived only in the past and in the future … Orpah is a kindred spirit in this respect. Hopefully together we'll discover how to live in the present' (Mda: 2007, 286). No less than quilt-making, Toloki's itinerant Professional Mourning, in which Orpah is his partner, expresses ecologically progressive and non-consumerist values, connects strongly with the past and is both universal and rooted in *this* American time, *these* American places. It is joyfully ludic, incorporating Orpah's performing talents as singer, sitar-player and graphic artist. Together Toloki and Orpah hope to design 'performances and exhibitions with which we'll celebrate the bereaved' (*Ibid*, 286) just as the quilt-makers, inspired by the past, move into new aesthetic freedoms. These not only carry memories but express a creative originality that speaks to the present as well as the future.

Chapter Six

Imaginary homelands: Diaspora and identity in *Cion*

The concept of diaspora

In this chapter, I consider several postcolonial theorists' use of the term 'diaspora' to interrogate its usefulness for Mda's novel. Discussions of 'diaspora' by Tobias Döring, Ania Loomba, Stuart Hall and Bill Ashcroft are considered and are interwoven with my own analysis of *Cion*.

Tobias Döring

I start with Tobias Döring's discussion of the term 'diaspora' in his *Postcolonial Literatures in English*. It opens up several important perspectives for Mda's fifth novel, *Cion*:

> *The term [diaspora], which literally means 'scattering' or 'dispersal', is traditionally used with reference to Jewish history where it describes the experience, predominant at least since the destruction of the temple in Jerusalem in 133 AD, of living outside the Holy Land: in foreign countries, with sometimes hostile … societies and often under acute forms of oppression. In such diverse conditions, to keep up elements which define a distinctly Jewish way of life — through rituals, prayers, language, dietary rules or clothing — requires extraordinary determination and the strong awareness that the current place of residence is just a stage in transit, a provisional abode before returning to the true homeland. And yet it is just such an attitude that has maintained Jewish communities through centuries of migration, wandering and violent persecution, by keeping alive cultural memories of their real place, beyond present predicaments, and by cultivating practices to mediate these memories to coming generations* (Döring: 2008, 30–1).

The central thrust of Döring's exploration of diaspora is on language and cultural identity. Jews dispersed in the Diaspora long for return to their true homeland; this quest for the discovery of origins is accompanied by profound nostalgia for the lost places from which they have been evicted. *Cion* enacts several versions of the search for origins: in the link to Africa that characterises the Abyssinian Queen's visual and narrative imagination, in the relationship between the WIN Americans of Kilvert and their indigenous ancestors and in Toloki's own understanding of his rootedness in South African customs.

Döring discusses the cultural fragmentation that has resulted from the colonial violence inflicted on dispersed people:

> *In general terms, the history of colonialism, with centuries of slavery, violent dislocation, enforced migration and actual genocides, has radically shaken up, if not eliminated, the traditional structures of belonging. As a result, people of African descent now find themselves in North and South America, in the Caribbean, Europe or wherever, in a diasporic situation where the only way to counter their condition and cultivate a feeling of togetherness is by means of cultural memory* (*Ibid*, 31).

Juxtaposing the present conditions of rural people living in the Appalachian areas of eastern Ohio against the history of their slave ancestors in the plantations of the American South, *Cion* is very much about violent dislocation, enforced migration and actual genocide in the Kilvertians' past structures of belonging. The novel is also about the communal coherence inspired by cultural memory. This togetherness is given tangible expression in the quilt-making of the Kilvert Community Centre and celebrated in the memory rituals enacted by the medium man, Mahlon Quigley, and his musically and artistically talented daughter, Orpah. Crucial to the identity formation of the Kilvert protagonists is the mediation of Toloki, the Professional Mourner whom Mda has transported from his first South African novel, *Ways of Dying*, set in the townships of South Africa, to the cities and countryside of eastern Ohio.

Toloki's achievement of cultural identity for the people he meets in Ohio is, however, constantly subject to change, recalling Döring's argument:

> *In a postcolonial perspective, 'identity', even ethnic identity, is less a fixed, inherited and given point of reference, which may subsequently be tested, confronted or disturbed in social interaction; it is rather the result of such disturbances, confrontations and ongoing interactions, possibly changing in their course and constantly transforming itself in response to them. Diaspora would thus be the prime site for notions of identity to be defined and defended* (*Ibid*, 32).

In *Cion*, Toloki has to learn several important new skills. He has to learn to take over the telling of his story from his creator, the Sciolist. And he has to learn, from his many interactions with the Kilvertians, that cultural identity is continuously in flux, continuously open to renegotiation. This is as much the case for himself as it is for those whom he meets.

Ania Loomba

Loomba discusses Paul Gilroy's book, *The Black Atlantic*, as highlighting the cross-fertilisations that resulted from the black diasporas or 'the movements of black people [from Africa to Europe and the Americas] not only as commodities but engaged in various struggles towards emancipation, autonomy and citizenship'. She explains that Gilroy defines 'a black Atlantic' as an intercultural and transnational formation that 'provides a means to re-examine the problems of nationality, location, identity and historical memory'. Gilroy's book shows the extent to which African-American, British and Caribbean diasporic cultures mould each other as well as the metropolitan cultures with which they interact (Loomba: 2005, 147). Loomba concludes that 'the task ... is not simply to pit the themes of migrancy, exile and hybridity against rootedness, nation and authenticity, but to locate and evaluate their ideological, political and emotional valencies' (*Ibid*, 153).

My reading of *Cion* seeks to bring out these valencies by exploring the novel's preoccupations with emancipation, autonomy and citizenship. The Kilvert community with whom Toloki interacts belongs to a socioeconomically marginalised rural constituency in Appalachian America. Descended from escaped slaves in the southern plantations and experiencing real poverty in relation to their better-off fellow citizens, the extent of the Kilvertians' emancipation and autonomy in contemporary America is contestable. What the novel shows, however, is that the Kilvert constituency of racial and cultural hybrids is more rooted — in the past, in community, in the values of an agricultural economy — than their more affluent counterparts elsewhere in the US. The Quigley family with whom Toloki lives are already engaged in rituals of historical memory on his arrival: Mahlon and Orpah as medium and spirit child recreate the stories of their slave ancestors. What the novel dramatises is the forward trajectory of the Quigleys' development that results from Toloki's presence in their midst. They move from nostalgically remembering the past to inhabiting the present. Equally, Toloki's understanding of his hosts and their social, psychological and cultural positioning informs his own development, both as Professional Mourner and as increasingly gifted storyteller as he learns to displace the Sciolist. Thus, as in the cross-fertilisation to which Loomba draws attention, Toloki and the Kilvertians mould each others' life-stories.

Stuart Hall

One of the most eloquent theorists of the meaning of diaspora for postcolonial studies is Stuart Hall, whose own Caribbean history is reflected in everything he writes. Hall believes that 'far from being grounded in mere "recovery of the past", which is waiting to be found and which, when found, will secure our sense of ourselves into eternity, identities are the names we give to the different ways we are positioned in and position ourselves within, the narratives of the past' (Hall: 1996, 112). Of the Caribbean's cultural hybridity Hall remarks:

> *The Dominican Republic is a place where it is possible to feel closer to Spain and to the Spanish tradition of Latin America than anywhere else I've been in the Caribbean. The melting-pot of the British islands produced everywhere you look a different combination of genetic features and factors, and in each island elements of other cultures — Chinese, Syrian, Lebanese, Portuguese, Jewish — are present. I know because I have a small proportion of practically all of them in my own inheritance. My background is African, also I'm told Scottish — of pretty low descent, probably convict — East Indian, Portuguese, Jew. I can't summon up any more but if I searched hard I expect I could find them* (Hall: 2001, 283).

Hall emphasises that cultural diversity cannot be understood outside of the framework of power. His writing thus seeks to empower the previously disempowered and to bring into focus their ideologically constructed images of Africa:

> *I want to … speak … of the peoples for whom on the whole there were no cultural models, the peoples at the bottom of the society. And as you can imagine, that always involved a renegotiation, a rediscovery of Africa. The political movements in the New World in the twentieth century have had to pass through the re-encounter with Africa. The African diasporas of the New World have been in one way or another incapable of finding a place in modern history without the systematic return to Africa* (Hall in Castle (ed): 2001, 286).

In *Cion*, the re-encounter with Africa is both parodically and seriously treated. On a comic level, Toloki is 'Ruth's African', a shamanistic figure who brings glamour into her humdrum life, driven as it is by poverty and constrained by fundamentalist beliefs. On a more serious level, Toloki's narration brings out the extraordinary power of the Abyssinian Queen, a slave on the Fairfield Farms who inspires her sons to escape to the North and teaches them the folklore of the old country. No less than Negro spirituals, her storytelling celebrates freedom.

A feature of diasporic identity in the New World to which Hall alludes is the role of religion. Religion gives voice to the voiceless through 'the distorted languages of the one Book that anybody would teach them to read'. From alienation and dispossession people of the Book can learn to imagine another kind of identity:

> *What they felt was, I have no voice, I have no history, I have come from a place to which I cannot go back and which I have never seen. I used to speak a language which I can no longer speak. I had ancestors whom I cannot find; they worshipped gods whose names I do not know. Against this sense of profound rupture, the metaphors of a new kind of imposed religion can be reworked, can become a language in which a certain kind of history is retold, in which aspirations of liberation and freedom can be for the first time expressed, in which what I would call the 'imagined community' of Africa can be symbolically reconstructed* (Hall: 2001, 289).

That Hall is talking about the Caribbean does not diminish the relevance of these words for the world which Toloki encounters in Kilvert, Ohio. That world is dominated by the fundamentalism of Ruth Quigley's Christian beliefs, which are as politically conservative as they are initially creatively repressive. The novel opens with the Halloween parades in which Ruth's son, Obed, impersonates a slave ancestor in a confused and derivative return to the past because he feels that he has no stake in the present. But by the end of the novel Obed has become a preacher, combining in 'hoofing' the performative talents that Toloki's Professional Mourning has taught him with the consolations of religion. Ruth's immersion in religion also moves forward as the novel progresses: by the end she has found a way to incorporate her quilt-making talents into the illustration of Bible stories, that is, to combine tradition with innovation. The novel's exploration of the real roles that religious beliefs can play in the lives of the Kilvert community is thus part-parodic, part-serious: religion expresses a communal identity that is both American and African.

For Hall, the Terra Incognita of America that marks the beginning of diaspora creates contexts of diversity and hybridity:

> *The diaspora experience as I intend it here is defined, not by essence or purity, but by the recognition of a necessary heterogeneity and diversity; by a conception of 'identity' which lives with and through, not despite difference; by hybridity. Diasporic identities are those which are constantly producing and reproducing themselves anew, through transformation and difference … It is because this New World is constituted for us as place, a narrative of displacement, that it gives rise so profoundly to a certain imaginary plenitude, recreating the endless desire to return to 'lost origins, to be once again with the mother, to go back to the beginning … And yet, this return … is like the imaginary of Lacan — it can neither be fulfilled nor requited, and hence is the beginning of the symbolic, of representation, the infinitely renewable source of desire, memory, myth, search, discovery'* (Hall in Mongia: 1996, 119–20).

The story that Toloki learns to tell, both as Professional Mourner and as Master Storyteller, marks his entrance into the symbolic, a realm that constantly demonstrates tension between the desire to recover lost origins and the recognition that cultural identity is provisional and elusive. In some ways, what Toloki must learn to do in *Cion* is a version of what Gates celebrates in *The Signifying Monkey* (1988): to develop the black voice using myths derived from Africa brought to America by slaves; to palimpsestically write new texts derived from other histories over existing texts. Toloki's story supplants the Sciolist's story, reminding the reader of the human quest to access desire and memory, a quest that is as universal as it is impossible to fulfil.

Bill Ashcroft

Examining postcolonial societies' engagement with imperial language and history, and responsive particularly to Aboriginal peoples' cultures of habitation and horizontality, Bill Ashcroft writes:

> *As soon as we begin to see the construction of place as a factor of a way of inhabiting we see how dense and how intense is the rhizomic pattern of relationships in which place is located* (Ashcroft: 2001, 159).

In *Cion*, the story-worlds of both past and present characters are intimately linked to the sycamore tree, an emblem of rhizomic relationship, not only in its own botanical structure (where roots and trunk are as important as leaves) but in its ability to connect the lives of the Fairfield slaves with their successors in modern Kilvert. Just as the Abyssinian Queen hid her boys' quilts and the tools they would need on their journey to freedom, so Orpah hides her drawings in the capacious boles of the sycamores to protect them from destruction by Ruth.

Drawing on the work of bell hooks, Ashcroft points out that

> *the very meaning of the term 'home', in terms of a sense of place, has been very different for those who have been colonized, and ... can change with the experience of decolonization. In times of estrangement, 'home is no longer just one place. It is locations ... One confronts and accepts dispersal and fragmentation as part of the constructions of a new world order that reveals more fully who we can become'. One might say that, ironically, one of the consequences of the disruptions and displacements of colonization has been that 'home', like 'place', becomes freed from a simple spatial concept of location. It becomes a way of seeing, a way of inhabiting and, ultimately, transforming global discourses of power by being 'at home' in them whatever local appropriations that may entail* (Ashcroft: 2001, 197).

In *Cion*, the Quigley family rely on Toloki to help them overcome the fragmentations that have marked their histories: Obed and Mahlon's over-dependence on the past; Orpah's inability to express her creativity; Ruth's acceptance of fundamentalist positions that inhibit her personality. Toloki's interactions with the Quigleys show them and the reader what they can become because he teaches them a new way of seeing. Toloki's way of being 'at home' in Kilvert is idiosyncratic. He leaves Ruth's house and takes up a nomadic lifestyle in the van in which he lives; later, he and Orpah will travel together in this all around the United States. Yet Toloki is 'at home' in Kilvert because of the important influence of the Kilvert Community Centre, where he learns to express his own creativity as he learns the skills of quilting. His way of inhabiting Kilvert is thus not dependent on a simple spatial concept of location. Through his influence the Quigleys, in turn, learn to be 'at home' in Kilvert by fulfilling their potentials: Obed to marry Beth and become a preacher; Orpah to plan a future travelling with Toloki; Ruth to design Bible quilts; Mahlon to grow flowers and vegetables again because Toloki has helped him to deal with his mother's memory by finding her grave. What all these stories demonstrate is what Ashcroft calls a new way of inhabiting space, a 'practice' that eludes the parameters of the purely visual, topographical or geographical, turning the location of Kilvert 'into home, into owned space' (*Ibid*, 159).

Narrating identity: South Africa and the United States

Toloki as storyteller must enter into the realm of the symbolic shown by Hall to be Janus-faced: to contain the hope of return to lost origins while showing this return to be impossible. On the material level, however — the level of geographical and social referents — Toloki's story as a black South African, new to America, makes evident a number of striking points of comparison between the culture he comes from and the one he is visiting. In the first chapter we find him startled by the 'celebration of a culture of death' that he witnesses in the colourful Court Street Parades at Halloween. Toloki exclaims: 'Even I who exult in death find the abundance of blood and bloody situations overwhelming' (Mda: 2007, 1). The Court Street processions demonstrate that in Bush's Republican administration economic growth and military aggression are alarmingly conflated: 'Stimulate the economy, start a new war. Stimulate the economy, bomb a third world country!' (*Ibid*, 10). So also are Christian fundamentalism with aggressive militarism and sexual violence with xenophobia: 'I elbow my way across the street, past a man who is holding a life-size inflated rubber doll upside down and is giving it a blow job between its legs; and a few Arabs in white robes and black Kaffiyehs being hustled at gunpoint by marines in camouflage' (*Ibid*, 12). The full moon during these Halloween parades is associated not with natural ecological cycles, but with violence, arrests, stabbings and shootings.

The novel opens with the aggression and violence of the Halloween scenes in which Americans masquerade as icons from the media or as politicians, inhabiting borrowed identities that are entirely derivative and that reflect US commodification and consumerism. Other repressive and regressive aspects of Republican policy — like supporting the death penalty or opposing gay rights — spur Toloki to remark to Ruth Quigley that the South African Constitution leads the world in protecting civil liberties in relation to gender and racial equity. Ruth replies contemptuously, 'Todoloo. Your country is Sodom and Gomorrah. I'm glad you came to the good ol' US of A to escape the death and pestilence that the Lord is surely gonna visit on Africa' (*Ibid*, 76).

The novel's opening Halloween scene foregrounds spectacle in highly visible rituals, which Toloki calls a celebration of death. The television programmes that enjoy mass viewing are more insidious: they turn 'our beautiful war' into a spectacle where death is made invisible as television renders the Iraq War no more frightening than sequences in comic books or movies. The accompanying commentary embodies xenophobia and insularity. Americans, Toloki observes, 'can afford to be ignorant about the world because they don't need the world!' (*Ibid*, 132). 'Family viewing' on television features bombings and live military action that are turned into exciting footage, complete with sound effects: 'Those were the days television screens lit up with big letters: *Operation Phantom Fury* to the background of suspenseful music' (*Ibid*, 210). The USA is depicted as a country driven by political extremism: 'Ruth's land is the land of powerful Christian ayatollahs, old Testament fundamentalists who serve a wrathful and vengeful god' (*Ibid*, 251). By contrast, South Africa, the nation that condoned the brutal crimes of apartheid against millions of its citizens, emerges post-apartheid as a state with a Constitution that protects its linguistic diversity, religious freedom and gender equality. Most surprisingly, the South African media are shown to have more freedom than their American counterparts. Toloki notes that in America, 'free and independent media are patriotic and will therefore not give all sides of the story. This last observation may appear commonplace to most American readers. They may even think it lowers the tone of my story. But it will certainly amaze those who are following my story from South Africa; they think that the media here are the freest ever and that journalists can report on anything without fear of being labelled unpatriotic' (*Ibid*, 132).

Where there are many striking divergences between the cultures of the USA and SA, there are also numerous convergences. Ruth Quigley challenges Toloki: '[D]id I know why she voted for George W. Bush? Because Bush was a man of God' (*Ibid*, 51). Ruth maintains that the 'old-timers know the truth, which was why the Republican Party was the party of them coloured folks' (*Ibid*, 59). There is a close analogy here with the history of the coloured (mixed-race, brown-skinned) nation in South Africa. Considered to be second-class citizens under white domination, when enabled to vote for change in the referendum that predated the black majority's landslide to victory, coloured people opted, in large numbers, to align themselves with the whites who had implemented apartheid. Like their WIN (mixed white, Indian and Negro) equivalents in Kilvert, Ohio, who feel politically marginalised in Bush's America, South African coloured people largely failed under the new ANC government to find a place for themselves in a post-apartheid South Africa ruled by a black government. Ruth remarks: 'We don't belong to nobody. Our race of people is different from any race of people that ever lived on earth' (*Ibid*, 28), to which Obed adds: 'Yeah, we don't belong nowhere. White people hate us because we ain't white enough.

Black people hate us too. They call us yellow niggers. They are jealous of our complexion' (*Ibid*, 28). Toloki's narrative brings home to the South African reader the similarity of the plight of 'coloured' people under an ANC government to the situation of poor mixed-race Appalachian communities under George Bush — a perspective not available to Ruth Quigley as an ardent Bush-supporter.

But Toloki's focalisation, as he reports his first impressions of the farm landscape through which he is travelling, again rings bells with the South African reader, accustomed to the stark poverty of the townships that exist on the edges of wealthy cities. Approaching the hamlet of Kilvert, Ohio, Toloki reports seeing 'run-down houses strewn with scrap metal, muddy gardens, broken down vehicles and rusty trailers'. These coexist with picturesque and colourful sights: big yellow pumpkins outside the houses, some of them turned into jack o' lanterns, and a country church that recalls patterns from quilt-making: 'We walk past a little church with a red roof. It looks like a toy. Or like a confectionery creation of dark brown and light brown chocolate bricks arranged in symmetric patterns' (*Ibid*, 23). We are in rural Appalachia, where the average household lives far below the breadline and 80 per cent of the population is unemployed. Yet as Toloki perceives, the graveyards here are carefully tended by people who 'obviously care for their dead' (*Ibid*, 23). When he asks Obed why his people don't move to better places, Obed replies: 'It's the pull of the ancestors [...] We don't move from here. Even those who leave to work in Columbus or Chicago, they come back all the time because the darn place pulls them back. You know why? It's where our race of people was moulded.' This connection with place because of the importance of ancestors surprises Toloki: 'It is my first time to hear an American talk of ancestors. I thought ancestor veneration was our sole preserve' (*Ibid*, 20). Equally, Americans protesting political detentions in Guantanamo Bay who demand 'Charge or Release Detainees' elicit from Toloki the comment, 'The slogan sounds very familiar. It takes me back to years ago. Protesters used to chant it during the detention-without-trial in South Africa' (*Ibid*, 26). The USA and SA react in similar ways to 'threats' to the state by denying civil liberties; the process is analogous to that which Toloki has experienced back home. But here — as in the many surprising overlaps Toloki discovers between how things are done in the States and SA — his process of discovery, which is also the reader's process of discovery about cultural differences, is partial and gradual. It takes the whole trajectory of the novel's development to make these similarities and differences clear to Toloki and to the reader.

Narrating identity through the narratives of the past

Toloki's narration, therefore, has particular resonances for a South African reader. These may not be fully apprehended by an American reader. A much more available perspective that his story unfolds to the American reader is the importance of the past in the cultural life of the Kilvert community today. 'Identities,' Stuart Hall reminds us, 'are the names we give to the different ways we are positioned in, and position ourselves within, the narratives of the past' (Hall in Mongia: 1996, 112). The narratives of the past most important to the Quigley family of Kilvert, Ohio, are those connected with the Negro traditions of their plantation slave ancestors and those connected with the Indian — Powhattan, Shawnee, Cherokee — traditions of their native American ancestors.

When we first meet the Abyssinian Queen at the heart of the plantation past, Obed's nostalgia for a lost heritage — wistfully shared by Toloki when he first hears Orpah's bluegrass music — is made graphic. (Toloki tells the reader that the sounds of Orpah's sitar induce a powerful longing in him 'for something I do not know — some place I have never known' (Mda: 2007, 26): we are perhaps meant to connect his strong emotion with his as yet unexpressed longing for a retrieval of African origins.) In the slave narrative, the Abyssinian Queen, as a seamstress gifted in quilting and sewing, starts by making shirts and dresses from food sacks — just as women do in South African townships today, creating clothing from the bags of the maize-meal that provides a staple diet for their families. From this functional sewing the Abyssinian Queen progresses to making 'crazy' patchworks, before learning the language of the quilts. (For a discussion of these 'crazy' designs, see Chapter Five). The Abyssinian Queen is multiply creative, and expresses this equally in storytelling, singing and quilting. Her boys sit under her quilting frame, listening entranced to stories of escape. Their mother tells them tales derived from African folklore — about 'Ananse, the wily spider who came with the ancestors from the old continent and whose bag was always full of tricks' (*Ibid*, 45). Able to assume protean forms, her stories travel through different time-frames, re-emerging in the contemporary memory rituals of Mahlon and Orpah.

The Abyssinian Queen's stories draw on a richly matriarchal African tradition. While the children in her audience participate in her stories, she tells them the originary myth of a female Sun, a principle of creation that gives light and life to the world. Her primeval creation story offends the plantation owner's wife, who wants her to tell Bible stories instead of 'voodoo'. But these 'voodoo' songs are socially as well as theologically transgressive. They break down divisions by mixing children who would normally be 'segregated and quartered according to their breed and pedigree' (*Ibid*, 47). These songs also teach the children about the natural world — foxes, buzzards, rabbits and wolves — so that, despite the hardships of their instrumentalised lives, they learn of an ecologically rich and magical story-world far removed from the rigid categories and constructions of the stories told by the plantation owner's wife. Equally, slaves labouring in the fields inspire one another by singing Negro spirituals — *Steal Away* or *Let My People Go.* The words of these songs proclaim the readiness of the Underground Railroad to facilitate escape. The tradition of quilting, as remarkably illustrated by the Abyssinian Queen, thus serves to bind individuals 'into a cohesive force, and remind them of their duty to freedom' (*Ibid,* 109). Quilts have in common with spirituals, adages and proverbs the capacity to jolt memories and record communal values: 'Like the stories the storytellers and the griots of the old continent told whose rhymes and rhythms forced people never to forget them and the history they contained, the patterns and colours and designs and ties and stitches of quilts were mnemonic' (*Ibid,* 109–10).

Inheriting the creativity of the Abyssinian Queen, Orpah — who refuses to work, but loves music and gothic romances — is unable to separate nature from culture. Treasuring the sycamore or 'ghost' trees because of their connections with slave history, she translates them through her designs into 'trees in dance'. As the Abyssinian Queen's stories assume protean shapes, so Orpah's sycamore designs assume any number of shapes under her adept but naïve hand. Orpah's paintings are worked into the ghost trees in ways that combine realism with symbolism: 'Two figures, one white in a black background and the other black in a white background sitting like foetuses in the stylised heart of a ghost tree' (*Ibid,* 125). Ruth fears the power of Orpah's creativity, just as Toloki's father, the blacksmith, had resented his son's inventiveness. Toloki defends Orpah against her mother's ire: 'Orpah has something to say to the world, let her work give her an unhampered voice' (*Ibid,* 130), as Orpah insists, 'I want to invent patterns that tell my own story'. Ruth's expert quilting, by contrast, produces all the traditional designs — Jacob's Ladder, Bow Tie, Drunkard's Path, Shoofly, Monkey Wrench, Wagon Wheel, Flying Geese, Crossroads, North Star, Log Cabin, Bear's Paw — but adds nothing of her own to these carefully executed patterns. Toloki, however, recognises, as an apprentice quilt-maker himself, that modern quilters create works of art that are based on traditional designs but venture into new directions.

Another dimension of alterity that informs identity in Toloki's narrative is the relationship between modern Kilvertians and the indigenous American peoples of the past. 'Our people', made up of white, Indian and Negro strains, trace their ancestry back to the Cherokee, Shawnee, Navajo and Powhatan tribes with whom their ancestors intermingled. Orpah believes that native American folklore will one day come to her rescue: 'She sees herself as a tortured soul that will one day be released by the return of a stranger mentioned in some North American tales'

(*Ibid*, 79). But which Indian legacy will come to her aid — given that her sitar originates from 'real Indians from India' (*Ibid*, 79) is never made clear. What is clear is that inter-marriage between Africans, Irish and Native Americans created 'a new race of people' in the history of Kilvert. Like the cosmology expressed in the storytelling of the Abyssinian Queen, the folk heritage of these Native Americans was matriarchal. When the escaped slave Abednego came to Tabler Town, as Kilvert was known before, he was taken in by the indigenous tribes who lived together harmoniously and whose deity was female:

> *For the first time Abednego got to know the meaning of freedom among the tribes — the Shawnee and the Cherokee and the Powhatan — that lived side-by-side in the region. He learnt about the God of the Shawnee, the Great Creator known as 'Our Grandmother', and paid his respects to Her, and gave his thanks for being brought to this beautiful place. Having been brought up by the graceful Abyssinian Queen, he found it comforting that the Creator was a woman. That was one thing the preachers of his Christian church that met in the Fairfield Farms big barn had failed to teach him* (*Ibid*, 112).

In addition to belongng to a matriarchal culture — like that which sustained the slaves on the Southern plantations — Native Americans celebrated ancestors. This is in contrast to contemporary America, where the Court Street Halloween masquerades (with the exception of Obed Quigley's impersonation of a dead slave) are rooted in the values and personalities of the present. Indigenous Americans — Shawnee, Cherokee, Powhatans — also lived in ecological balance with their surroundings, unlike the contemporary city-dwellers of Ohio, who participate in an economy of waste. It is only amongst the poorest of Americans, those living in rural Appalachia, that the values of indigenous Americans — celebrating ancestors or practising ecologically sustainable lifestyles — are demonstrated. But the Quigleys' ancestry mixes the strains of Shawnee, Cherokee and Powhatan tribes in ways that make it impossible to revive the belief systems and life practices of these native Americans. In contemporary America, the Eastern Shawnee tribe of Oklahoma is active in campaigning for 'aboriginal possessory land rights' (*Ibid*, 227): they lay claim to more than 93 000 acres of northwest Ohio. They want hunting, fishing and gathering rights in large sections of Ohio as well, and insist also on their right to establish casino gambling in these contested areas. Obed Quigley's support of the Shawnee claim is based on his ambition to force the US government into proclaiming a Shawnee reservation, a project that requires the total exclusion of the Cherokee and Powhatan peoples who have historically co-existed with the Shawnee in Ohio. Cultural links with the Shawnee are all but erased; what remains is a social and political alliance with Bush's America that denies the rights of other indigenous Americans. There are now no stories, paintings, quilts or songs that continue to represent Indian traditions. By contrast, what anchors the past culture of the southern slaves in the memory of present-day Kilvertians is performance — of stories, of music, of dancing, of quilt-design, which continue to influence their daily lives — and it is to this performative dimension of cultural identity that I now turn.

Performing identity

Toloki is a Professional Mourner, a profession that he has designed for himself in the poverty-ridden and death-haunted townships of South Africa. Coming to America for the first time, he discovers that other peoples throughout the ages have also devised ceremonies to mourn death and celebrate memory, and his repertoire of professional mourning increases. But in order to practise his profession he needs Americans, the majority of whom are schooled in fundamentalist Christian beliefs, to understand that the role of a Professional Mourner is necessary to honour the dead. In this project, he has a powerful ally in Obed Quigley who explains to the congregation in Brother Michael's church that they should turn to Toloki 'the African shaman' because 'every one of them was totally inept at handling grief. That was just how human beings were created. Hence the need for a Professional Mourner' (*Ibid,* 184). Obed even finds a biblical quotation from Jeremiah 9:17: 'Thus says the Lord of hosts: Consider the call for the mourning women, that they may come; and send for skilful wailing women, that they may come. Let them make haste and take up wailing for us, that our eyes may run with tears, and our eyelids gush with water.' The reading of this passage immediately spurs Toloki to produce mourning sounds, while Ruth's eyes swell with tears. The context is now prepared for Toloki and Orpah by the end of the novel to become itinerant Professional Mourners, travelling around the States producing 'the performances and exhibitions with which we'll dazzle the bereaved' (*Ibid,* 286).

This performance of mourning links back insistently to the Abyssinian Queen, whose stories are staged in the ghost trees or singing sycamores so precious to Orpah's designs. The singing sycamore becomes a symbol of regeneration, as celebration and memory bring back the voices of children from the past:

> *The singing sycamore was haunted. Not because it was a ghost tree but for the well-known fact that it harboured in its soul the spirits of little children who once sat under it listening to stories and telling their own [aeons] before the world was killed. These were spirits waiting to be reunited with all the children from the tribes of the universe on a regenerated earth that would be free of sickness and death; an earth where man, woman, and child would roam free, owned by no one* (*Ibid,* 86).

The hollowed and hallowed sycamore trees are not only repositories of stories from the past; they also prepare for the future by storing the quilts, tools and provisions that runaway slaves such as Abednego and Nicodemus will need in their flight from the Fairfield Farms. And in the contemporary chronotope these trees play a crucial role in stimulating memory and keeping alive the hopes and dreams that sustained the slaves' lives and that still give meaning and purpose to lives otherwise instrumentalised.

When Toloki and Obed combine to mourn at the grave of Obed's ancestor, Niall Quigley, they produce a two-part harmony and a call-and-response pattern that 'transports us to another place, another realm, another time' (*Ibid*, 157). The narrative now moves back into the past to reproduce Quigley's bizarre story. Performing stories collapses time and space boundaries: Niall Quigley as a slave on the Fairfield Farms finds that he can identify with the singing of the field slaves because it reminds him of folk stories he had heard as a child back in Ireland.

Folk memories and the stories told to children anticipate the narrations, in the present story, of the medium man Mahlon Quigley, who combines with his spirit child daughter Orpah to enact, in full costume — he's 'a knight in armour one night, and a sultan in flowing robes on another' (*Ibid*, 196) — the stories passed on from the slave days. But this celebration of memory contains anomalies. Mahlon is haunted by the fact that he has never properly mourned the memory of his own mother. It is only when Toloki helps him to do this, by finding and naming her grave, that Mahlon is enabled to move into a new creative space, returning to growing things whereas before he could only collect garden gnomes.

When towards the end of the novel Orpah plays in public for the first time in her life, taking the stage with her sitar, the effect is immediate and electrifying, transfixing the audience. Others join her: a guitar, a flute, a lap dulcimer, a fiddle and a banjo: 'And soon the impromptu band is giving bluegrass standards a tone that has never been heard before' (*Ibid*, 215). The musical talent of the spirit child is matched by the storytelling talents of her father Mahlon, the medium man to whom the sycamores tell their stories. Like Orpah's bluegrass-inspired improvisation, Mahlon's storytelling derives from the time of the slaves: 'Memories of how an Abyssinian Queen flapped her wings and swooped to the ground and of how the sun was once lonely because it had no one to play with. His body soaks in these memories, so that his mouth may retell them later' (*Ibid*, 220). In these performances, old memories beget new patterns —just as Toloki learns to sew and his fingers become more adept '[his] quilt becomes art ... like a sculpture' (*Ibid*, 224). Together, as Professional Mourners working 'for fulfilment rather than remuneration' (*Ibid*, 231), Toloki and Orpah live in his RV, which has been elaborately decorated with dogwood quilts. Toloki likes to sleep on an Irish

Chain quilt, while Orpah declares of her collages: 'I want them pictures to tell a story. Like back in them days if something happened there'd be a song wrote about it' (*Ibid*, 234). Toloki remarks: 'These collages are a song'. He promises, as he becomes more skilled, to translate them into quilts.

To perform his stories, Mahlon needs both costumes and movement: to tell the story of Massa Blue Fly, who comes back to the Abyssinian Queen to assure her that her boys are safe, he flies around Orpah's room and makes buzzing sounds. But the question of who owns these cultural memories so precious to Mahlon and his children vexes Orpah, who becomes possessive and territorial, closing Toloki out of the storytelling rituals: 'He can't take no part in our memories' (*Ibid*, 243). Toloki's plea to Orpah that these stories and the memories they enact be shared, foregrounds the community role of memory. The ethical dimension of memories becomes insistent: can there be such a thing as private memory? Toloki remarks of Mahlon's gentle storytelling: 'No one who tells such wonderful stories can kill anybody' (*Ibid*, 252). Toloki's own practice of professional mourning brings together the community meaning of mourning — which he now recognises to be related to the ancient Aztecs and to both the historical and continuing traditions of public mourning at Irish wakes — and the movements that Mahlon performed in enacting his memories. It appears also that the work of the Virginia Mourners, which Toloki wishes to study, is anecdotal, cast in the oral tradition and based on a matriarchal culture like that of the Negro and Indian ancestors of the Kilvertians.

Toloki and Orpah, now lovers, come together to combine the erotic with the tragic in their somatic mourning partnership. Meanwhile, Obed's 'hoofing' — the singing and dancing he loved as a child — has paved the way for his future spiritual performances as a pastor after he finishes training at Bible School. By the end of the novel, even Ruth — Ayatollah Ruth, Tsunami, Taliban in the House — has learned to balance new artistic inputs — she wants to learn how to make Bible quilts — against her religious fundamentalism and her skill as a traditional quilter. The dénouement of *Cion* thus celebrates the performative dimension as key to creative self-individuation. Toloki breaks free from his creator the Sciolist so that, like Orpah, he can 'tell his own stories'. Having assisted his American family to move towards greater independence, Toloki and his partner Orpah, on the last page of the novel, triumphantly take possession of the present: 'Before I came to Kilvert I lived only in the past and in the future. I therefore found the present a very lonely place to be. A very boring place. Orpah is a kindred spirit in this respect. Hopefully together we'll discover how to live in the present. And we'll do so without the aid of the sciolist' (*Ibid*, 286).

My final comment on the importance of performance for *Cion* is satirical. Orpah buys, at an auction, a 'Bush gnome' for her father Mahlon, which she wants Toloki to give him 'because he don't like you and you want him to like you' (*Ibid*, 213). Toloki describes this curious icon:

> *It is a famous George W. Bush gnome invented by one Sam Girton, an Athenian no less, and it sells internationally on e-bay and always creates a flurry of bidding. It comes with accessories: if you love Bush then you place an American flag in his hand. If you hate Bush you make him hold a bag of money with a dollar sign on it or a machine gun. The gnome is popular with Bush haters and Bush lovers* (*Ibid*, 213).

What I have discussed in this section is the importance, for the Appalachian Americans of Kilvert, Ohio, of the memories of ancestors. These, mediated by Toloki, continue to invigorate their cultural practices — in storytelling, quilting, music-making and ecological inventiveness. The 'Bush Gnome' anecdote is an indication that even among the wealthiest Americans, for whom commodification and consumerism have long replaced creativity, it is necessary to retain some illusions of choice and agency — although these are forced into constricted, reactionary modes.

Toloki takes over from the Sciolist

When Mda — via the Sciolist, 'author' of Toloki's tale — moves his Professional Mourner from *Ways of Dying* in the townships of South Africa to the rural poverty of Appalachia in the eastern USA, he simultaneously dramatises several perspectives. Through Toloki's experience of living in the diaspora, he gains new insights into his own profession of mourning, as well as a new understanding of the complex relationships between the contemporary Kilvert community and the plantation slave ancestors whose storytelling, music and quilt-making still dominate their cultural horizon. Toloki has another learning curve to master: to question, mock and finally discard the literary authority of his creator, the Sciolist. *Cion*, then, uses the worldly context of diaspora and the literary context of metafiction to enable Toloki's individuation.

Metafiction is usefully described by J. U. Jacobs and David Bell:

> Cion *can perhaps be described as a work of historiographic metafiction, in which, to quote Linda Hutcheon, 'the notion that history's problem is verification, while fiction's is veracity' (1988, 112) is confused. The respective 'truth' values and 'authenticity' of history and of fiction are contrasted and complicated through the combination of historiography with metafiction and their mutual influence. Both fiction and history are exposed as narrative genres, their productions as constructs, and the line between them blurred* (Bell & Jacobs: 2009, 358).

Cion's metafictional discourse is, as Jacobs and Bell note, captured in the terms of 'cion' and 'sciolist', which play on the 'self-reflexive relationship between the fictional Toloki and his implied author, Zakes Mda ... as Mda's fictional offspring, Toloki becomes not his "scion" or descendant, but merely the eponymous "cion", the verb referring, in its Middle English spelling without an "s" to a twig, runner or offshoot, a cutting for grafting' (*Ibid*, 359). Combining as it does African with American roots and forms, *Cion* 'provides a creative textual collage that makes a statement about the contemporary world and the role of the writer within it' (*Ibid*, 366).

The relationship between Toloki and the Sciolist is ironic from the start. On the opening page Toloki remarks: 'The Sciolist has delusions of grandeur. At his whim I find myself walking among colourful creatures that are hiding in stolen identities'. Why the Sciolist has decided to begin Toloki's story amid this inauthenticity — this Halloween hiding behind others' identities — is not disclosed. In any case, it is Toloki, not the Sciolist, who opens this novel with rueful remarks about a self-deluded author. 'Every year at this time, I am told, the natives go wild and invoke their pagan gods, who descend upon the earth in the guise of these Court Street creatures.' Combining participant observation with reliance on others' accounts of this opening spectacle, Toloki recognises the Halloween masquerade as 'a celebration of blood'. Unlike Bakhtinian Carnival, which expresses a folk culture that interrogates the 'authoritarian voice' of dominant orthodoxy, the Court Street revels with which the novel opens echo the commercialism that characterises George Bush's Republican America. Masquerading as media-created figures or as American public figures, the Court Street revellers adopt stolen identities that are highly derivative.

Toloki's identity emerges from his attempts to disentangle himself from the Sciolist's numerous 'abandonments' of the character for whom he is supposed to be responsible. These 'abandonments' Toloki uses to explain how he came to be in Kilvert, Ohio. The Sciolist comes across to the reader as lacking resources, his actions driven by others' suggestions, whereas Toloki's story reveals an increasing versatility as his actions in the present emerge from his understanding of the past. Explaining that the Sciolist has been commissioned to write a play in Durham, UK, he mentions that the Sciolist has brought with him the hero of his first novel, *Ways of Dying*. In that novel, Toloki began to cultivate the asceticism of the monastic life lived by the *aghori sadhu* of India. Now, in Durham, he connects his own history to that of the tombs in Durham Cathedral. He explains to the reader that his Professional Mourning has fallen into a rut in South Africa since AIDS, the number-one killer amongst his people, became a taboo subject in the South African media and press: 'People died of silence. Of shame. Of denial' (*Ibid*, 3).

Disillusioned both because he is discovering that professional mourning is not his invention but has been practised through the centuries by the ancient Greeks and Romans (and in more recent times in Spain, Italy, India, Ireland and Zambia), and that his chosen profession has come to a stalemate in his own country, Toloki decides to take up the challenge issued to the Sciolist by Sam Crowl, a Shakespearian professor at Ohio. Crowl had mooted that the Sciolist should take Toloki to another culture, and suggested Durham. In Durham, Toloki is in his element in the Chapel of the Nine Altars, which contains the tomb of St Cuthbert, on whose open hands birds came to nest, and he holds 'erudite conversations with the Venerable Bede whose bones lie buried in a splendid tomb in the Galilee Chapel on the opposite end of the cathedral' (*Ibid*, 3). In Durham, Toloki thrives on Crowl's idea of becoming an itinerant mourner. But the Sciolist 'could not find a story that would go with my wanderings [in Durham]' and so decides to dump Toloki at the cemetery belonging to the mental asylum at The Ridges in Athens, Ohio — presumably because Crowl is from Ohio. Here once again Toloki is in his element, welcoming the challenge of mourning 'the unwanted people from society': the indigent, the homeless, the loveless.

Remarking that 'the richness of re-inventing deaths lies in the fact that you first have to re-create the lives of the deceased before they died' (*Ibid*, 30), Toloki sets to work inventing the histories of the nameless occupants of rows of undated tombs, signalling hereby his understanding of the social construction of 'madness' as a category that he, as author, can escape or transcend. In this initial chapter of *Cion*, then, the Sciolist emerges as marginal to the story that will be told, whereas his creature Toloki responds to the challenges of his diasporic displacement with imagination and creativity. Thus, when Toloki first meets Ruth Quigley, with whose family in Kilvert, Ohio, he will stay for nearly a year, he introduces himself without reference either to Sam Crowl or the Sciolist — as though he were entirely the author of his own story: 'I came in search of mourning'. The first chapter of the novel ends with the Sciolist relegated to the margins, as Toloki takes over the story that 'is told by the earthy scent of the quilts' (*Ibid*, 30). By the time the second chapter opens, moving back in time to the history of Fairfield Farms, the Sciolist is definitively absent. The story is told by an omniscient narrative voice that foregrounds the role of folklore, as in the matriarchal world of the Abyssinian Queen: 'In the folk tales that were told when work was done and fires were roaring the sun was king and the moon was queen'. The Fairfield Farms narrative about slave-owning is brutal in its distinction between love and ownership — with slave mothers not allowed to lay claim to their disallowed children. But these oppressive perspectives are undone by the talents of the Abyssinian Queen — storyteller, singer, artist. Her love for her sons, the runaway slaves Abednego and Nicodemus, will be at the centre of their narrative and accorded a central place by the omniscient narrator. The Abyssinian Queen is the true heroine of the slaves' story and leaves no narrative space for the Sciolist.

The best the Sciolist can manage when consulted by Toloki on 'how to deal with the ghosts of the past in rural America' is a portentous aphorism: '[M]emory thrives on transforming the past to palliate the present.' But once again it is Toloki who explores this maxim in relation to the characters in his story-world, informing the reader that both Ruth and her son are trapped in a past with which they are obsessed: '[T]he past is all they ever talk about with joy and pride in their eyes' (*Ibid*, 55). As architect of the story-world, the Sciolist should have scripted a summer escape for the slaves Nicodemus and Abednego, given the hazards and difficulties of a winter escape through snow and ice. But the boys, driven by pressing personal motives, decide to escape in winter, against the counsel of the Abyssinian Queen, whose quilts have taught them to follow the North Star (taking a northerly direction), the Drunkard's Path (following a zigzag route) and the Monkey Wrench (being prepared and equipped for escape). But they have ignored the Flying Geese pattern, since this illustrates flight 'in spring or summer'. All that the Sciolist can do is 'acquiesce' in this winter escape, foregrounding his passivity and loss of agency in relation to his fictional characters.

Although the Sciolist enters into Toloki's dreams, reminding him of his mission, he never plays a central part in ordering the narrative. Toloki continuously escapes his control, hinting at a future in which he will radically destabilise the Sciolist's plans. Thinking about Africa, Toloki recognises that there are 'hundreds of cultures on the [African] continent', so that his search for mourning 'should have started there'. Because the Sciolist 'had other plans for me', this project has been delayed. But Toloki insists: 'I will do it. One day I will do it' (*Ibid*, 119). In this contest between the Sciolist and Toloki, the reader wants to hear more from Toloki about how he is going to expand his African horizons. This is a project not available to his American interlocutors, who use African heritage to falsify their cultural constructions. Toloki, a true African, has a role to play in this deconstruction that the Sciolist does not share. Even when Toloki refers from time to time to the Sciolist's master plan for the novel (for instance when he signals that he does not yet know the full story of the performances enacted by the medium man and spirit child because 'the Sciolist kept these secrets close to his chest') it is Toloki, not the Sciolist, who takes over narration about and commentary on the novel's story-world from a perspective of gathering sophistication, which cues the attentive reader in to the novel's developments. Therefore when, at the end of the novel, Toloki describes the Sciolist as being in the God business and exacting love from his creatures, his insistence on his own independence comes as no surprise to the reader.

Finally...

This chapter has attempted to link several concepts implicit in the term diaspora — geographical dispersal, cultural fragmentation, search for 'origins', the importance of memory in reconceptualising culture — to *Cion*, a novel in which the chief protagonist Toloki is a South African who goes to America in search of a new cultural identity. His self-identification is enabled by his interactions with the Quigley family in Kilvert, Ohio, who are themselves shaped by their descent from their slave ancestors on the Southern plantations.

Toloki's experience of the American art of quilt-making as transformative art-form accompanies his metafictional development. The concept of diaspora historically refers to 'a range of cultural and ethnic groups held together by shared cultural or religious commitments and [sharing] some sense of exile from a place or state of origin and belonging' (Hawthorn: 2000, 78). The term changes in current postcolonial theorisations, when it becomes 'decoupled from an actual or desired homeland and understood instead, in more post-structuralist vein, to describe a dynamic network of communities without the stabilizing allusion to an original homeland or essential identity' (Peter Brooker, quoted by Hawthorn: *Ibid*, 71). This dialectic between the search for origins and the recognition that cultural identiy is always provisional and dynamic informs Toloki's story as Professional Mourner and as Master Storyteller.

Chapter Seven

'Our only physical and psychic home'[1]: Ecology and community in *The Whale Caller*

In this chapter I filter Mda's fictional preoccupations in *The Whale Caller* through the arguments of other writers who explore ecological issues, because I believe that in this novel Mda has designed a powerful ecological allegory.[2] My theoretical frameworks are recent ecological debates both in South Africa and in America, since Mda as writer and academic is linked to both traditions. American universities — and Mda is Professor of Creative Writing at Ohio — have experienced a recent flowering of cross-disciplinary ecological criticism and environmental scholarship, the aim of which is 'to bridge the gaps between scholars, artists, students and the public'.[3] Moving from framing debates to a discussion of the novel itself, I will focus on the consciousness and reactions of the main protagonist. The richness and complexity of his story invites comparison with the stories of other contemporary writers who are concerned with communicating the urgency of environmental issues. I argue that *The Whale Caller*, for all its satire and humour, is the bleakest of Mda's novels because it depicts a dysfunctional human community that ensues in ecological catastrophe. While *The Madonna of Excelsior*, *The Heart of Redness*, and *Cion* all reflect Mda's interest in environmental issues, these novels are far less pessimistic than *The Whale Caller* since all three affirm the possibility of communal action, which this novel denies.

1 The phrase is William Kittredge's.

2 Brian McHale points out that in the last quarter of the twentieth century 'the romantic prejudice against allegory has been lifted, and it has once again become possible to call a work allegorical without being pejorative' (McHale: 1987, 140). He notes that 'the revival of allegory in postmodernist writing can … be related to postmodernist poetics … Like metaphor … allegory offers itself as a tool for exploring ontological structure and foregrounding ontological themes, so in a sense we should hardly be surprised at the contemporary resurgence of allegory' (*Ibid*, 141).

3 This phrase occurs on the inside cover of the journal *ISLE — Interdisciplinary Studies in Literature and Environment* — connected with the Department of English at the University of Nevada, Reno, and edited by Scott Slovic. Jacklyn Cock emphasises that America has become the centre of ecological studies that link the environment to social justice.

The South African theoretical framework for this chapter originates in three recent journal editions of *The English Academy Review*, *Current Writing* and the *Journal of Literary Studies*. All three editions are dedicated to ecological issues; they attest to the burgeoning of ecological discourse in South Africa.[4] The American theoretical framework I adopt originates in a conference I attended in October 2009 at Goedgedacht Farm, near Malmesbury in the wheatlands of the Cape. Titled 'The Literature and Ecology Colloquium', it was attended by a small number of delegates in a beautiful and inspiring agricultural setting.[5] One of the plenary speakers was the American ecologist Scott Slovic, whose book *What's Nature Worth? Narrative Expressions of Environmental Values*, co-edited with Terre Satterfield, I have used in the American debates section of this chapter. In my reading, Slovic and Satterfield's book raises many ecological challenges dramatised in *The Whale Caller*. *What's Nature Worth* contains interviews with 12 writers working in the genres of non-fiction essay, short story and poetry (and making reference to novels). The book is about 'biologically significant systems, treasured landscapes and/or threatened species' (Slovic & Satterfield: 2004, 5). Its editors point out that ethicists 'have led the effort to counter the trend towards monetary expressions of value by defining both anthropocentric

4 South African environmentalists emphasise that ecological discourse in this country, though expanding, has yet to attain the sophistication of its equivalents in Britain, Europe and America. Sandra Swart remarks, 'The "animal turn" in the southern African social sciences, and within the historical guild in particular, is still very small' (Swart: 2007, 280). Dan Wylie notes that 'the words "ecology" and "ecocriticism" are notably absent from [the papers he has collected]' and remarks 'nationally, we are apparently still at a stage of considerable theoretical naïvety' (Wylie: 2006, 5). Julia Martin comments: '[Q]uestions of ecology, place and situatedness [are discussed] by a growing body of teachers and researchers internationally, although [they remain] ... marginal in South Africa' (Martin: 2003, 108). Yet the number of special journal editions recently devoted to ecological issues, with hundreds of pages of discussion, indicates that South Africa is rapidly catching up with international peers.

5 As a venue, Goedgedacht is a remarkable example of social interconnection. A working olive farm, it uses its resources from harvesting olives and running its conference centre to improve the lives of farm-workers' children in this very poor area. The Goedgedacht Trust provides children with a square meal every day and a place to do their homework so that they can remain at school. Inspired by the collective efforts of the poorest of the poor — the slum dwellers of Mumbai in India — Goedgedacht's educational commitment is reaching far beyond the immediate area in which it is located, launching community initiatives in education all over South Africa. When I spoke to Mda about Goedgedacht, knowing his commitment to combining writing with community involvement, he replied that he had been invited to visit Goedgedacht on several occasions and was looking forward to going there when his schedule between the USA and SA allows.

and ecocentric theories of worth' (*Ibid*, 7). The 12 writers interviewed explain why they think the language of story is more effective in dramatising ecological issues than other forms of discourse.[6] In the conclusion of this chapter I draw on the work of South African sociologist Jacklyn Cock, another of the speakers at the Goedgedacht Conference. The title of her book, *The War Against Ourselves: Nature, Power and Justice*, announces its argument that nature is not external to the world of people and that ecological issues are linked to social justice and peace, as Mda eloquently demonstrates in *The Whale Caller*.

An eco-criticism for South Africa

Perhaps the best place to start with the South African eco-critical debates reflected in Mda's fiction is with Mda himself. In 'The Pink Mountain: Landscapes and the Conception of a Literature of Public Action' (2009) Mda speaks of how place or setting in his works inspire his community initiatives — like the beekeeping project that he set up on the Pink Mountain. Storytelling, he insists, begins with landscapes, because they are replete with memory and trauma. These landscapes he brings to the reader's attention through focalisation. His preoccupation with the environment has elicited strong critical response:

> *My enthusiasm for visual pleasures in general, and for what eco-critics variously refer to as 'nature', 'the wilderness', 'ecology' and 'the environment', in particular, has been seen in a number of discussions as a departure for black South African literature which is largely set in urban spaces ... The cradle of Sesotho literature is in Lesotho and the northeastern Free State province in South Africa. isiXhosa literature is rooted in the Eastern Cape. In these regions, and in others that continue to produce literatures in the indigenous languages, writers have not yet been alienated from natural environments and landscapes* (Mda: 2009a).

6 Critics' responses to *The Whale Caller* curiously neglect the novel's connection with ecological issues. They foreground the novel's relation to the 'new' South Africa, with its allusions to truth and reconciliation, its 'insatiable expectations' and its 'precarious euphoria of a society in transition' (Maya Jaggi, *The Guardian*, 27 August 2005). Or they complain that 'the characters' behaviour is at best merely eccentric, at worst insane' and deplore the lack of a Márquez-like magic realism that might transform its meaning (Madison Smartt Bell, *New York Times*, 8 January 2006). Or they have read the novel as 'a simple love triangle between a rigid and ritualised man, a captivating town drunk and a spectacular whale', using satire 'to lampoon all the banalities, constraints and tribulations of standard romantic love'. One reviewer writes that *The Whale Caller* is about 'the beauty of imperfect love ... its deeper, darker concern is not so much the fragility of love, but the fragility of life itself when one surrenders wholly to the foolish heart' (Steve Amick, *The Washington Post*, 11 December 2005). Amick's emphasis on 'the fragility of life itself' begins to suggest the context in which I discuss the novel.

Commenting on the perception that 'black people have adopted an antagonistic stance to conservation', Mda criticises the neo-liberalism of post-apartheid South Africa because of its enslavement of 'wilderness' to market forces. He points out, however, that 'some members of the urban black elite now seek to develop a new relationship with the land, be it the conserved spaces that dot all provinces and earn tourist dollars, the natural landscapes of the Valley of a Thousand Hills in KwaZulu-Natal, or the highly developed and mechanised commercial farms of the Free State' (*Ibid*, 11). He concludes: 'Caring about animals and telling stories about them cannot be a "white thing" because these are the very animals that featured as characters in the stories that my grandmother told me when I was a little boy; stories that had been passed to her by previous generations of grandmothers long before white people came to South Africa' (*Ibid*, 12). Mda maintains that in the 'new' South Africa environmental issues have been presented in ways that alienate black South Africans: 'the problem … is not that blacks don't care about the environment', but that the 'discourse on environmental justice is not framed in a manner that relates directly to their lives' (*Ibid*, 12). He concludes: 'Black South Africans … do care about our environment … that is why environmental issues in general, and landscapes in particular, are a crucial part of my fiction … One thing that I attempt to do in my storytelling is to frame the discourse on environment in a manner that relates directly to our lives; to show how our very humanity is intractably entangled with nature' (*Ibid*, 13). *The Whale Caller*, I would argue, is a sustained and moving fictional exploration of that intractable entanglement.

At the centre of South African responses to ecological issues is J. M. Coetzee's *Elizabeth Costello*. In 'The Lives of Animals', already quoted in this book's epigraphs, Costello reflects on the interconnectedness of life on earth:

> *In the ecological vision, the salmon and the river weeds and the water insects interact in a great, complex dance with the earth and the weather. The whole is greater than the sum of the parts. In the dance, each organism has a role: it is these multiple roles, rather than the particular beings who play them, that participate in the dance* (Coetzee: 2006, 98).

Taking up a metaphor that echoes Coetzee's 'dance' analogy of ecological interconnection, Mariss Everitt coins the phrase 'net of energy': 'Hopefully, the relatively new science of ecology will permeate human consciousness and make us understand and respect nature as a "net of energy" which sustains life on the planet' (Everitt: 2006, 92–3). Similarly, Jayne Glover quotes the phrase 'web of being' to figure the interconnection of species and life-forms on earth: '[T]he science of ecology has provided additional support for a world-view that perceives all of life as an interconnected web or single living being' (Glover: 2006, 130). This is reminiscent of the trope used by American writer

Rachel Carson, who refers to 'a web of life that binds together all organisms' (quoted in Cock: 2007, 37). To be unaware of our participation in that dance, net or web of life is to promote uneven ecological relations, to jeopardise our own peace as well as the equilibrium of the planet. Harry Sewlall quotes Wangari Maathai, a Kenyan Nobel Peace Prize winner. When asked, 'What's the world's biggest challenge?', she replied, 'The environment. We are sharing our resources in a very inequitable way ... And that is partly the reason why we have conflict' (Sewlall: 2007, 386). Anthony Vital, discussing South Africa's environmental justice movement, expresses the hope that the founding of Earthlife Africa, an organisation that combines progressive politics with environmental concerns, may '[develop] an environmentalism that could be called postcolonial, asserting the need for a "people-centred" interest in the environment while being alert to South Africa's colonial legacies and its peripheral position within a globalised economy' (Vital: 2005, 298).

In the following section I summarise the ecological debates currently taking place in South Africa under the headings 'Dismantling dualisms', 'The sympathetic imagination/Becoming animal' and 'Storytelling'. There are, of course, many points of correlation between these South African discussions and those taking place in America, which are the subject of the next section. Both sections on ecological discourse are linked to my analysis of *The Whale Caller*.

Dismantling dualisms

Investigating the biologist-writer Douglas Livingstone's attribution of subjectivity and agency to animals, Wendy Woodward cites ecological critic Patrick Murphy. Murphy reconceptualises traditional ontology: '[I]nstead of thinking in terms of "I" and "other", we [should] conceptualise interconnection between "we", a communal notion of the self, and "anothers"' (Woodward: 2003a, 46). Woodward also draws on the work of Val Plumwood, who seeks to build a non-instrumental relationship to nature: '[T]he only way to dismantle dualism and the Cartesian "dream of power" is to develop a non-hierarchical concept of difference'. Livingstone, Woodward concludes, is a poet with ecological vision. His writing moves towards dismantling some of the dualisms on which Cartesian dreams of power depend, although in some respects he reasserts dominant masculinity.

Julia Martin, discussing her teaching practice, shares Woodward's hope that the dualisms on which our knowledge has traditionally been built can be deconstructed: 'Drawing on the extensive ecological, feminist and other analyses of the exploitative consequences of binary thinking and ideology of hierarchic dualism, I would hope in the learning environment to articulate the value of treading a middle way between the dualisms according to which we habitually construct our lives, and in particular our academic work' (Martin: 2003, 111). Mike Marais, however, believes that the project of overturning the epistemological and ethical dualisms on which power turns is utopian. Given what he sees as humankind's 'ineluctable anthropomorphism', he argues that 'the only hope for an ethical response to the environment lies in the interruption, rather than sublation, of the opposition between human subject and objective world' (Marais: 2003, 69). Marais argues that Cartwright's novel, *White Lightning*, takes a pessimistic view of human capacity to 'be with' other species. Literature can only 'represent nature ... from the perspective of human subjects' (*Ibid*, 84); the reconfiguring of the binaries on which Western power/knowledge depends cannot be achieved.

Does *The Whale Caller* dismantle or reiterate the dualisms on which Western master discourses depend? I would suggest that it does both. In creating a relationship of equality between the Whale Caller and the whale Sharisha, the novel undoes the opposition between human and animal subjects. But in the tragic dénouement of Sharisha's death, it highlights the Whale Caller's failure of accountability to the creatures in his care. The master narrative of male domination is once again reiterated, with tragic consequences for human and non-human subjects alike.

The sympathetic imagination/Becoming animal

Once again, it is Coetzee's novel *Elizabeth Costello* that provides the phrase that stands behind much ecocritical thinking. In her talk on 'The Philosophers and the Animals', Costello tells her audience that 'there is no limit to the extent to which we can think ourselves into the being of another. There are no bounds to the sympathetic imagination ... If I can think my way into the existence of a [fictional] being who has never existed, then I can think my way into the existence of a bat or a chimpanzee or an oyster, any being with whom I share the substrate of life' (Coetzee: 2004, 80). The same argument emerges in 'The Poets and the Animals', where Costello describes Ted Hughes' creation of the jaguar: 'By bodying forth the jaguar, Hughes shows us that we too can embody animals — by the process called poetic invention that mingles breath and sense in a way that no one has explained and no one ever will. He shows us how to bring the living body into being within ourselves. When we read the jaguar poem, when we recollect it afterwards in tranquillity, we are for a brief while the jaguar. He ripples within us, he takes over our body, he is us' (*Ibid*, 97–8).

Pat Louw, writing about nature documentaries, quotes Karla Armbruster's ecocritical philosophy, which, like Costello's, turns on the imaginative possibilities that the study of literature can release: 'I can influence people to develop more sustainable relationships with the natural world by exploring, critiquing, and re-envisioning the worldviews found in literary and other cultural texts — especially views of human relationships with nature' (Louw: 2006, 147). Mariss Everitt also advocates the unifying power of the human imagination '[that] offers a possibility of synthesis between the intuitive and the rational ... [and] ... could lead to an authentically ecological sensibility'. Human beings she believes must learn to reconnect with animals through the 'elusive but powerful human imagination' (Everitt: 2006, 91) which is both an intellectual and a creative faculty. This faculty is similarly acclaimed by Wendy Woodward:

> *That imagination is a positive attribute in the representation of animals is also acknowledged when J.M. Coetzee has Elizabeth Costello define 'sympathetic imagination' as 'sharing ... the being of another'. According to Buddhist ethics, 'Seeing others as being like yourself ... means that you cannot kill them'* (Woodward: 2007, 300).

A further step in the process of imaginative extension described above is a protagonist's learning, through 'new practices of witnessing'

> *the multisensual business of becoming animal — a relational process in which animal subjects are configured through particular social bonds, bodily comportments, and life habits that are complicated, but neither originated nor erased, by the various ways in which they may be enmeshed in the categorical and practical orderings of people* (Shirley Brooks, quoting Whatmore and Thorne: 2006, 21).

Literary texts can dramatise this process; Costello quotes Hughes' poetic creation of the jaguar, which allows the reader to feel at one with the animal. Wendy Woodward discusses the 'ontological shift' required to participate in 'becoming-animal':

> *Shamanistic practice demands an ontological shift, one which is described in Deleuze and Guattari's concept of 'becoming-animal' ... they stress that becoming-animal is not a metaphoric process but one in which identities become 'deterritorialised' through a radical sense of immanence ... For the human, becoming-animal eradicates subjectivity and its duality, and does not include guilt* (Woodward: 2006, 33).

The ways in which Mda presents the sympathetic imagination or the ability to 'become animal' are figured particularly in the Whale Caller's somatic and kinetic relationship with the whale Sharisha. This relationship entirely avoids the crypto-anthropomorphism risked by the human signifying systems embodied in language. It is discussed in some detail in the next section.

Storytelling

The role of literature to dramatise ecological issues is foregrounded in the work of the South African writers considered here. Tracy Morrison remarks:

> *Storytelling is an important social activity through which identities — individual or collective — are constructed and maintained. Though it may be individuals who tell stories, their stories are composed of larger cultural stories that are passed on, handed down, told and retold. Therefore, our narratives are located within a particular place and time and are shaped by the larger stories available to us — the 'factual' and the fictional, the conventional or the subversive. We draw off these in order to create our own coherent narratives* (Morrison: 2008, 57).

According to Morrison, we should perceive of our humanity 'as belonging in the world, rather than it belonging to humans ... If we see ourselves as interconnected and interdependent, then we will be able to see that "what I do to the other I do to myself"' (*Ibid*, 71). Thinking also about this interconnection, Anthony Vital asks: '[H]ow do we begin to tell the story of animals and humans, drawing the distinction in such a way that the lives of both can be opened to a fullness of being, while acknowledging both the deprivations of colonial pasts and the power exerted by an ever more dominant global civilisation linked historically to European and American cultures and practices?' (Vital: 2005, 306).

Introducing a special edition of *Current Writing* with an article titled 'Animal presences, animal geographies', Dan Wylie comments:

> *The symbiosis between the physical orientations of these sometimes astonishingly autonomous, coherent individual creatures around us — animals, wild and domestic — and their literary and psychological presences and effects in all our lives, is a relationship which holds the promise of endless avenues for reassessment of those lives. Any close reassessment is likely to confront us with, at the very least, our own troubling animality, our accelerating destruction of most other species, and our potential for redemptive compassion. And what is the role of the written word — literature — in forging and expressing these relationships?* (Wylie: 2006, 1).

Mariss Everitt takes up Wylie's challenge:

> *I pin my hopes on the elusive but powerful human imagination. Perhaps literature can be used to persuade where environmental facts fail. After all, stories have been used as a didactic tool from the beginnings of human civilization. To put it another way, it is not knowledge of our biological and evolutionary heritage but, rather, our uniquely human capacity to make art which may reunite humankind with the rest of the natural world* (Everitt: 2006, 91).

Robert Bieder, discussing stories that 'humanise' animals, comments:

> *[In these tales about bears] are situated cultural themes touching on origins, ancestors, taboos, identity, metamorphosis, greed, duty, spiritual power, breakdown of social order, respect for nature, cycle of life, and rebirth. They are tales that both bridge the boundaries between humans and bears and give cultural meaning to the bear. They also bridge the boundary between the past and the present* (Bieder: 2006, 165).

These stories, then, impinge on the lives of human beings because they

> *[h]elp us understand the world and our place in it; they help us imagine ourselves and our relationships with the world around us. In these stories ... bears are powerful, sacred spirits; ancestors; healers; shape shifters; lovers and mates. The stories ... are also about cultures exploring and reshaping environment* (*Ibid*, 172).

On a somewhat bleaker note, discussing animals in Mda, Honwana, Coetzee and Cartwright, Wendy Woodward argues for these texts' capacity to capture readers' attention in ways which, if they cannot prevent the killing of animals, will at least make humans aware of their complicity in these killings. These texts 'encourage the reader to imagine sharing the being of another, who is condemned to death ... Constrained socially from quitting tables laden with the corpses of dead animals, we can, at the very least, tell stories of their deaths' (Woodward: 2007, 310).

The creative processes of storytelling, therefore, can dismantle dualisms, engage the sympathetic imagination and celebrate the interconnection between humans and non-humans. Mda, in *The Whale Caller*, dramatises all these interactions in telling a story of love between a human and a non-human that challenges readers' responses to the natural world. American ecocritics also foreground the role of literature in achieving a transfigured ecological consciousness that breaks down barriers between humans and non-humans, and to these writers I now turn.

Storytelling as political activism

Starting with the central question of the political dimension of storytelling, Slovic and Satterfield quote Barry Lopez's hope that nature writing 'will not only one day produce a major and lasting body of American literature, but might also provide the foundation for a reorganisation of American political thought' (Slovic & Satterfield: 2004, 15). This conviction is reiterated by several of the contributors to *What's Nature Worth?* Speaking as an activist concerned to influence public policy-making, Terry Tempest Williams remarks: 'I keep thinking literature, art, paintings, dance and music are offerings for the policy world. These media slow you down and make you think' (*Ibid*, 76). Alison Hawthorne Deming also sees storytelling as valuable in breaking down the static polarities of politicians' decision-making, because 'stories are a reflective enterprise, not a persuasive enterprise' (*Ibid*, 104) and thus challenge readers to participate in stories rather than receive them passively. She remarks: 'Art can serve activism by teaching an attentiveness to existence and by enriching the culture in which our roots are set down' (*Ibid*, 122). Ofelia Zepeda, a member of the Tohono O'Odham (formerly Papago) tribe of Arizona, believes that 'everyone is a storyteller' (*Ibid*, 102) and that 'stories can be made out of anything' (*Ibid*, 130). Zepeda echoes Deming's confidence that stories can serve activism. She recounts the efforts of Indian tribes to achieve federal recognition through storytelling. Terre Satterfield, in her conclusion to the book, gives this example of a successful use of an indigenous oral tradition to document the rights of Native Americans:

> *In a recent land-claims-related decision in British Columbia, Canada's supreme court (Delgamuukw v. B.C.) hereditary chiefs from the Gitksan and Wet'suwet'en First Nations presented their legal arguments in narrative form in deference to long-standing oral traditions. They did so in a manner that followed the necessary legal arguments at stake, and yet also enacted 'narratives, songs and dances that had formerly been performed only within a community context, presenting these as statements linking history … and land' (Ibid,* 286).

Where do we situate *The Whale Caller* in relation to these positions? I believe that this novel is designed to make South African readers aware of the urgency of the ecological issues that both South African and American ecocritics dramatise. In this sense Mda, as a South African writer, shares the activist agenda of his American colleagues. Mda's commitment to the performing arts as challenging received thought and enabling creativity, a commitment shared by Williams, is evident everywhere in his fiction. *The Whale Caller* opens with Acknowledgements that celebrate the performances that have become 'blessings' that mark the birth of the novel:

> *And now the blessings:*
> *If Wilson Salukazi (the real-life whale caller of Hermanus) really did call the whales to himself; if one special person in my life, Gugu Nomcebo Nkosi, was not dead scared of the dark, if young Lungu Tubu had not sung arias in his unbroken voice, bringing tears to my eyes; and if my then four-year-old daughter Zenzi had not invented the names Saluni, Sharisha and Mr Yodd, there would be no story to tell* (Mda: 2005, Acknowledgements).

In this novel, the Whale Caller's intimate knowledge of the Southern Rights, humpback whales, Bryde whales, blue whales and orcas — gained over 35 years of observing them along South African seashores — makes him especially responsive to the songs of the Southern Rights.[7] To Sharisha's breaching,

7 Whereas the Whale Crier of Hermanus locates groups of Southern Rights to inform tourists of their whereabouts so that they can be watched and photographed, the Whale Caller summons the she-whale Sharisha to himself in an ongoing and personal relationship. The phenomenon of real-life, as opposed to fictional bonds between human beings and wild animals is documented by the biologist Lyall Watson. He tells of dolphins brought to the shore by a dreaming porpoise-caller in Kuna Village, on the Gilbert Islands, and of a giant leather-backed turtle, *penju kulit,* summoned by a *djura* (an expert in locating marine life underwater) on a remote island in the Banda Sea. The giant turtle breached, swam closely past the onlookers on a coral reef, and gently nibbled at the *djura*'s fingers, before swimming back into the deep sea (Watson: 1979, 210 and 213).

lobtailing and spyhopping he responds by blowing his kelp horn and dancing. The Whale Caller's response to Sharisha is centred in the 'attentiveness to existence' discussed by Deming. When Sharisha designs a new display for her calf, the Whale Caller participates in this display, the purpose of which he understands although he has never seen it before:

> *When they get close enough Sharisha teaches the child a new trick: tail-sailing. Although this is a display especially for the Whale Caller, it is quite different from the tail-slapping ... mating ritual that used to be a crucial form of bonding between the Whale Caller and Sharisha* (*Ibid*, 136).

Just as writers in *What's Nature Worth?* believe in the political effectiveness of nature writing, I would argue that Mda's parable about the relationship between the Whale Caller and his non-human Other, the she-whale Sharisha, dramatises for the reader the degradation of community in a post-apartheid South Africa. Consumerism gives rise to new forms of the gender, social and racial inequities that plagued South Africans under apartheid. The Whale Caller, naturally ascetic and non-social, is unusually sensitive to the environment, deploring the mindless accumulation of human wealth at the expense of non-human species that he sees in the tourists and citizens of Hermanus. Yet his story ends in an all-too-familiar dénouement in which nature, gendered feminine, becomes the prey of the male explorer. Both the human and the non-human females whom he has desired and courted, but failed to protect, are exterminated. His story thus links the individual to the social, for unless human beings work together to protect the environment, they will end up as lonely and disconnected as the Whale Caller. At the end of his story, he is cut off from his kind and from the sea that has delighted and sustained him all his life.

The sensorium of storytelling

The importance of making readers sensorily aware of the natural world is frequently alluded to by the writers in *What's Nature Worth?* John Daniels exhorts us to *feel* our connectedness to the natural world, in order to know it (Slovic & Satterfield: 2004, 161). William Kittredge undertakes an annual autumnal quest to achieve sensory contact with the physical world. The editors comment that this is a form of 'imaginative "sustenance", a way of supporting and vivifying his mind during the coming winter' (*Ibid*, 21). Mda's Whale Caller stores up all year the experiences of his interactions with the Southern Rights during the months they spend in the seas off Hermanus. Kittredge believes that the energies of nature constitute 'our only physical and psychic home', because 'the kind of creature we are cannot exist for long anywhere else' (*Ibid*, 23). Richard Shelton remarks: 'I don't think that without the direct sensory existence of nature one can be human. One cannot value what one has not experienced' (*Ibid*, 156). Stephen Trimble writes that his father first taught him to 'listen to the landscape'. After many interactions with Native Americans in the West, he has learned to adopt a 'native' way of looking at the land (*Ibid*, 186).[8]

Because story works through suggestion rather than assertion, stories about nature are important for people to learn about their landscape; they inculcate 'attention' to what we see and hear. This attention is necessarily centred in the consciousness and experience of the observer; it will be different for each individual. Stories teach us, therefore, according to Gary Nabham, to register the value of our own particular places: '[L]oving the weirdness of our backyards and not the backyards in *Sunset Magazine* or whatever is trendy. The values that I have that make me want what is right here, what is distinct from anywhere else in the world' (*Ibid*, 260). 'People really love where they live: it's what sings to us,' remarks Terry Williams (*Ibid*, 68).

The Whale Caller, from the beginning of his story, feels his connection to the natural world and Mda's processes of focalisation make the reader see the 'blue, green, yellow and red boats' visible off the slipway as, in the first paragraph, the Whale Caller descends the cliffs in search of Sharisha. Reunited with her, he joyously celebrates her distinguishing features: 'She is the queen of all southern rights. See her white callosities! See the regal wave of her flippers! See the bonnet of callosity on the tip of her snout!' (Mda: 2005, 51). His attention to the singularity and individuality of the animals with whom he interacts connects with his closeness to his surroundings. Gary Nabham speaks of the pleasures of being in touch with the local and specific: 'True hedonism resists commodification of the natural world. It's manifest in people who delight in the sensory pleasures of hearing the mockingbird vespers in the spring evenings in Tucson, as opposed to what mockingbirds sound like in some other part of the world or what a generalised mockingbird might sound like' (Slovic & Satterfield: 2004, 260). The Whale Caller makes us aware that Southern Right whale songs are different from the songs of humpback

8 Discussing the ways in which indigenous people's knowledge of the environment differs from Western knowledge of the environment, Barbara Bender remarks:

> The Inuit track animals, the Micronesians track the night skies, the Western Apache track people. They 'shoot them' with stories, they 'stalk them' with places. The Western Apache also, like the Inuit, remark that 'Whitemen need paper maps: we have maps in our minds'. Their historical stories are anchored spatially (Bender: 1999, 41).

Similarly, Claire Smith comments:

> It is extensively documented that the cultural life of Native Americans, in its spiritual as well as its economic aspect, is closely connected with the earth and specifically to the features and qualities of their indigenous landscape (Smith: 1999, 246).

or orca whales, and so the songs of the Southern Rights off Hermanus, to which he responds, will be different from the songs of the Southern Rights in Australian waters.

From the beginning of his story, the Whale Caller's life is firmly rooted in Hermanus. When Saluni, in preparation for radio stardom, boasts of being destined for Hollywood, the Whale Caller grieves:

> *If Saluni does go, what will happen to him? How is he going to live without Saluni? And if she does become a star she will surely forget about him. He can't leave Hermanus. He can't follow Saluni to Hollywood. He will be out of place there without the sea and the whales and the seagulls and the hot smells of rotting kelp and the salt air brushing against his silver-grey beard and the southeaster lashing against his body and the Wendy house and Hermanus* (Mda: 2005, 159-160).

His attunement to the local and specific in turn enables the interactions that his story dramatises. When he and Sharisha perform together, their 'dance' lasts all night, long after spectators have gone to bed:

> *The spectators went to their homes and to their hotels to sleep. Sharisha and the Whale Caller continued their dance unabated. Deep in the night the wails of his horn could be heard, sometimes sounding like a muted cornet and at others like a Last Post bugle, and then picking up again in the fast-paced scatting of a demented jazz-singer* (*Ibid*, 59).

Somatically engaged in their interspecies 'dance', Sharisha and the Whale Caller fuse nature and culture. Saluni, however, has no desire to enter into this nature-culture interaction. Although her physical link to the Whale Caller — particularly through her 'mouldy yet sweet smell' — is strong, she will not enter into the sensorium that links the Whale Caller with Sharisha. Intensely jealous of Sharisha's power over her lover, because he forgets her in his liaisons with the she-whale, Saluni declares that she 'refuse[s] to be forgotten'. But the place in which she chooses to sit, amid the tablets commemorating the dead of Hermanus, links her to history in an increasingly negative way. The memorial commemorates not only the victims of Hermanus who died in the two World Wars, but also those 'who were killed in some war that is not mentioned'. Their panel is described as 'The Republic of South Africa Roll of Honour (1973–1979)'. The war is not named because these citizens 'died on the border defending apartheid' (*Ibid*, 44). Saluni's life-story as a 'love child' and instrumentalised object of male desire is very much a legacy of apartheid, as are the lives of the Bored Twins with whom she likes to associate. The twins are left to wander around the derelict mansion where they live — ruins of the once-fashionable and opulent ostrich industry — and its surrounding countryside by parents who work long hours as exploited migrant labourers; the children amuse themselves by torturing the fauna of the surrounding marshes and grasslands — insects, frogs and snakes. They will finally also cause Saluni's death by throwing stones at her head as she wanders off in a drunken stupor to find the Whale Caller. Their sadism towards both human and non-human creatures contrasts sharply with the Whale Caller's capacity for interaction with 'earth others'. The reader cannot escape the implication that a society that neglects so many of its citizens is also a society indifferent to the interconnectedness of life, which the Whale Caller affirms.

Stories' 'emotional hue'

'Storytelling,' William Kittredge tells us, 'invites readers to make up a story of their own, to use the story they're being told as a mirror in which to view their own responses to their own concerns' (Slovic & Satterfield: 2004, 13). He believes that narrative 'invites readers to participate emotionally in the events and processes they're learning about' (*Ibid*, 20). Alison Hawthorne Deming speaks of the 'emotional hue' of story: 'There's a tone to story and so when you're engaged emotionally you're more likely to want to reciprocate with a story. In the end, it's pretty hard to tell a story without it having an emotional hue' (*Ibid*, 105).

'Emotional hue' suggests the intense processes of focalisation — making the reader *see* the story — that Mda uses throughout his fiction. These are apparent from the first paragraph of *The Whale Caller*, where the reader strains to see and hear Sharisha's response to the Whale Caller's blowing of his kelp horn as he stands on the cliffs staring into the distance, willing the whale's return. This sequence leads swiftly from the physical to the visionary, as the narrator moves from the protagonist's looking at these boats to his imagination of the recent past, and then to a past now lost in myth:

> *When the Whale Caller is in a happy mood he can see the weather-beaten fishermen shrouded in the mists of time, taking to sea in their fleet of small boats. Some are rowing back with their catch, while others are gutting the fish or drying it on the rocks. He can see even deeper in the mists, before there were boats and fishermen and whales, the Khoikhoi of old dancing around a beached whale* (Mda: 2005, 2).

Narrative and emotion meet in the creation of such pictures, real or imagined: '[I]mage works because it's a kind of embodied presence. Image feels sensory. It's as if you're experiencing it with your senses, not your intellect. We know it to be a primal way of processing our experience. We know it through dreaming and through fantasy' (Deming, in Slovic & Satterfield: 2004, 105). As the reader responds sensorily and emotionally to this strange story of interspecies love[9] (s)he is drawn into the story-world. Like many of the writers

9 Terre Satterfield uses the phrase 'charismatic megafauna' to denote memorable animal species, citing a grizzly bear and a spotted owl. Sharisha the Southern Right surely qualifies for this phrase, both for her size and for her remarkable songs and dances.

in *What's Nature Worth?* Mda explores 'the poetics, politics and erotics of place' by creating a protagonist who is 'in spiritual and physical dialogue with landscape' (Slovic & Satterfield: 2004, 28).

What that dialogue requires is a strong sense of connection between the human and the non-human world: 'I think what we are desperate for, as human beings, is a world where there is no separation ... if we can't become shape-shifters, then we are destined for loneliness, impoverishment. Lonely policies, impoverished politics, and sterile art' (Terry Tempest Williams in Slovic & Satterfield: 2004, 67). Kittredge similarly states that '[b]eauty in nature is that which encourages us to feel at home in the weave of energies, and not isolated. It is connected, obviously, to solace and religious feelings' (*Ibid*, 27). Creating the 'emotional hue' that enables an individual's recognition of feeling 'at home in the weave of energies' presupposes an egalitarian society. In *The Whale Caller* Mda exposes various socially destructive profitmaking practices that undermine the 'weave of energies'. The illegal abalone trade is a case in point:

> *Coloured folk sell their harvest to white men who pay about two hundred rands a kilogram. The white men sell to the Chinese men for about a thousand rands a kilogram. The Chinese ship the abalone to the Far East where they get about two thousand five hundred rands a kilogram for it. And these are the old prices* (Mda: 2005, 175).

Or there is the practice, in Zwelihle Township, by 'the city fathers and mothers' of disqualifying poor families from social relief and forcing them to pay for utilities and municipal services:

> *The city fathers and mothers are quick to disqualify a family as soon as it owns a fridge, a geyser or some other appliance that may be deemed a luxury* (*Ibid*, 78).

Thus post-apartheid social 'improvements' fail to alter the lives of South Africa's poorest citizens.[10] No wonder, then, that in Hermanus — playground of the rich — the politically fashionable phrase 'Rainbow People' rings so false. Individuals sporting colourful arrays of clothes, hairstyles, tattoos and tans secretly nurse a sense of betrayal:

10 That such abuses occur throughout South Africa, impacting on the lives of millions of its poorest citizens, is made clear in the chapter 'Privatising Nature' in Jacklyn Cock's book. Writing about the privatisation of water services in the huge informal settlement of Orange Farm in Gauteng, Cock quotes Dule T McKinley:

> We want to emphasise that the ongoing struggles in Phiri are but part of a much longer struggle that is taking place across South Africa against the neo-liberal policies of the ANC government — over land, education, health care, water, electricity and housing. The repression and arrogance being meted out by the ANC government and Johannesburg Water have not, and will not, halt the struggle for basic human dignity and rights of the poor in Phiri and indeed, in innumerable poor communities across the breadth of South Africa. The collective resistance of the poor is not ephemeral — it is both necessary and never-ending for as long as the barbarism of capitalism exists (in Cock: 2007, 98).

> *Hair. It is a blight they must carry on their heads, exposing the position each head occupied in the statutory hierarchies of the past. The troubles of humanity are locked in the hair. Yet the people have managed to disguise their shame by painting it in the colours that designate them all a people of the rainbow. Without exception. Without a past. Without rancour. Without hierarchies. Only their eyes betray the big lie. In these eyes you can see a people living in a daze. Rainbow people walking in a precarious dream that may explode into a nightmare without warning* (*Ibid*, 15).

Gregory McNamee discusses the politics of short-term gain at the cost of long-term ecological equilibrium: 'I think that the enemy, the real enemy in our lives, is the politics of the short term, of the immediate return. It's a world-destroying vision that lets us get in and out as quickly as we can. It lets us extract and then say "the hell with it!"' (Slovic & Satterfield: 2004, 86). Against the politics of short-term gain, the Whale Caller's story enacts the hope of long-term ecological connection. But this connection cannot be sustained in the absence of a cohesive community.

Towards an ecological sublime

The realisation of an interconnectedness of life that opposes 'the politics of the short term, of the immediate return' brings into play a numinous or religious dimension.[11] In *What's Nature Worth?* Terry Williams sees storytelling as both holistic and holy: 'I think [that in storytelling] … we see the world whole again, even holy. Even for a moment' (*Ibid*, 71). Kittredge similarly describes the ecological imagination as 'a system of energies that we call "sacred" because we are part of it, where we feel whole and intuit that we are part of holiness' (*Ibid*, 25). John Daniels speaks of the religious sense of nature that he finds in American Indian cultures and that our culture once possessed. He discusses how the Christian mystical tradition — Julian of Norwich, Hildegard of Bingen, Saint Francis of Assisi — affirms the oneness and sacredness of nature. Daniels contends that 'the sacred family is not something new and unattained. It is a latent possibility in us all'. Withdrawing from the sacred family as we have done in modern, technological, secular society has led to a loss of responsibilities, but also to a loss of privileges: '[T]he cost is the loneliness of our disconnected state, the great bereavement of no longer knowing ourselves at home in the natural matrix that gave us birth. True power comes from relatedness' (*Ibid*, 184).

11 On the relationship between nature and religion, Jacklyn Cock quotes the director of the United States Parks Services:

> [W]ilderness is a religious concept. Religion is the recognition of the limits of human competence in the presence of the unknowable and the uncontrollable before which humans recoil in awe. Wilderness has this in common with the sacred: we accord to it … reverence and we act towards it … with restraint (Cock: 2007, 147).

Surely this is the tragedy that the Whale Caller's story enacts: '[T]he great bereavement of no longer knowing ourselves at home in the natural matrix that gave us birth' (Slovic & Satterfield: 2004, 184). That story is charged with the numinous from the beginning, when the Whale Caller's closeness to nature is linked to his need for Mr Yodd as confidant and confessor, and to his need for mortification. The Whale Caller's consciousness makes him a good candidate for what in Kant's analytic of the sublime may be termed an ecological sublime, in which closeness to nature is connected to the subject's sense of separation from nature. Sabine Wilke, writing in *ISLE* about the role of aesthetic experience in dialectical conceptions of nature, explains: '[t]he point of the analytic of the sublime in [Kant's] third critique is to analyse what happens in the human being (mentally, physically) when he/she is confronted by something that is larger than what can be processed by the human mind' (Slovic: 2009, 101). The somatic nature of this response is communicated, in the original German, using 'erotically charged language to describe the feeling of the sublime as an orgasmic outpouring of our vital powers after a momentary inhibition' (*Ibid*, 100). The Whale Caller's music-making and dancing with Sharisha are nothing if not erotic and orgasmic: he is as physically exhausted after a night with the she-whale as he would have been after a night's love-making with a human partner. Kant's analytic of the sublime is apposite here. Sabine Wilke explains:

> *Many ecocritics ... refer to Kant as one of the most important theorists who guides our thinking about the relationship between the subject and nature, particularly his notion of the sublime* (*Ibid*, 100).

She continues:

> *Kant defines the concept of the sublime by outlining its difference from the concept of the beautiful. While the beautiful is tied to a form, the feeling of the sublime 'is a pleasure that arises only indirectly, being generated, namely, by the feeling of a momentary inhibition of the vital powers and ... the more powerful outpouring of them'* (*Ibid*, 100).

Wilke points out that in his analytic of the sublime Kant does not really talk about the sublime at all but focuses on our reaction to the sublime ... 'the sublime is ... not to be sought in the things of nature but only in our ideas' (*Ibid*, 101). Thus Kant's analytic of the sublime is not a philosophy of nature, but relates to the mental and physical processes in human beings.

For a character to apprehend the sublime, therefore, (s)he must have an imaginative conception of nature. This is why the Whale Caller's 'discussions' with the rock rabbit, Mr Yodd, work for the reader as projections of his own complex psychic states — his feelings of shame, anger, anxiety or triumph — and why Saluni's 'discussions' with Mr Yodd fail to convince. Nothing in Saluni's characterisation as a *femme fatale* intent on pleasure and enjoyment make this kind of morbid introspection — even in the cause of regaining the attention of the Whale Caller — ring true for the reader. Above all, Saluni refuses mortification: she will not be made humble. In 'Toward an Ecological Sublime' (*Ibid*, 105), Sabine Wilke concurs with Christopher Hitt that in encountering nature the human subject must experience humility. This is surely central to the Whale Caller's obsession with confession and mortification. Finally, Wilke traces the connection of Kant's aesthetic and ethical thinking with the philosophy of history developed by Teodor Adorno: '[T]he path of modern progress, in essence, is a path toward destruction, certainly a path of devastation and nature, among other things, is a victim of this process'. She remarks that it is Adorno's mission to vindicate what capitalism has oppressed: '[A]nimal, landscape, woman' (106). This trio is also what *The Whale Caller* addresses, but in this novel, 'animal, landscape, and woman' cannot be defended against the incursions of a capitalism driven by short-term monetary gains.

Rethinking language

How do we promote ecological consciousness, given the human-centred focus of our language? This is a central problematic for the writers in *What's Nature Worth?* and one that preoccupies Mda in *The Whale Caller*. Terry Tempest Williams speaks of the lyrical, mysterious and even chaotic language of story (Slovic & Satterfield: 2004, 63). Kittredge remarks, in response to the question of why nature values are so difficult for many people to express:

> *Naming is an attempt to fix processes in place, to hold them static. Ezra Pound said only verbs are real, not nouns. Processes won't hold still. We have to falsify incessantly in order to sift processes through the scrim of our subject-verb-object language. Narrative as a technique tries at least partway to avoid this problem by inciting readers toward constantly re-forming stories out of what has been written or told. The audience is invited to form their own value systems out of their responses to experience. In this way narrative attempts to be less coercive than any other form of language* (*Ibid*, 26).[12]

12 Lyall Watson similarly observes: 'In all European languages, there is a predominance of nouns, whose function is largely static'. He explains that words designated by nouns become things, or physical objects: 'We can see a Cheshire cat with or without a grin, but not a grin without a cat. For, in our language, "a grin" is an act, which requires an agent, who must be a permanent entity. We literally talk ourselves out of a whole range of possible experience' (Watson: 1979, 372). Watson points out that the languages of Australian Aborigines do not contain 'parts of speech' comparable to ours. Since their main words are ones of action, like our verbs, their emphasis on a series of related acts frees their expression from 'the strict and purely metaphysical logic of our language, which insists that things must be either true or false, real or imaginary' (*Ibid*,

The Whale Caller is irritated by the politics of naming in the 'new' South Africa, which have reduced the place name of Hermanuspietersfontein to the more touristic 'Hermanus'. Official place names conferred by the state distort original names, silencing the voices of people who have lived in these places; changing place names is another form of appropriation or control. A member of the crowd watching the Whale Caller and Sharisha dance explains to onlookers about the Whale Caller's unfamiliar name for this place, Hermanuspietersfontein: 'He means us ... It is what this town used to be called ... after the shepherd and teacher who came down the mountain past the Hemel-en-Aarde valley and set up camp here almost two hundred years ago ... before the land was stolen from the Khoikhoi' (Mda: 2005, 60). Naming and renaming are processes that inscribe human perspectives on to geopolitical spaces. When place names are dictated by the state, people living in these places lose their connection with their own history and consequently their ability to tell their own stories.

If the politics of naming falsifies history and short-circuits community, the description of non-human consciousness in terms of human consciousness privileges the human above the non-human. Mda avoids this anthropomorphism by omitting any account of Sharisha's thought processes; they are not articulated in words at all. We are shown instead her actions as she responds to the music of the Whale Caller playing his kelp horn. The semiotic system in which the Whale Caller and Sharisha communicate is thus kinetic and musical rather than linguistic. On a semiotic level, this interaction recalls Bakhtin's notion that a novel can resemble a musical score: 'Within a novel perceived as a musical score, a single "horizontal" message (melody) can be harmonised vertically in a number of ways, and each of these scores with its fixed pitches can be further altered by giving the notes to different instruments. The possibilities of orchestration make any segment of text almost infinitely variable' (Bakhtin: 1981, 431). On a realistic level, the songs of whales have been well documented by biologists:

> *Roger Payne's recordings of the humpback whale* Megaptera novaeangliae *off Bermuda show that it has a song which contains about two hundred notes, ranging from high-pitched squeaks to low and resonant rumbles, which lasts for ten minutes or more. This is certainly a signal specific to the species and must be characteristic also of the individual singer who can, under certain circumstances where there are temperature inversion layers in the ocean, communicate over distances of several thousand miles. The recordings include examples of one whale picking up on the song of another and*

371–2). My point in this section is that Mda's depiction of the Whale Caller-Sharisha relationship attempts to bypass language altogether, using neither the linguistic categories of Western languages nor the more ecologically attuned concepts of indigenous languages.

returning it note-perfect, but with the embellishments of rhythm and cadence that suggest individual creative activity. It has even been suggested that the acoustic memory of whales is so elaborate that they could perhaps listen to an entire symphony just once and then have a mental playback later, remembering not only every phrase but also the way they felt when hearing it for the first time (Watson: 1979, 140–1).

If Sharisha's songs are as complicated as human music, the Whale Caller's kelp horn is superior to most musical instruments:

He played [the kelp horn] so celestially that His Eminence decided to do away with harps and tambourines, for they seemed to dilute the innocence of the horn. This caused an argument whose proportions had never been seen before at the Church. The Elders of the Church said that harps were by nature heavenly. Angels sang to harps and tambourines. To do away with them was playing into the hands of the Prince of Darkness. But His Eminence stood his ground. A kelp horn, he said, was a natural musical instrument that took the congregation back to its roots. It was an instrument that celebrated the essence of creation. God would lend a sharper ear to the prayers of those who praised Him to the accompaniment of an instrument that was shaped by His own hand through the agency of the seas (Mda: 2005, 6).

Not only do the Whale Caller and Sharisha communicate through music rather than through language, but that music derives from nature. It is fundamentally disconnected with the culture-generated rhetoric used by a commodifying society to communicate its values.[13]

The freedom that the Whale Caller and Sharisha enjoy in their non-linguistic interactions is not, however, a freedom natural to human beings, who can only survive in social contexts. Here Bakhtin's notion of the centrality of dialogue to establish meaning and identity comes into play:

Dialogism is the characteristic epistemological mode of a world dominated by heteroglossia. Everything means, is understood, as a part of a greater whole — there is constant interaction between meanings, all of which have the potential of conditioning others. Which will affect the other; how it will do so and in what degree is what is actually settled at the moment of utterance. This dialogic imperative, mandated by the pre-existence of the language world relative to any of its current inhabitants, insures that there can be no actual monologue (Bakhtin summarised by Holquist: 1981, 426).

The Whale Caller's story culminates in his fatal instrumentalisation of Sharisha when his anger at his human lover, Saluni, causes him to summon Sharisa on his

13 Saluni and the Whale Caller initially develop a 'virtual' language that mocks commodification: they 'taste' food in restaurants with their eyes or 'buy' food in supermarkets without touching it. This imaginative sharing recalls Noria and Toloki in *Ways of Dying*. They live together in a shack, the interior and garden of which are created by their imaginations. But by the end of *The Whale Caller* Saluni has abandoned the imaginary dimension she created with her lover for the real-life enticements of Hollywood.

kelp-horn because he yearns for the companionship of 'she who never calls him names or yells at him' (Mda: 2005, 196). But this inadvertent betrayal — when Sharisha beaches herself after a freak tidal wave in which the sea has turned black, making it impossible to distinguish the blue depths from the green shallows — is a cumulative result of the lack of reciprocity or mutuality between the Whale Caller and the human beings with whom he interacts. His loneliness, intensified by the failure of his relationship with Saluni, makes him over-dependent on a non-human environment that is actually dependent on him. Sharing no values with the tourists of Hermanus or with the other human inhabitants on whom his story turns, he will finally also become parted from 'the rocks and the waves and the moon' (*Ibid*, 210) on which he has built his life. Without communication between human beings, there can be no community; without community, there can be no protection of the environment. Human beings need dialogue. Here my reading of the novel overlaps with Ralph Goodman's: '*The Whale Caller* points to the isolated quality of individuals and the fractured nature of community which are part of the aftermath of apartheid — an isolation which is crucial to the final inability of both the Whale Caller and Saluni to recuperate their pain and loss' (Goodman: 2008, 109).

In *What's Nature Worth?* Ortiz insists on the value of the oral tradition: '[E]ven though I may say that writing is important, I have always said the most common and immediate and intimate language is the oral tradition. Story, and especially spoken story, is where language is our most immediate contact. I mean, it doesn't have to just be by the voice, not by writing, but by how we behave toward each other' (Slovic & Satterfield: 2004, 43). Knowing how to behave towards each other includes knowing how to behave towards non-human others. Berger explains this ethical stance as requiring us to understand 'the value of other creatures for their own sake, rather than ours; what Schweitzer called "respect for life"' (*Ibid*, 241). In this parable about the interdependence of the human and the non-human worlds, Mda's written text foregrounds the importance of the speech that connects people, our 'most common and immediate and intimate language'. In the absence of this communication, human beings lose the knowledge of how to behave toward one another and toward the non-human world. The results of this loss are tragic, for individuals and communities and for the ecosystems that sustain them.

Finally...

Jacklyn Cock's book, *The War Against Ourselves: Nature, Power and Justice*, demonstrates the relation between the abuse of nature and issues of social justice in contemporary South Africa: 'Justice involves changing the distribution of power, resources and opportunities in the world' (Cock: 2007, 22). Mda's social and ecological parable, *The Whale Caller*, dramatises this equation. The novel exemplifies Rachel Carson's notion of a 'web of life that binds together all organisms' where 'the implication of this interconnectedness is that even small change in one area or species will reverberate throughout the ecosystem. It is a web of life or death' (*Ibid,* 37). Recognition of interconnection enables the elimination of racism and sexism and the celebration of communal values. But this process centrally involves redressing social inequality — 'the unsustainable consumption patterns of the rich and the exclusion of the poor from livelihoods' (*Ibid,* 202). These have resulted in post-apartheid South Africa's overtaking Brazil 'to become the most unequal society in the world' (*Ibid,* 203). As a sociologist, Cock points out that 'much of what are experienced as personal, individualised problems are rooted in social processes' (*Ibid,* 215). Mda's novel graphically illustrates these social processes. *The Whale Caller* creates awareness in the reader of what the novel's characters — apart from the main protagonist — do not recognise as their own complicity in lifestyles that deny human dignity as they ignore ecological balance. Cock writes:

> *My conceptual anchor … has been Carson's notion of a 'web of life' in which we are all embedded. We are a part of nature, part of a continuous and interrelated pattern of living things and natural processes. Now this 'web of life' is unravelling, with fatal consequences for us all, unless we act* (Ibid, 214).

To remain part of the 'web of life' that *The Whale Caller* dramatises, it is essential to draw on the power of community to rescue and support individuals: 'We cannot challenge this process of commodification as atomised, isolated individuals. We may pick up the pieces, but to stop the breakage we have to join with others. An appreciation of our place in nature has to be translated into collective action … Alone we are powerless, but together we can develop our collective strength to end what Rachel Carson called "the war against ourselves"' (*Ibid,* 217). Mda's *The Whale Caller* is a moving and powerful exposure of this war and its catastrophic effects on human beings and their environment.

I close with these moving words by Mike Nicol:

> *What the whales have to tell us has everything to do with ritual and place. I think that their lives demonstrate the complexity of living and the importance of where they live. For they bring to the seas and the coastlines and the bays the ritual of their history. Unlike us they are unaware of it; unlike them we have demeaned what it is to live in this place. Here [in South Africa] the whale is part of a larger narrative, part of the story that is our conversation with ourselves and the land and the seas. In this we try to describe the awe that is struck in us at the play of lightning in approaching storms, or the arrangement of rocks on a barren plain, or a formation of vultures upon a midday sky. In this we recount our being. It is the story of who we are and what we mean. In it is stored our wisdom. But, more significantly, I think that from our rhythms come our dreams. And perhaps by telling and retelling we may come to know how we should live* (Nicol: 1995, 202, 205).

Chapter Eight

'The trenches are the boardrooms of South Africa': *Black Diamond*

Stereotypes and formulae

To understand Mda's depiction of black economic empowerment (BEE) in *Black Diamond* we need look no further than the novel's chapter headings. These jaunty titles throw the reader into a parodic potpourri derived from numerous sources like the liberation movement during apartheid ('Free the Visagie brothers', 'Comrades and lovers', 'An injury to one is an injury to all' 'Cadres in the trenches'). These escalate into the unashamed capitalism of comrade Molotov's mantra ('Accumulation cannot be democratised, comrades') and combine with the banal colloquialisms of detective fiction, gangster movies, women's magazines and television advertising. So we have 'Somehow the bitch must pay', 'The cat that caused all the trouble', 'Stevo has a dream', 'An intruder in the house', 'Blonde bombshell', 'Shootout', 'See how she glows' and 'The big jol'. Designer labels mix with popular psychology in the plot's trajectory ('The curse of the Zara Man', 'Smart okes use psychology'); there are faint intertextual resonances in 'Widows' long march to freedom' and 'Hell hath no fury' and finally the novel thuds to a potentially nasty dénouement in the last chapter, 'The final dance', which ends in near disaster, with the black protagonist Don Mateza in hospital, telling his lover, the white magistrate Kristin Uys, that he and his cat are moving into a new dimension: 'Me and Snowy … we can no longer be kept' (Mda: 2009, 207).

The opening page is equally illuminating about how this novel works. The first sentence is spoken by a narrator who jumps in whenever the reader needs the plot explained: 'No one will blame you if you think Kristin Uys is dressed for a funeral'. The narrator's second sentence introduces the sartorial parody that will attach to designer labels and the people who like to be seen in them throughout the novel: 'Not the black folks' kind of funerals where women give the dead a glorious send-off in the same Versaces, Sun Goddesses and Givenchys that are a staple of such horse racing events as the Durban July Handicap or the J&B Met' (*Ibid*, 1). So here are the upwardly mobile black women who dominate former whites-only events such as the Durban July Handicap. At funerals they sport expensive designer clothing so as to impress the other mourners. Their mood is celebratory, giving the dead 'a glorious send-off'. In this black culture 'the living crack jokes about the dead, and get sloshed and dance to loud music at those marathon parties known as "after-tears"'. In stark contrast to such gaudy and loud celebrations of mourning are 'the sad and sombre affairs that pass for funerals in white communities'. This is what the novel is about: aspirant black BEE excecutives and the white executives with whom, post-apartheid, they share the same urban space. This urban space, in the formerly whites-only suburbs in which the upwardly mobile protagonists live, lacks any kind of cultural identity. Townhouses, streets and interiors have no individual features, whereas the Soweto townships to which BEE executives nostalgically retire every weekend bustle with life: food, music, nightclubs and community vibe. Lest the reader should lose track of these sociological complexities, an intrusive narrator continually intervenes to provide orientation, addressing the reader directly: '[The magistrate's] black gown will soon disabuse you of any notions of bereavement, and will place you squarely in a courtroom'. The courtroom setting signals the detective-novel storyline, for Kristin Uys, the white magistrate, is hearing the case of the Visagie brothers, accused of running a brothel. As the storyline develops, it transpires that Kristin is on a campaign to eradicate prostitution, although in the privacy of her townhouse she dresses as a tart and performs a prostitute's dance because her former husband, Barend, loved prostitutes.

Black Diamond's dust-jacket claims: 'Zakes Mda tackles every conceivable South African stereotype, skilfully (and with the lightest touch) turning them upside down and exposing their ironies, often hilariously'. The opening chapter certainly exposes the ironies of stereotypes and formulae — the (white) Visagie brothers are supported by their white mother, Ma Visagie, and their coloured ex-nanny, Aunt Magda, who has carefully studied struggle literature to marshall its rhetoric so that she can publicly defend the boys. Ma Visagie and Aunt Magda are in bitter competition for the boys' affection, and the white magistrate Kristin Uys abuses her power by sentencing Stevo to six months' imprisonment for contempt (when the maximum sentence for this offence is three months). The narrator establishes all of the important plot details such as Aunt Magda's canniness in telling reporters that 'the government has failed the widows of this country', and shows the reader the drabness of Kristin's suburb, Weltevreden Park. This is no longer a paradise for Afrikaans white-collar workers but is now inhabited by black 'middle management apparatchiks of big corporations, and chief executives of smaller corporations' (*Ibid*, 5). The narrator also establishes that the interior of Kristin's townhouse lacks distinguishing features such as paintings, though Vivaldi's *Four Seasons* constantly plays on the hi-fi. Kristin herself is described as having a sense of humour — 'So she *can* laugh, after all'. But this narrator — unlike the communal narrators of *Ways of Dying* or *The Madonna of Excelsior* — doesn't belong to any of the cultures he describes. He functions more like a fly on the wall — or a camera eye — seeing everything, explaining everything, except his own position in relation to the story-world he recounts. This, then, is what we get from *Black Diamond*'s first chapter.

Can a novel that satirises and parodies literary conventions by exposing their formulae escape becoming formulaic itself? And if it becomes merely a collection of formulae, will it not lose the reader's interest and cease to be able to engage with serious social issues? These are, I think, real problems for *Black Diamond.* But there are two areas of the novel that arguably escape this reductionism: the depiction of Soweto, which is in places rich and various, and the depiction of cookery, particularly Don's, as a genuine expression of creative cultural interaction between individuals and their environment. I start with these, and then go on to look at the problems that *Black Diamond*'s story-world demonstrates. Can this novel elicit the collaborative performativity that Mda creates so powerfully in his prior novels?

Soweto and cookery

Chapter Four moves to the novel's heart: Orlando West in Soweto, the township to which Don Mateza of VIP Protection Services and his girlfriend, Tumi, who runs a modelling agency, return for nostalgic visits. Before this we go to Don's and Tumi's Three Oaks townhouse in North Riding. Like Kristin Uys's house in Weltevreden Park, the Three Oaks townhouse lacks any distinguishing features. It is expensively furnished in the style dictated by 'new money', with 'charcoals/ acrylics of township art' on the walls. As in the opening chapter, the narrator is intrusive in explaining the characters' motives and behaviour: he tells us that Don 'used to be Molotov's commander back in the bush'; he speaks of Tumi's anger with Don's former comrades, who are now successful beneficiaries of the government's black economic policy, and of her indignation that Molotov and his wife Cathy 'addressed the bodyguard as "comrade" as if they were all equal' (*Ibid*, 10). Tumi practises her mantra — 'Positive thinking' — on Don, hoping to persuade him to become a Black Diamond; Krish Naidoo, the Indian prosecutor with whom Kristin works in court, invites her home for *matter paneer*; and then we come to the Soweto chapter, ironically framed by Molotov's mantra, which gives the chapter its title, 'Accumulation cannot be democratised, comrades'.

Now we move to a world that is as vibrant as the white suburbs are arid — a world of food and soccer and gossip:

> *The Sowetans make regular visits back home just for the smells, the tastes and the noises: for the Sunday lunch of* chakalaka, *curried chicken,* dombolo *steamed bread*

> *soaked in tomato and onion gravy, fried cabbage, mashed pumpkin, green beans cooked with potatoes and grated carrots, beetroot salad, custard and jelly; and to be fussed over by aunts and uncles and neighbours; and to talk soccer with people who really know something about the 'beautiful game'; and to enjoy the latest gossip in the taverns; and to have their gaudy Hummers and Lamborghinis admired by urchins playing soccer on dirt streets with tennis balls* (*Ibid*, 21–2).

Soweto provides not only the physical satisfactions of cooking and eating, but the emotional satisfactions of community gossip and the pleasures of soccer for those passionate about the game. Kids admire the visitors' expensive motorbikes but continue to be engrossed in their 'soccer' games, played with tennis balls in the streets. The pleasures of Soweto, therefore, are as much emotional as material, as the narrator insists:

> *More than anything else, former Sowetans return to Soweto for the homeliness as well as the nostalgia: being in Soweto is like being enveloped in the ample bosom of a much-loved matriarch* (*Ibid*, 22).

Don and Tumi return to Soweto for 'homeliness as well as nostalgia', but much of the magic they experience is rooted in the past — in the days when the shapely Tumi often appeared in *Drum* and *Bona*, so that now kids in the street recognise her and greet her with excitement. Also magical were the schooldays when Don and Tumi met buying *vetkoek* and *snoek* at the Mokgetha Supermarket, their friendship cemented by the fact that he always had lunch money and would buy her *amagwhya vetkoek* with mango *atchaar*, as well as special luxuries like French polony, Russian sausages and chips when he had stolen money from his mother's purse.

Memories of the past are followed by a brief encounter with the drunk 'Oupa' who used to be one of Tumi's suitors. Seeing him as a sad reflection of the deterioration of many of their childhood friends, Don and Tumi guiltily give him a ten-rand note. In return he promises them that 'the good *Amadlozi* — the ancestors — will bless them with more Jaguars than they already have' (*Ibid*, 25). Now we move to the architecture of the new Soweto, where small municipal houses have been extended 'from the uniform, matchbox design of the past, to different shapes and sizes, some of which would not be out of place in the suburbs. Only the small yards stop further extension' (*Ibid*, 25). Here a novel satirising popular formulae overlaps, in its depiction of township life, with popular journalism. On a plane journey to Gauteng on the budget airline, 1Time, in June 2010, I picked up the airline magazine distributed free to passengers. One of its feature articles, titled 'Millionaires in the ghetto: South Africa's upwardly mobile townships' ('story and pix by Joost Bos and Allard de Witte/Tos'), begins:

> *South Africa's townships have long been known for their poverty and violence. But the situation in Soweto is changing fast. The number of shacks is decreasing and a new generation of rich black South Africans are moving in and building mansions there. Soweto is now hot, and even millionaires are proud to call the township home.* (Bos & De Witte: 2010)

The article focuses on 31-year-old Sibusiso Nkosi, who started life in Soweto as a street child but now works as a consultant in a platinum mine. He talks about how he and a generation of young South Africans who were earning well left the township: 'Nobody wanted to live in Soweto as it meant you were poor. Leaving was a sign that you were doing well' (*Ibid*, 86). However, life in the fashionable white Johannesburg suburb in which Sibusiso bought a house turned out to be disappointing. He 'hung plasma TV screens in every room, and filled his wardrobe with expensive clothing. But he didn't enjoy life'. Sibusiso explains: 'Everyone in the suburbs of Johannesburg locks themselves in behind high walls and barbed wire. I didn't even know my neighbours and I became utterly miserable. As a result I found myself returning more and more often to visit my friends and family here. In Soweto I know pretty much everyone' (*Ibid*, 86). Documenting the township's history as dormitories for black workers from the nearby gold mines, the writer of this article contrasts the daily stream of workers from Soweto, who in the past poured into the city on public transport, with the current executives in their BMWs or Mercedes-Benzes heading for their offices:

> *A black middle and upper class nouveau riche is emerging rapidly in the new South Africa. Here they are known as black diamonds, and they own a growing number of homes in Joburg's wealthier suburbs. But not everyone with money leaves. Many work in the city, but live in the townships. Life is more sociable here, and there isn't 10 000 Volts running through your gate. Neighbours still watch out for each other's houses and feel responsible for one another* (*Ibid*, 88).

Weekends, trendy young Sowetans gathering 'to see and be seen' are joined by black diamonds from the suburbs: 'They come to show off their new cars and expensive clothes. In the suburbs they don't stand out: everyone has a large car. But in the townships they are recognised by old friends and appreciated for their money and success' (*Ibid*, 88). The article now moves to the pastel-painted palm-befronded villa of jazz musician 'Hotstix' Mabuse: 'On the wall are gold discs and photographs of packed concert halls, and of Mabuse with jazz legends like Miriam Makeba and Hugh Masekela'. Mabuse comments:

> *Despite the dust, I'd far rather live here than in a boring suburb of Johannesburg. Soweto is where we all started out together … We were all oppressed and none of us had money. The house where I grew up had one bedroom. My father and mother slept there. I slept with my three brothers under the dining table in the living room. The past binds the people of Soweto, whether they are rich or poor now* (*Ibid*, 88).

Black Diamond introduces jazz through Tumi's father, Rre Molefhe. A figure of the 1960s, he is sitting on a rocking-chair on the *stoep* and smoking a pipe, dressed in his eight-piece Ayres cap and his Florsheim shoes, both from the 1960s: 'Don observes with satisfaction that the jazz generation has not yet died out in Soweto', remarks the narrator, who reminds the reader that in the past 'people sat out on the black, red or green *stoeps* listening to John Coltrane, Charlie Parker, Sonny Stitt, Milt Jackson, Duke Ellington, Count Basie, Sonny Rollins, and Dizzy Gillespie'. These, the narrator tells us, 'were the big names that every jazz collection in the township would have'. *Rre* Molefhe is an avid collector, with 'stacks and stacks' of LPs. What people continue to enjoy is the human drama of the songs:

> *When Jack Dupree sang of how his mother-in-law was the ugliest woman anyone had seen, and that she was so skinny she could hide behind the broom, they laughed heartily and ribbed each other about their mothers-in-law. Even though they had heard those lyrics over and over again and knew them by heart, they still found them hilarious* (Mda: 2009, 26).

How does the airline magazine's account of life in contemporary Soweto differ from Mda's? The answer lies surely in *Black Diamond*'s recreation of a past life now registered simply as nostalgia: 'You cannot but feel better when you are in Soweto. It is a place of nostalgia, and nostalgia does have a healing effect. Nostalgia is analgesic — it numbs you into a world where things were better, even though no one realised it at the time' (*Ibid*, 114). What the 'Millionaires in the Ghetto' piece foregrounds are the current changes in Soweto that spell the beginning of a vibrant and creative black environment. This largely economic transformation to more affluent lifestyles is applauded by the writer of this piece, as one might expect from an airline's commodity-focused, popular magazine. But in Mda's novel everything vibrant in Soweto belongs to the past: Tumi's and Don's childhood romance, Rre Molefhe's jazz collection, the closeness of neighbours in the township, even the famous nightclub Wezile's, once visited by Mandela and Tutu in *Black Diamond* produces only the crooks Bova and Fontya, embittered ex-liberation fighters who now attempt to rob a bank. True, *Black Diamond*'s protagonists, like the businessmen described in the airline article, retreat to Soweto to escape the mindlessness of life in white suburbia. But these retreats can only be temporary. Tumi, for instance, resolutely refuses to cook the *tsholo* (pulled beef brisket) and *ting*, a Setswana dish, prepared by her mother in Soweto, and a delicacy that Don wants to learn to cook. Tumi admonishes him: '[W]e eat this kind of stuff in Soweto and not in North Riding. Here, as far as everyone knows, we eat sushi and the like. Plus, you know, Don, I don't like my man to stand in an apron in the kitchen cooking' (*Ibid*, 45). Rather than returning to tradition, Tumi and her friends assert their modernity by keeping in shape at their Virgin Active Classic Club and wearing brand-name clothes.

Tumi's commitment to her modelling agency removes any incentives to further her education, for BEE desiderata create commodified women.

If 'the trenches are the boardrooms of South Africa', these boardrooms offer Black Diamonds no alternative cultural space. They live in a present that is disconnected from the past and that will continue to generate values that will make the future as barren as the present. The only exception to this uncreative impasse is cooking, which links individuals to one another and to their environment in surprising and unpredictable ways. Don and Kristin, though from opposing racial and cultural backgrounds, are kindred spirits. Neither is comfortable with group attitudes. Don hates Tumi to call him a Black Diamond and resists her 'positive thinking' formula; Kristin has overcome the racism of her Afrikaans apartheid upbringing and is impervious to designer clothes, preferring to wear what she likes. Both Don and Kristin love cats. Where they connect most strongly is in enjoying cooking together. Through Don's influence, Kristin moves from the dutiful cooking she has learned since her divorce to the seductive cooking that they both practise when surprising each other with candlelit dinners. In their culinary collaborations Don and Kristin celebrate the 'cross-pollination' of Indian, Xhosa, Afrikaner and Cape Malay dishes that reflect the diversity of South African cultural traditions. This genuine 'cross-pollination' is in stark contrast to the culturally garbled appropriations of a protagonist like Aunt Magda who, in her campaign to free the Visagie brothers, borrows from Zulu protest songs that 'zulufy' the names of apartheid figures such as Verwoerd and Malan, as well as from Xhosa freedom songs. But since Aunt Magda doesn't understand either African language her borrowings can only be treated parodically.

'Camera eye' narration: ideological considerations

I asked Mda why in *Black Diamond* he uses an authorial narrator who knows everything, sees everything, but is not part of the story-world he narrates. He replied that in this novel, which will be turned into a film, he wanted to draw on the techniques of 'camera eye' narration: that is, to tell the story from the perspective of a camera filming the characters and their actions. Jeremy Hawthorn notes that 'camera-eye narrative ... is generally taken to imply some sort of neutrality in the narrative determinations — as if a camera were left in a room to record anything that took place in front of it. Those familiar with the complexities of film narrative have tended to react against the somewhat simplistic assumptions lying behind the usage' (Hawthorn: 2000, 258). The narrator in *Black Diamond* doesn't just see and report on what he sees; he also frequently introduces value judgements, pieces of information and satirical remarks. To describe his narration as 'camera eye' is thus misleading. Here are some examples from the first three chapters of the narrator's ideological interventions: 'In the same way that mass action brought the apartheid government to its knees, it was bound to bring the post-apartheid justice system to its senses' (Mda: 2009, 3); 'In the tradition of South African criminals who have become folk heroes in their communities, the Visagies often operate on a semblance of the Robin Hood principle' (*Ibid,* 4); 'So [Kristin] can laugh, after all!' (*Ibid,* 6); 'You see, [Don Mateza] used to be Molotov's commander back in the bush, until Molotov bungled a mission to bomb a power station in Pretoria; and was arrested and sent to Robben Island' (*Ibid,* 8); 'None of the youth knows that A.K. Bazooka was in fact Don Mateza's nom de guerre' (*Ibid,* 9); '[Tumi] found it ridiculous that both Molotov and his white wife Cathy addressed the bodyguards as "comrade" as if they were all equal, whereas the bodyguards called him "chief"' (*Ibid,* 10); 'Don realises that he would be bringing nothing to the corporate table since he has no political clout that can be converted into capital' (*Ibid,* 13) and

> *[Kristin] believes she is racing against time. The new government of the post-apartheid South Africa has already shown tendencies of being too liberal on issues of morality. The government has legalised homosexuality; sexual orientation is in the constitution. Gay people can marry. Now there is talk of legalising prostitution ... Even if she cannot stop that tide by herself, she is determined to make life hell for prostitutes and their pimps before the new age of utter degradation is visited upon the upright citizens of the land* (*Ibid,* 18).

So what Mda has described as 'camera eye' narration is a form of authorial control over the novel's story-world — whether in characters' thoughts, plot elements or the reader's response to the novel's socio-political world as laid out by the author. How exactly this authorial control will 'translate' into film narrative when the novel is filmed is an interesting problem — using voice-over, perhaps? — but certainly 'camera eye' narrative techniques cannot render the perceptions, judgements and values transmitted to the reader by *Black Diamond*'s narrator. Ironically, film theorists like Baudry and Metz have discussed the cinema as 'an apparatus destined to obtain a precise ideological effect, necessary to the dominant ideology' (Jay: 1993, 475). For them the cinema viewer is like a voyeur because (s)he is isolated in the audience and sees a scene that cannot look back at him or her: 'In the spectator's voyeurism there is no need ... to be seen (it is dark in the cinema, visibility is confined entirely to the screen), no need for a knowing object, or rather an object that wants to know, an object-subject to share in the activity of the component drive' (*Ibid,* 481). If the viewer confronted with cinema-eye narrative in film is rendered passive, the reader of *Black Diamond* is even more passive, since his or her reactions are limited by an authorial frame that allows for no interpretation other than its own.

The Economist of 5–11 June 2010 compiled a 14-page special report on South Africa. This included an article ('A new kind of inequality: Black economic empowerment has had unintended consequences') that speaks directly to Mda's concerns in *Black Diamond.* The article notes that black economic empowerment was introduced by the ANC (with the collaboration of the white business world) in order to benefit the mass of poor blacks disadvantaged under apartheid. But BEE 'has resulted in "a few individuals benefiting a lot", as Mr Zuma admitted earlier this year. He should know; he and many of his family members are among the lucky few. He has now vowed to make the scheme much broader' (*The Economist,* 9). BEE's impact on the majority of South African blacks has been minimal:

> *For the poor black masses ... the scheme has been a dismal failure. Moeletsi Mbeki, an analyst and entrepreneur (and brother of the former president) says that BEE has proved a 'parasitic drag' on economic growth, having struck a 'fatal blow against the emergence of black entrepreneurship by creating a small class of unproductive but wealthy black crony capitalists'. John Kane-Berman, head of the South African Institute of Race Relations, argues that the scheme has discouraged self-reliance and encouraged a debilitating sense of entitlement among blacks, as well as putting off foreign investors. It has also led to a lot of public tenders being awarded, often at inflated prices, to family and friends of politicians and officials* (*Ibid,* 9).

These are the issues that *Black Diamond* addresses. Mda has insisted, in interview with me, that his preoccupations in this novel are not only satirical or ironising, but also serious. In my last section I consider the issue of whether a novel can succeed in making serious socio-political statements in the absence of agency on the part of its protagonists or interpretative challenges on the part of its readers.

Riding the tiger

There was a young lady from Riga
Who smiled as she rode on a tiger
They returned from the ride
With the lady inside
And the smile on the face of the tiger.[1]

1 I wrote most of this chapter while staying with my good friend Ed French at his house in Clarens in the Free State, overlooking the distant Maluti Mountains. The landscapes around Clarens are very like those depicted in the paintings of Frans Claerhout, with their vibrant, saturated colours. While discussing my work in progress, Ed came up with the tiger limerick, which he has used in his own work. I asked him to write a paragraph to explain this connection:

> Since 1990, radicals have at times tried hard to convince themselves that they could somehow use and manipulate the mechanisms of the triumphant market to fulfil their aspirations for a better, more just society. Whether in the quest for redistribution of wealth or for 'authentic' educational alternatives, they rather desperately attempted to use conservative ideologies of accounting, accountability and bottom lines in ways they hoped would promote radical change. In various contexts I have found it useful to quote the limerick about the young lady from Riga in talking about this hope. In the 1990s it seemed possible (cautiously) to think that the tiger might take the young lady to a good place. We seem now to have reached a place where the young lady has been devoured (or is in profound trauma). At the same time, the tiger has no reason to smile. When Gail Fincham was outlining the problem of *Black Diamond* to me, it seemed a related case where the message was devoured by the medium.

Mda has claimed that he wants *Black Diamond* to be seen as a serious commentary on the contemporary socio-political situation in South Africa and the novel's satire clearly registers his contempt for BEE ideology. But this novel differs from Mda's previous fiction in that it erases the possibilities of either meaningful community or effective agency. The reader is left recoiling from the final chapter, in which the pimp Stevo Visagie attempts to avenge himself on the magistrate Kristin Uys, who sentenced him to imprisonment: he plans to murder her after she has performed her prostitute's dance for him. The writing here degenerates into a chilling combination of sadism and banality. It would seem, therefore, that Mda's anger at the idiocies of BEE political realities has destroyed his ability to empower his protagonists, whatever their situation, and to allow his readers to fruitfully enter into the imaginative possibilities of the places in which his fictional protagonists live. Most puzzling (especially in a novel that will be turned into a film script) is the fact that the rich and varied techniques of focalisation, which Mda's fiction has always provided for its readers, are almost non-existent. In this novel BEE has the last laugh, not the author; as did the tiger and not the lady from Riga.

Black Diamond and Jacob Dlamini's *Native Nostalgia*

In the section 'Soweto and cooking', I focused on Mda's depiction of Soweto and on his description of the nostalgia experienced by BEE executives who return to Soweto sporadically to escape the drabness of life in the white suburbs of Johannesburg. But I also pointed out that nostalgic returns are fundamentally disconnected from BEE executives' present lives, since they have now bought into lifestyles where they must constantly demonstrate wealth and status. In the section 'Riding the tiger', I suggested that Mda's indignation at BEE betrayals of working-class black people has resulted in a novel that is weakened by the loss of agency and community on the part of the protagonists, and by the lack of interpretative challenges offered to the reader.

A powerful antidote to *Black Diamond*'s sense of stagnation is *Native Nostalgia*, a book published in 2009 that combines the genres of memoir with acute sociological analysis. Jacob Dlamini writes about growing up in Katlehong, a black township about 30 kilometres east of Johannesburg, bringing to the reader's attention 'shattered fragments of memory' from a township childhood. The model he adopts — after Svetlana Boym, whose book is tellingly called *The Future of Nostalgia* — is that of 'reflective nostalgia', which 'lingers on ruins, the patina of time and history, in the dream of another place and another time' (Dlamini: 2009, 17–18). The irony that Dlamini insists upon, in relation to nostalgia, is 'that it is essentially about the present. It is about present anxieties refracted through the prism of the past' (*Ibid*, 16). Equally, Dlamini is concerned to counter 'the distorting master narrative of black dispossession that dominates the historiography of the struggle' because this narrative misleadingly assumes that the oppressed black masses 'experienced apartheid the same way, suffered the same way and fought the same way against apartheid' (*Ibid*, 18). Not only does such an account fail to register 'gender, class, ethnic, age and regional differences' between people, it also 'blinds us to a richness, a complexity of life among black South Africans, that not even colonialism and apartheid at their worst could destroy' (*Ibid*, 19). Dlamini writes:

> *I challenge facile accounts of black life under apartheid that paint the forty-six years in which the system existed as one vast moral desert ... as if blacks produced no art, literature or music, bore no morally upstanding children or, at the very least, children who knew the difference between right and wrong — even if those children did not grow up to make the 'right' moral choices in their lives* (*Ibid*, 19).

'Struggle' rhetoric presents an implicit denial of agency amongst blacks under apartheid that seems to Dlamini as insulting as the assumption made by the anthropologist Bronislaw Malinowski in the 1930s, that Africans living in cities had abandoned the coherence of rural African tribal life without having achieved the material requirements and hygienic standards of European city life (*Ibid*, 151). Dlamini's memories of Katlehong show the reader how falsifying are portrayals of townships merely 'as places of crime, squalor and disease — hopeless places awaiting development by a benevolent government' (*Ibid*, 156).

Several issues are at stake in Dlamini's important and illuminating work. Firstly, the difference between subjects and objects. Black people under apartheid were treated as objects but remained subjects because they continued to demonstrate the distinctive subjectivity that Dlamini's book celebrates. Secondly, what Dlamini calls 'reflective nostalgia' never becomes monodimensional or merely sentimental. Instead it 'can be ironic and humorous. It reveals that longing and critical thinking are not opposed to one another, as affective memories do not absolve one from compassion, judgement or critical reflection' (Boym, quoted by Dlamini: 2009, 18). Finally, people's experience of place is strongly inflected by the role of imagination: 'Katlehong is more than just a township made up of houses and basic amenities. Katlehong is also a world that exists in the imagination, a world where the metaphorical is as important as the material' (*Ibid*, 107). The nostalgia analysed by Dlamini in relation to township life in the evil days of apartheid is not an emotion frozen in the past. Rather, it springs from the situation of the present: '[I]t is usually when people feel themselves adrift in a world seemingly out of control that they come down with nostalgia' (*Ibid*, 16). Thus the terms that Dlamini's book restores to the reader via the notion of reflective nostalgia are irony, complexity, agency, community, subjectivity and the multiple links between the past and the present. All these have lost their power in *Black Diamond*, where the BEE present is as arid as the worst features of the apartheid past. The reader loses the sense of connection between past and present that Mda has created so powerfully in all the novels up to *Black Diamond*. Also lost in this novel are the concrete sensoria of sight and sound powerfully evoked in earlier Mda novels (and evoked also by Dlamini in *Native Nostalgia*) as well as the sense of lived community, which has given to Mda's previous novels new, surprising and moving angles. All these dimensions *Native Nostalgia* restores.

Finally...

In this chapter, I have sketched the formulaic elements that accompany Mda's satirical treatment of BEE executives in *Black Diamond*. These, I feel, reduce the novel's scope by shortcutting the performative dimension usually so central to Mda's fiction — particularly the role of the reader. In his most recent work *Sometimes there is a Void*, an autobiography, Mda's linking of place with memory and agency is very powerful. Since he always has ideas for three or four new novels as he finishes a book, it is to be hoped that his next novel will avoid the conceptual and narratological impasses to which *Black Diamond* falls prey.

Chapter Nine

Some concluding thoughts

We shall not cease from exploration
And the end of all our exploring
Will be to arrive where we started
And know the place for the first time.

— T. S. Eliot, *Little Gidding*

I have learned a great deal from working on Mda's novels and from the theorists whose ideas have enabled mine. But my explorations are beginnings rather than conclusions. I hope readers will build on these beginnings, in the performative spirit that animates this book. For *Dance of Life* is all about the performative in Mda's fiction writing — in relation to author, characters and readers.

In the autobiographical mode which sits next to his fiction, this dimension is suggested in the story of 'Zakes the Artist', who as a child paints a picture of the Zulu warrior uPhosozwayo and wins an essay competition for his first story while still at primary school in Lesotho. In adulthood, Mda moves from writing plays about democracy for a largely non-literate audience to writing fiction about the new post-apartheid South Africa. He has developed increasingly sophisticated techniques of juxtaposition that link the past with the present, the imaginary with the real and the individual with the social. Crucial to these depictions is his evocation of place and setting, which animate his characters and which reflect an indigenous concept of landscape as opposed to Western notions of landscape.

All Mda's writing demonstrates generic instability and narrative innovation. Characteristic also is his deployment of intertextuality, based on his familiarity with other writers' texts, and his use of an African resource base derived from oral traditions. Typically, Mda's texts enact the performative in their textual strategies and their orchestration of divergent voices. I have argued, as have other critics, that Mda's awareness of the dynamics of performance evolved out of his earlier experience of working with the Maratholi Travelling Theatre in Lesotho.

Mda's characters are all involved in performance. When his first protagonist, Toloki in *Ways of Dying*, learns to become a Professional Mourner, his performances enable psychological and geographical mastery as the performativity of his art establishes a new territoriality. In *The Heart of Redness* a whole cast of characters demonstrates, through storytelling, singing and dancing, their historical connection with — and contemporary independence from — the Xhosa nation in the nineteenth century. In *The Madonna of Excelsior*, protagonists — 'ordinary people doing ordinary things' — are rescued from the political oppressions of the Miscegenation Trial by their involvement in the visionary world of Claerhout's paintings. *Cion* plays with metafictional tropes to illustrate the coming of age of Toloki, both as Professional Mourner and as Master Storyteller, while the Whale Caller's singing and dancing with the Southern Right whale, Sharisha, dramatises the challenges and problems of ecological connection in a political world that forbids community. And what of *Black Diamond*? Despite its deployment of multiple modes and its reliance on the media, I have argued that the performative dimension enacted by protagonists and demanded of readers throughout Mda's fiction is largely absent in this parable of the 'new' South Africa. Whereas Mda's previous vivid settings have staged dances of life, *Black Diamond*'s bland settings culminate in a dance of death.

But it is the response of readers to Mda's texts that best illustrates the performative dimension. I have tried to demonstrate that Mda's depiction of individuals always brings collective contexts into play. In exploring written texts and oral storytelling devices, I have assumed readers' cultural flexibility in their conversations both with literature and orature, with social realism and magic realism. The notion of a 'cross-border' readership assumes an ability to move between geographical, cultural and political horizons, to identify with African humanism or *ubuntu* and to recognise the hybridity of the author's styles. Since Mda's deployment of intertextuality (demonstrated in Chapters Two and Three) is essential to his writing, his ideal reader must also be prepared to grapple with Bakhtin's heteroglossia, to register contrasts between Conrad's and Mda's depictions of Africa and to respond to the 'singularity' for which I argue both in *The Heart of Redness* and in Peires' *The Dead Will Arise*. Equally, Mda's ideal reader will be receptive to the visual and perceptual repertoires enacted in his techniques of focalisation, 'seeing' the juxtaposed worlds of Claerhout's colourful paintings as opposed to the black-and-white of the media reporting of Excelsior's Miscegenation Trial (see Chapter Four).

Readers of Mda's texts as interpreted in this book are asked to consider the 'mesh' between theoretical paradigms and textual analysis. How useful are the postcolonial frameworks provided by Döring, Loomba, Hall and Ashcroft in interpreting Toloki's narration in *Cion* (Chapter Six), as he defines himself both as Professional Mourner and as Master Storyteller? How central to the narrative and thematic preoccupations of *The Whale Caller* (Chapter Seven) are recent cross-cultural environmental debates in South Africa and America? Readers are also invited to critique the assessments that I, and other critics, make. How does Mda 'position' his readers? To what extent is the performativity created in his earlier fiction absent or present in his most recent novel, *Black Diamond*? How well do Mda's gender politics fit his narrative strategies? What is the significance of the fact that his most striking and most transgressive female characters — Noria in *Ways of Dying*, Nongqawuse and Qukezwa in *The Heart of Redness*, Niki and Popi in *The Madonna of Excelsior*, Orpah in *Cion* and Kristin Uys in *Black Diamond* — are all voiced by a controlling male narrator? Equally, what is the significance of Mda's insistence on separating his critical from his creative faculties? Doesn't this separation undermine his own narratological achievements as he learns to combine the limited perspectives of a communal narrator with the authoritative perspectives of an omniscient narrator, a combination illustrated in the transition from *Ways of Dying* to *The Madonna of Excelsior*? What new directions might Mda's fiction take after *Black Diamond*? These are open questions. One of the pleasures of writing about a living author is the unpredictability of his texts in the future. Another is the unpredictability of readers' responses. The reader of this book is invited to assess both Mda's fictional worlds and my readings of them, to act therefore as metacritic, enabling new interpretations.

In a recent review of new South African writing, Shane Graham remarks:

> *With the end of apartheid, long-ostracised South Africa opened itself up to the rest of the world. South African literary studies has begun to move away from the restrictive lens of South African exceptionalism, to consider how the country's literary production has always taken place within a context of global migration and exchange.*

Graham discusses Helgesson's new book on transnationalism:

> *Helgesson's central questions are, 'how has African literature challenged the tyranny of place? ...[U]nder what conditions have black and white African writers positioned themselves in what Pascale Casanova has dubbed world space?' Implicit in this latter question is the issue of newness in African literature: how do writers negotiate the tension between needing to prove their mastery of Western literary discourses, and needing to create something new in order to take their place in Casanova's 'world republic of letters?'* (Graham: 2010, 152).

He concludes:

> *The result of Helgesson's ... 'discomfort with reductive, totalising explanations' is a thorough debunking of the kind of binarism and Manichean thinking that has often inhibited and restricted South African literary studies. He shows us how, at least in southern African literatures, it is impossible to draw close distinctions between African versus European, local versus transnational, traditional versus modern,*

> *orality versus literacy, inner versus outer realms of cultural life and high culture versus mass culture* (*Ibid*, 154).

This book has attempted to demonstrate the ways in which Mda has 'challenged the tyranny of place' and 'created newness in African literature' by positioning himself in world space. His story-worlds transcend binarism and refuse Manichean oppositions.

Above all, *Dance of Life* has argued for the central importance of the work of the reader. Attridge remarks:

> *I am suggesting ... that the attempt to do justice to literary works as events, welcoming alterity, countersigning the singular signature of the artist, inventively responding to invention, combined with a suspension of all those terms that constitute the work as an object, is the best way to enhance a vital critical practice* (Attridge: 2004, 137).

My hope, as author of *Dance of Life*, is that Zakes Mda will in the future create new literary events to which we, as his readers and critics, may respond with the joyful singularity he has taught us.

Bibliography

Allison, John (1999) 'Self-determination in cultural resource management: Indigenous peoples' interpretation of history and of places and landscapes'. In Ucko, Peter J. & Layton, Robert (eds) *The Archaeology and Anthropology of Landscape: Shaping Your Landscape.* London and New York: Routledge.

Amick, Steve (2005) 'Review: *The Whale Caller*'. *The Washington Post,* 11 December.

Anderson, Benedict (1983) *Imagined Communities: Reflections on the Origin and Spread of Nationalism.* London: Verso.

Ashcroft, Bill (2001) *Post-Colonial Transformation.* London and New York: Routledge.

Ashcroft, Bill, Griffiths, Gareth & Tiffin, Helen (eds) (1995) *The Post-Colonial Studies Reader.* London: Routledge.

Attridge, Derek (2004) *The Singularity of Literature.* London and New York: Routledge.

Attwell, David (2005) *Rewriting Modernity: Studies in Black South African Literary History.* Pietermaritzburg: University of KwaZulu-Natal Press.

Bainbridge, James (ed) (2009) *The Lonely Planet Guide: South Africa, Lesotho and Swaziland* (8 ed). USA and UK: FSC.

Bakhtin, M. M. (1981) In Holquist, Michael (ed) *The Dialogic Imagination: Four Essays.* Translated by Emerson, Caryl & Holquist, Michael. Austin: University of Texas Press.

Bal, Mieke (1997a) *Introduction to the Theory of Narrative* (2 ed). Toronto: University of Toronto Press.

Bal, Mieke (1997b) *Narratology: Introduction to the Theory of Narrative* (2 ed) Toronto: University of Toronto Press.

Barker, Derek Alan (2008) 'Escaping the tyranny of magic realism? A discussion of the term in relation to the novels of Zakes Mda'. *Postcolonial Text,* 4 (2).

Barnard, Rita (2004) 'On laughter, the grotesque and the South African transition: Zakes Mda's *Ways of Dying*'. *Novel,* 37 (3).

Barnard, Rita (2007) *Apartheid and Beyond: South African Writers and the Politics of Place.* Oxford: Oxford University Press.

Bell, David (2003) 'The persistent presence of the past in contemporary writing in South Africa'. *Current Writing,* 15 (1).

Bell, David (2007) 'The intimate presence of death in the novels of Zakes Mda: Necrophilic worlds and traditional belief'. In Ronning, Anne Holden &

Johannessen, Lene (eds) *Readings of the Particular: The Postcolonial in the Postnational.* Amsterdam and New York: Rodopi.

Bell, David (2009) 'A theatre for democracy'. In Bell, David & Jacobs, J. U. (eds) *Ways of Writing: Critical Essays on Zakes Mda.* Pietermaritzburg: University of KwaZulu-Natal Press.

Bell, David & Jacobs, J. U. (eds) (2009) *Ways of Writing: Critical Essays on Zakes Mda.* Pietermaritzburg: University of KwaZulu-Natal Press.

Bell, Madison Smartt (2006) Review. *New York Times.* 8 January. Available at: www.nytimes.com.2006/01/08/books/review/08bell/html?_r =1

Bender, Barbara (1999) 'Subverting the Western Gaze: Mapping alternative worlds'. In Ucko, Peter J. & Layton, Robert (eds) *The Archaeology and Anthropology of Landscape: Shaping Your Landscape.* London and New York: Routledge.

Beukes, Lauren (2008) In *Book Southern Africa News.* 22 July. Available at: http://book.co.za/blog/2008/07/22

Bieder, Robert (2006) 'The Imagined Bear'. *Current Writing: Text and Reception in Southern Africa.* April.

Boehmer, Elleke (1995) *Colonial and Postcolonial Literature.* Oxford: Oxford University Press.

Bos, Joost & De Witte, Allard (2010) 'Millionaires in the ghetto: South Africa's upwardly mobile townships'. *AbouTime.* June.

Bradford, Helen (1996) 'Women, gender and colonialism: Rethinking the history of the British Cape Colony and its frontier zones'. *Journal of African History,* 37.

Brooker, Peter (1999) *Cultural Theory: A Glossary.* London: Arnold.

Brooks, Shirley (2006) 'Human discourses, animal geographies: Imagining Umfolozi's white rhinos'. *Current Writing: Text and Reception in Southern Africa.* April.

Chapman, Michael (1998) 'The aesthetics of liberation: Reflections from a Southern perspective'. *Current Writing,* 10 (1).

Chatman, Seymour (1990) *Coming to Terms: The Rhetoric of Narrative in Fiction and Film.* Ithaca: Cornell University Press.

Cock, Jacklyn (2007) *The War Against Ourselves: Nature, Power and Justice.* Johannesburg: Wits University Press.

Coetzee, J. M. (1992) In Attwell, David (ed) *Doubling the Point: essays and interviews.* Cambridge, Massachusetts and London: Harvard University Press.

Coetzee, J. M. (2004) *Elizabeth Costello.* London: Vintage Books.

Conrad, Joseph (1946, first published in 1898) *Heart of Darkness.* London: J. M. Dent and Sons.

Cooper, Brenda (1998) *Magical Realism in West African Fiction: Seeing with a Third Eye.* London: Routledge.

Cosgrove, Denis (1988) *The Iconography of Landscape: Essays on the Symbolic Representation, Design and Use of Past Environments.* Cambridge: Cambridge University Press.

Courau, Rogier (2004) 'Re-imagining community histories in the South African fiction of Zakes Mda'. Unpublished MA dissertation. University of KwaZulu-Natal.

Courau, Rogier & Murray, Sally-Ann (2009) 'Of funeral rites and community memory: Ways of living in *Ways of Dying*'. In Bell, David & Jacobs, J. U. (eds) *Ways of Writing: Critical Essays on Zakes Mda.* Pietermaritzburg: University of KwaZulu-Natal Press.

Dannenburg, H. P. (2009) 'Culture and nature in *The Heart of Redness*'. In Bell, David & Jacobs, J. U. (eds) *Ways of Dying: Critical Essays on Zakes Mda.* Pietermaritzburg: University of KwaZulu-Natal Press.

Darian-Smith, Kate, Gunner, Liz & Nuttall, Sarah (eds) (1996) *Text, Theory, Space: Land, Literature and History in South Africa and Australia.* London and New York: Routledge.

Deacon, Janette & Foster, Craig (2005) *My Heart Stands in the Hill.* London, Cape Town, New South Wales, New Zealand: Struik Publishers.

D'Haen, Theo L. (1995) 'Magic realism and postmodernism: Decentering privileged centers'. In Zamara, Lois Parkinson & Faris, Wendy B. (eds) *Magic Realism: Theory, History, Community.* Durham and London: Duke University Press.

Dlamini, Jacob (2009) *Native Nostalgia.* Johannesburg: Jacana.

Döring, Tobias (2008) *Postcolonial Literatures in English.* Stuttgart: Klett Lernen und Wissen.

Dowson, Thomas (1996) 'Re-production and consumption: The use of rock art imagery in Southern Africa today'. In Skotnes, Pippa (ed) *Miscast: Negotiating the Presence of the Bushman.* Cape Town: University of Cape Town Press.

Driver, Dorothy (1990) 'Women as mothers, women as writers'. In Trump, Martin (ed) *Rendering Things Visible: Essays on South African Literary Culture.* Johannesburg: Ravan Press.

Driver, Dorothy (1992) 'Women and nature, women as objects of exchange: Towards a feminist analysis of South African literature'. In Chapman, Michael, Gardner, Colin & Mphahlele, Es'kia (eds) *Perspectives on South African English Literature.* Johannesburg: Ad Donker.

Duggan, Carolyn (2009) 'Betrayal and the search for empowerment in the early plays'. In Bell, David & Jacobs, J. U. (eds) *Ways of Writing: Critical*

Essays on Zakes Mda. Pietermaritzburg: University of KwaZulu-Natal Press.

Durrant, Sam (2005) 'The invention of mourning in post-apartheid literature'. *Third World Quarterly*, 26 (3).

The Economist 'A new kind of inequality: Black economic empowerment has had unintended consequences'. 5–11 June 2010.

The English Academy Awards 1997. *EAR* 14, December.

Everitt, Mariss (2006) 'On humans and animals: Sparring with the beast in Douglas Livingstone's poem *Descent from the Tower*'. *Current Writing: Text and Reception in Southern Africa.* April.

Fanon, Frantz (1993, first published 1967) 'On national culture'. In Williams, Patrick & Chrisman, Laura (eds) *Colonial Discourse and Post-Colonial Theory: A Reader.* Hemel Hempstead: Harvester Wheatsheaf.

Farred, Grant (2000) 'Mourning the post-apartheid state already? The poetics of loss in Zake Mda's *Ways of Dying*'. *Modern Fiction Studies*, 46 (1).

Fincham, Gail (ed) (2001) *Conrad at the Millennium: Modernism, Postmodernism, Postcolonialism.* Boulder: Social Science Monographs and Lublin: Marie Curie-Sklodowska University.

Fincham, Gail (2003) '*Heart of Darkness* and Plato's *Republic*: A reverse parable'. *L'Epoque Conradienne*, 29.

Fincham, Gail (2009) 'Community and agency in *The Heart of Redness* and Joseph Conrad's *Heart of Darkness*'. In Bell, David & Jacobs, J. U. (eds) *Ways of Writing: Critical Essays on Zakes Mda.* Pietermaritzburg: University of KwaZulu-Natal Press.

Fothergill, Anthony (1989) *Heart of Darkness.* Milton Keynes: Open University Press.

Frielick, Stanley (1992) 'Deep ecology, the environment and African literature'. In *Literature, Nature and the Land: Ethics and Aesthetics of the Environment: Collected AUETSA Papers.* Durban: University of Natal.

Gates, Henry Louis Jr. (1988) *The Signifying Monkey: A Theory of African-American Literary Criticism.* New York: Oxford University Press.

Gaylard, Gerald (2005) *After Colonialism: African Postmodernism and Magical Realism.* Johannesburg: Wits University Press.

Glover, Jayne (2006) 'The metaphor of the horse in Doris Lessing's *The Marriages Between Zones Three, Four and Five*: An ecofeminist question?'. *Current Writing: Text and Reception in Southern Africa.* April.

Goodman, Ralph (2004) 'De-scribing the centre: Satire and postcolonial strategies in *The Madonna of Excelsior*'. *Journal of Literary Studies*, 20.

Goodman, Ralph (2008) 'The Man, the woman and the whale: Exploring the politics of the possible in Zakes Mda's *The Whale Caller*'. *Current Writing*, 20(1).

Goodman, Ralph (2009) 'Race, satire, and post-colonial issues in *The Madonna of Excelsior*'. In Bell, David & Jacobs, J. U. (eds) *Ways of Writing: Critical Essays on Zakes Mda*. Pietermaritzburg: University of KwaZulu-Natal Press.

Graham, Shane (2009a) 'Burdened by the scars of history: Zakes Mda's *The Heart of Redness*'. In *Southern African Literature after the Truth Commission: Mapping Loss*. New York: Palgrave Macmillan.

Graham, Shane (2009b) 'Mapping memory, healing the land: *The Bells of* Amersfoort'. In Bell, David & Jacobs, J. U. (eds) *Ways of Writing: Critical Essays on Zakes Mda*. Pietermaritzburg: University of KwaZulu-Natal Press.

Graham, Shane (2010) Review of Stefan Helgesson's *Transnationalism in Southern African Literature: Modernists, Realists, and the Inequality of Print Culture. The English Academy Review*, 27 (2) October.

Gray, Stephen (2009) 'Copy rites and wrongs'. 1 October. Available at: http://www.andrewoffenburger.com/mailandguardian

Gribble, Jill (2000) 'Motifs of transformation in four novels of Margaret Atwood'. Unpublished MA thesis. University of Cape Town.

Hall, Stuart (1996) 'Cultural identity and diaspora'. In Mongia, Padmini (ed) *Contemporary Postcolonial Theory: A Reader*. London: Arnold.

Hall, Stuart (2001) 'Negotiating Caribbean identities'. In Castle, Gregory (ed) *Postcolonial Discourses: An Anthology*. Oxford: Blackwell.

Hawthorn, Jeremy (1996) *Cunning Passages: New Historicism, Cultural Materialism and Marxism in Contemporary Literature*. London, New York and Sydney: Arnold.

Hawthorn, Jeremy (2000) *A Glossary of Contemporary Literary Theory* (4 ed) London: Arnold.

Helgesson, Stefan (2004) *Writing in Crisis: Ethics and History in Gordimer, Ndebele and Coetzee*. Pietermaritzburg: University of KwaZulu-Natal Press.

Holloway, Myles (1988) 'Zakes Mda's plays: The art of the text in the context of politics'. Master's thesis. University of Natal.

Holstein, Jonathan (1973) *The Pieced Quilt: An American Design Tradition*. Boston, Massachusetts: New York Graphic Society.

Hutcheon, Linda (1980) *Narcissistic Narrative: The Metafictional Paradox*. New York and London: Methuen.

Jacobs, J. U. (2000) 'Zakes Mda and the (South) African Renaissance: Reading *She Plays with the Darkness*'. *English in Africa*, 27 (1).

Jacobs, J. U. (2002) 'Zakes Mda's *The Heart of Redness*: The novel as *umngqokolo*'. *Kunapipi*, 24 (1 and 2).

Jacobs, J. U. (2005) 'Flying in the face of convention: *The Heart of Redness* as rehabilitative of the South African pastoral literary tradition through the frame of universal myth'. *Journal of African Studies*, 1 (3).

Jacobs, J. U. (2009) 'Towards a South African expressionism: *The Madonna of Excelsior*'. In Bell, David & Jacobs, J. U. (eds) *Ways of Writing: Critical Essays on Zakes Mda*. Pietermaritzburg: University of KwaZulu-Natal Press.

Jaggi, Maya (2005) Review. *The Guardian*. 27 August. Available at: www.guardian.co.uk/theguardian/2005/aug/27/guardianreview

Jay, Martin (1993) *Downcast Eyes: The Denigration of Vision in the Twentieth Century French Thought*. Berkeley, Los Angeles and London: University of California Press.

Killam, Douglas & Rowe, Ruth (eds) (2000) *The Companion to African Literatures*. Oxford: James Currey.

Kissack, Mike & Titlestad, Michael (2009) 'Invidious interpreters: The postcolonial intellectual in *The Heart of Redness*'. In Bell, David & Jacobs, J. U. (eds) *Ways of Writing: Critical Essays on Zakes Mda*. Pietermaritzburg: University of KwaZulu-Natal Press.

Koyana, Simhokazi (2003) 'Qholorha and the dialogism of place in Zakes Mda's *The Heart of Redness*'. *Current Writing*, 15.

Lazley, Chris (2008) 'Space and place in the novels of Zakes Mda'. Unpublished MA thesis. University of Cape Town.

Levin, David Michael (ed) (1993) *Modernity and the Hegemony of Vision*. Berkeley, Los Angeles and London: University of California Press.

Lloyd, David (2001) 'The modernization of redness'. *Scrutiny*, 26.

Lombardozzi, Litzi (2005) 'Harmony of voice: Women characters in the plays of Zakes Mda'. *English in Africa*, 32 (2).

Loomba, Ania (2005) *Colonialism/Postcolonialism*. London: Routledge.

Lothe, Jacob (2001) 'Cumulative intertextuality in *Heart of Darkness*: Virgil, Dante, and Goethe's *Faust*'. In Fincham, Gail (ed) *Conrad at the Millennium: Modernism, Postmodernism, Postcolonialism*. Boulder: Social Science Monographs and Lublin: Marie Curie-Sklodowska University.

Louw, Pat (2006) '"Nature documentaries" eco-tainment? The case of MM + M (Mad Mike and Mark)'. *Current Writing: Text and Reception in Southern Africa*. April.

MacDonald, T. Spreelin (2009) 'Twinship and humanism in *She Plays with the Darkness*'. In Bell, David & Jacobs, J. U. (eds) *Ways of Writing: Critical Essays on Zakes Mda*. Pietermaritzburg: University of KwaZulu-Natal Press.

Marais, Michael (2003) "'We know bugger-all about baboons": Nature and exile in Justin Cartwright's *White Lightning*'. *The English Academy Review*, 20, December.

Martin, Julia (2003) '"This is where I am coming from": Gangsters, thatched roofs and cheese boys in an undergraduate classroom'. *The English Academy Review*, 20, December.

Mazibuko, Nokuthula (2007) 'Mothers, madonnas and musicians: A writing of Africa's women as symbols and agents of change in the novels of Zakes Mda'. PhD thesis. University of the Witwatersrand.

McHale, Brian (1987) *Postmodernist Fiction*. London and New York: Routledge.

Mda, Zakes (1990) 'Maratholi Travelling Theatre: Towards an alternative perspective of development.' *Journal of Southern African Studies* 16(2) June.

Mda, Zakes (1994) 'Learning from the ancient wisdom of Africa: In the creation and distribution of messages'. *Current Writing*, 6 (2).

Mda, Zakes (1995a) *She Plays with the Darkness*. Florida, RSA: Vivlia Publishers.

Mda, Zakes (1995b) *Ways of Dying*. Oxford: Oxford University Press.

Mda, Zakes (1997) Acceptance speech for the Olive Schreiner Prize. *English Academy Review*, 14.

Mda, Zakes (2000) *The Heart of Redness*. Oxford: Oxford University Press.

Mda, Zakes (2002) *The Madonna of Excelsior*. Oxford: Oxford University Press.

Mda, Zakes (2005) *The Whale Caller*. London: Penguin Books.

Mda, Zakes (2007) *Cion*. Johannesburg: Penguin Books.

Mda, Zakes (2008) 'Justify the enemy: Becoming human in South Africa'. *Boston Review*, May/June. Available at: http://bostonreview.net/BR33.3/mda.php

Mda, Zakes (2008a) 'A response to "Duplicity and plagiarism in Zakes Mda's *Heart of Redness*" by Andrew Offenburger'. *Research in African Literatures*, 30.9.

Mda, Zakes (2008b) 'A charge disputed'. 17 October. Available at: http://www.mg.co.za/article/2008-10-23-a-charge-disputed

Mda, Zakes (2009) *Black Diamond*. Johannesburg: Penguin Books.

Mda, Zakes (2009a) 'The pink mountain: Landscapes and the conception of a literature of public action'. Address delivered at the African Literature Association Conference in Burrington, Vermont. 18 April.

Mda, Zakes (2009b) 'Of pink mountains, bees and writing'. Unpublished interviews with Gail Fincham, Johannesburg.

Mda, Zakes (2011) *Sometimes there is a Void: Memoirs of an Outsider*. Johannesburg: Penguin Books.

Mervis, Margaret (1998) 'Fiction for development: Zakes Mda's *Ways of Dying*'. *Current Writing*, 10 (1).

Miller, J. Hillis (1996) In Hawthorn, Jeremy (ed) *Cunning Passages: New Historicism, Cultural Materialism and Marxism in Contemporary Literature.* London, New York and Sydney: Arnold.

Miller, J. Hillis (2002) 'Should we read *Heart of Darkness*?' In Fincham, Gail (ed) *Conrad at the Millennium: Modernism, Postmodernism, Postcolonialism.* Boulder: Social Science Monographs and Lublin: Marie Curie-Sklodowska University.

Morris, Pam (ed) (1994) *The Bakhtin Reader: Selected Writings of Bakhtin, Medvedev, Voloshinov.* London: Arnold.

Morrison, Tracy (2008) '"Our place in the family of things": A story of animals, (re)connection and belonging in the World'. In Wylie, Dan (ed) *Toxic Belonging? Identity and Ecology in Southern Africa.* Newcastle: Cambridge Scholars Publishing.

Naidoo, Venu (1997) Interview with Zakes Mda. *Alternation*, 4(1).

Ndebele, Njabulo S. (1991) *Rediscovery of the Ordinary: Essays on South African Literature and Culture.* Johannesburg: COSAW (Congress of South African Writers).

Ndebele, Njabulo S. (1998) 'Memory, metaphor and the triumph of narrative'. In Coetzee, Carli, & Nuttall, Sarah (eds) *Negotiating the Past: The Making of Memory in South Africa.* Cape Town: Oxford University Press.

Ngara, Kudzayi (2009) 'The itinerant flâneur: Toloki as a migrant in time and ideological space in *Ways of Dying*'. *English Academy Review*, 26 (2).

Ngugi wa Thiong'O (1993, first published 1986) 'The language of African literature'. In Williams, Patrick & Chrisman, Laura (eds) *Colonial Discourse and Post-Colonial Theory: A Reader.* Hemel Hempstead: Harvester Wheatsheaf.

Nicol, Mike (1995) *The Waiting Country: A South African Witness.* London: Gollancz.

Nkosi, Lewis (1994) 'Constructing the "cross-border" reader'. In Boehmer, Elleke, Chrisman, Laura & Parker, Kenneth (eds) *Altered State? Writing and South Africa.* Sydney: Dangaroo Press.

Nuttall, Sarah (2004) 'City forms and writing in the "now" in South Africa'. *Journal of Southern African Studies*, 30 (4).

Offenburger, Andrew (2008) 'Duplicity and plagiarism in Zakes Mda's *The Heart of Redness*'. *Research in African Literatures*, 39 (3), Fall.

Pechey, Graham (1998) 'The post-apartheid sublime: Rediscovering the extraordinary'. In Attridge, Derek & Jolly, Rosemary (eds) *Writing*

South Africa: Literature, Apartheid and Democracy 1970–1995. Cambridge: Cambridge University Press.

Peires, J. B. (1989) *The Dead Will Arise: Nongqawuse and the Great Xhosa Cattle-Killing of 1856–7.* Johannesburg and Cape Town: Jonathan Ball Publishers.

Radhakrishnan, R. (1996) *Diasporic Mediations: Between Home and Locations.* Minneapolis: University of Minnesota Press.

Robbins, Bruce (1994) 'Secularism, elitism, progress, and other transgressions: On Edward Saïd's "voyage in"'. *Social Text,* 12 (3).

Rogers, Susan (2008) 'Multi-culltural mixed media: Byatt and Mda expropriate paint'. *The English Academy Review,* 25 (2) October: *Voice and Gaze in Metropolitan and Postcolonial Writing and Film.*

Saccaggi, C. (2008) 'The reinvention of historical discourse in Zakes Mda's *The Heart of Redness* and Mike Nicol's *This Day and Age*'. *Journal of Colonial Discourse,* 12 (1) 3.

Saïd, Edward (1983) *The World, the Text and the Critic.* Cambridge, Massachusetts: Harvard University Press.

Saïd, Edward (1984) 'The mind of winter: Reflections on a life in exile'. *Harper's Magazine,* 269.

Saïd, Edward (1986) 'Intellectuals in the post-colonial world'. *Salmagundi,* Spring/Summer 70–71.

Saïd, Edward (1993) *Culture and Imperialism.* London: Chatto and Windus.

Saïd, Edward (1994) *Representations of the Intellectual: The 1993 Reith Lectures.* London: Vintage.

Samuelson, Meg (2009) 'Nongqawuse, national time and (female) authorship in *The Heart of Redness*'. In Bell, David & Jacobs, J. U. (eds) *Ways of Dying. Critical Essays on Zakes Mda.* Pietermaritzburg. University of KwaZulu-Natal Press.

Schama, Simon (1996) In Darian-Smith, Kate, Gunner, Liz & Nuttall, Sarah (eds) *Text, Theory, Space: Land, Literature and History in South Africa and Australia.* London and New York: Routledge.

Scheub, Harold (1996) *The Tongue Is Fire: South African Storytellers and Apartheid.* Madison, Wisconsin: The University of Wisconsin Press.

Schwager, Dirk & Schwager, Dominique (1994) *Claerhout: Artist and Priest.* Maseru: Visual Publications.

Selden, Raman, Widdowson, Peter & Brooker, Peter eds (1985) *A Reader's Guide to Contemporary Literary Theory* (4 ed) Hemel Hempstead: Prentice Hall/Harvester Wheatsheaf.

Sewlall, Harry (2007) '"Portmanteau biota" and ecofeminist interventions in Zakes Mda's *The Heart of Redness*'. *Journal of Literary Studies,* 23 (4) December.

Slemon, Stephen (1995) 'Magic realism as postcolonial discourse'. In Zamara, Lois Parkinson & Faris, Wendy B. (eds) *Magic Realism: Theory, History, Community.* Durham and London: Duke University Press.

Slovic, Scott (ed) (2009) *ISLE – Interdisciplinary Studies in Literature and Environment.* 16 (1), Winter. Oxford: Oxford University Press.

Slovic, Scott & Satterfield, Terre (eds) (2004) *What's Nature Worth? Narrative Expressions of Environmental Values.* Salt Lake City: The University of Utah Press.

Smith, Claire (1999) 'Ancestors, place and people: Social landscapes in Aboriginal Australia'. In Ucko, Peter J. & Layton, Robert (eds) *The Archaeology and Anthropology of Landscape: Shaping Your Landscape.* London and New York: Routledge.

Sofianos, Konstantin (2004) 'Formal politics and informal settlements: The realism of Zakes Mda's *The Heart of Redness*'. Unpublished senior research project. University of Cape Town.

Spivak, Gayatri Chakravorty (2003) *A Critique of Postcolonial Reason: Toward a History of the Vanishing Present.* Cambridge, Massachusetts: Harvard University Press.

Spurr, David (1993) *The Rhetoric of Empire: Colonial Discourse in Journalism, Travel Writing, and Imperial Administration.* Durham and London: Duke University Press.

Steinmayer, Elke (2003) 'Chanting the song of sorrow: Threnody in Homer and Zakes Mda'. *Current Writing,* 15 (2).

Strydom, Leon (1983) *Frans Claerhout: Catcher of the Sun.* Cape Town: Tafelberg Press.

Swart, Sandra (2007) '"But where's the bloody horse?": Textuality and corporeality in "The Animal Turn"'. *Journal of Literary Studies.* 23 (3) September.

Ucko, Peter J. & Layton, Robert (1999) 'Introduction: Gazing on the landscape and encountering the environment'. In Ucko, Peter J. & Layton, Robert (eds) *The Archaeology and Anthropology of Landscape: Shaping Your Landscape.* London and New York: Routledge.

Vale, Peter & Maseko, Sipho (1998) 'South Africa and the African Renaissance'. *International Affairs,* 74 (2).

Van der Vlies, Andrew Edward (2007) *South African Textual Cultures: White, Black, Read All Over.* Manchester: Manchester University Press.

Van Wyk, Johan (1997) 'Catastrophe and beauty: *Ways of Dying,* Zakes Mda's novel of the transition'. *Literator,* 18 (3).

Verdon, Timothy & Henderson, John (1990) *Christianity and the Renaissance: Image and Religious Imagination in the Quattrocento.* Syracuse, New York: Syracuse University Press.

Vital, Anthony (2005) 'Situating ecology in recent South African fiction. J. M. Coetzee's *The Lives of Animals* and Zakes Mda's *The Heart of Redness*'. *Journal of Southern African Studies,* 31 (2).

Walker, Alice (1983) *The Color Purple.* London: Phoenix, Orion Books Limited.

Warner, Marina (2000) *Alone of All Her Sex: The Myth and Cult of the Virgin Mary.* London: Vintage.

Warnes, Christopher (2009) 'Chronicles of belief and unbelief: Zakes Mda and the question of magical realism in South African literature'. In Bell, David & Jacobs, J. U. (eds) *Ways of Writing: Critical Essays on Zakes Mda.* Pietermaritzburg: University of KwaZulu-Natal Press.

Watson, Lyall (1979) *Lifetide: A Biology of the Unconscious.* London: Hodder and Stoughton.

Weber, Rebecca L. (2004) 'The Africana QA: Zakes Mda'. 25 May. Available at: http://www.rebeccalweber.com/zakes.html

Wenzel, Marita (2009) 'Zakes Mda's representation of South African reality in *Ways of Dying, The Madonna of Excelsior* and *The Whale Caller*'. *Word and Image in Postcolonial Literatures.* Amsterdam: Rodopi.

Wessels, Michael (2010) *Bushman Letters: Interpreting /Xam Narrative.* Johannesburg: Wits University Press.

White, Hayden (1996) In Hawthorn, Jeremy (ed) *Cunning Passages: New Historicism, Cultural Materialism and Marxism in Contemporary Literature.* London, New York and Sydney: Arnold.

Woodward, Wendy (2003) '"Jim comes from Jo'burg": Regionalised identities and social comedy in Zakes Mda's *The Heart of Redness*'. *Current Writing,* 15 (21).

Woodward, Wendy (2006) 'Lions, leopards and liminal spaces: Representations of biosociality in the writings of Katy Payne, Linda Tucker and Gillian van Houten'. *Current Writing,* 18 (1) April.

Woodward, Wendy (2007) 'The killing (off) of animals in some Southern African fiction, or "Why does every animal story have to be sad?"'. *Journal of Literary Studies,* 23 (3) September.

Woodward, Wendy (2009) 'Whales, clones and two ecological novels: Zakes Mda's *The Whale Caller* and Jane Rosenthal's *Souvenir*'. In Bell, David & Jacobs, J. U. (eds) *Ways of Writing: Critical Essays on Zakes Mda.* Pietermaritzburg: University of KwaZulu-Natal Press.

Worton, Michael & Still, Judith (eds) (1990) *Intertextuality: Theories and Practices.* Manchester: Manchester University Press.

Wylie, Dan (2006) 'Animal presences, animal geographies'. *Current Writing*, 18 (1).

Yeats, William Butler (1961) *The Collected Poems of W. B. Yeats.* London: Macmillan.

Zamara, Lois Parkinson & Faris, Wendy B. (eds) (1995) *Magic Realism: Theory, History, Community.* Durham and London: Duke University Press.

Index

www.ingramcontent.com/pod-product-compliance
Lightning Source LLC
Chambersburg PA
CBHW061617100726
47898CB00002B/703

* 9 7 8 0 8 2 1 4 1 9 9 3 9 *